The Real
Guy Fawkes

The Real
Guy Fawkes

Nick Holland

PEN & SWORD
HISTORY

First published in Great Britain in 2017 by
PEN AND SWORD HISTORY
an imprint of
Pen and Sword Books Ltd
47 Church Street
Barnsley
South Yorkshire S70 2AS

ISBN 978 1 52670 508 2

Printed and bound in the UK
by T J International, Padstow, Cornwall, PL28 8RW

Typeset in Times New Roman by
CHIC GRAPHICS

Pen & Sword Books Ltd incorporates the imprints of Pen & Sword
Archaeology, Atlas, Aviation, Battleground, Discovery,
Family History, History, Maritime, Military, Naval, Politics, Railways,
Select, Social History, Transport, True Crime, Claymore Press,
Frontline Books, Leo Cooper, Praetorian Press, Remember When,
Seaforth Publishing and Wharncliffe.

For a complete list of Pen and Sword titles please contact
Pen and Sword Books Limited
47 Church Street, Barnsley, South Yorkshire, S70 2AS, England
E-mail: enquiries@pen-and-sword.co.uk
Website: www.pen-and-sword.co.uk

Contents

Acknowledgements

Writing a book is never a solitary endeavour, and there are many people and organisations I would like to thank for making The Real Guy Fawkes possible. I'd like to give particular thanks to my family and friends for their unflinching support and encouragement. Fulsome thanks must also go to everyone at Pen and Sword Books, particularly Jonathan Wright and Lauren Burton, who have been a pleasure to write for, and my editor Barnaby Blacker.

In addition to the above I would like to single out the generous help and advice I've had from Sister Ann Stafford and everyone at the Bar Convent, York; Liesbeth Corens of the Catholic Record Society; Michael Baxter and the Caro Archaeological Society; Ruth Somerville and the team at York's St. Michael-le-Belfrey church.

Many thanks also go to the British Library, the National Archives, St. Peter's School, York, the Royal Armouries Museum, Leeds, Historic Royal Palaces, the Royal Archives, Brussels, City of York Council Libraries and Archives, York Minster, Hatfield House, Coombe Abbey (whose afternoon teas I particularly recommend), and the Guy Fawkes Inn, York.

Final, and heartfelt, thanks go to you – the reader. I hope you enjoy reading the story of Guy Fawkes as much as I enjoyed researching and writing it.

Prologue

Dark clouds hung overhead on a cold winter's afternoon, but little could dampen the enthusiasm of those assembled in Westminster Yard. Approaching them, led by the arms, was a man who had once been tall, now stooped and walking with great difficulty. A man who had once been proud and defiant, now humble and defeated. This was the star attraction of the day: the devil in human form they'd come to see and jeer. It is 31 January 1606. The crowd are about to witness the final moments of a man who would have torn down the fabric of English society, one who would have killed the King, his heir, and all his lords and bishops: the man who would have reduced Parliament itself, and all it stood for, to dust and ashes, Guy Fawkes.

The capture of Guy Fawkes on a famous November night in 1605 led to celebrations across the country, and these celebrations continue today over four centuries later. November the fifth will forever be 'Guy Fawkes Night', with today's bonfires a reminder of ones that were spontaneously lit across the capital four centuries ago, and with the explosion of fireworks an echo of the explosion that Guy was within hours of creating beneath the House of Lords.

Today's fireworks, however, bear little relation to the explosion Guy would have wrought. He had assembled enough gunpowder to blow up the House of Lords twenty-five times,[1] and the blast would have devastated the Westminster area costing hundreds, perhaps thousands, of lives. What kind of man would willingly light a fuse and bring about human suffering on such a scale?

Guy Fawkes remains a controversial and in many ways misunderstood character, so just what was he: a fanatic, a fool, or a freedom fighter? He was certainly a product of his time, and many of the events of his day, which will be related in this book, seem almost too barbarous for a modern mind to comprehend: heads sliced off and

PROLOGUE

left to rot for years in a public marketplace; a woman stripped naked and crushed to death under sharp stones; genitals cut away and burned in front of a man's face as a crowd cheers.

This is the world that Guy lived in, but if we look below the surface we may find it's not so different to our world after all. Tracing Guy's life, and examining his role in the gunpowder plot, was a difficult task but one that I found thrilling and rewarding. Many documents have been lost or destroyed, and some events were deliberately obscured. Nevertheless, by looking at source materials that are still extant, and examining the confessions and letters of Guy and his fellow conspirators, we can get a fascinating insight into the man.

The gunpowder plot can be a confusing story, but my aim in this book is to cut through the complexity and make it accessible to all. To aid this, I have modernised some of the spellings contained within Tudor and Stuart documents and letters, and standardised the use of names (the spelling of names could vary from one document to another in the sixteenth and seventeenth centuries, so that we see Rokewood and Rookwood, and Faux and Fawkes for example).

It's time to step back to the year 1570 on the mud-strewn streets of York, where we begin our search for the real Guy Fawkes.

Chapter 1

By the Grace of God

Thy sight was never yet more precious to me;
Welcome, with all the affection of a mother,
That comfort can express from natural love:
Since thy birth-joy – a mother's chiefest gladness
After sh'as undergone her curse of sorrows –
Thou wast not more dear to me, than this hour
Presents thee to my heart
Thomas Middleton, *Women Beware Women*

York is a beguiling city with a long history, one filled with conquest, bloody battles, and rebellion. Today it is a hive of activity, its charming streets full of tourists, students, families and workers, but if we look closely we can still catch glimpses of the Tudor city that Guy Fawkes grew up in.

By the late sixteenth century, the population of York stood at between ten and twelve thousand souls, a slight increase on the number living there a century earlier. With the population of England as a whole increasing substantially at this time, it could be expected that York would have grown more dramatically than that, as it was to do in later centuries building up to a figure of around two hundred thousand today, but in fact it was a city that had entered decline.

York had long been famous for its woollen trade, with the hills and dales surrounding it proving perfect sheep pastures, and the rivers Ouse and Foss that flow through the city being ideal conduits to carry produce in and out. In Tudor times, however, smaller scale wool trading centres began to gain popularity across Yorkshire and

Lancashire. They were less cumbersome, with smaller overheads and offering cheaper prices.

Tudor York was also famous for its cathedral, the Minster. Then, as now, it dominated the heart of the city, but to many York dwellers by the mid-sixteenth century it had become a symbol of oppression rather than a source of pride. Even before its completion in 1472 it had been used as a centre of Catholic worship, with liturgies read in Latin that few of the congregation could understand, and an emphasis placed upon mysteries that had been passed down from generation to generation. In 1517, in a city over eight hundred miles away, an act took place that would change that for ever, and set in motion events that would lead to an attempt on the life of the King and all of England's ruling class.

Tradition states that on 31 October 1517, a priest nailed a letter to the door of All Saints' Church in Germany.[1] The priest was Martin Luther and the letter became known as the 'ninety-five theses'. In short, Luther was proclaiming his desire to see the Roman Catholic church reformed, and replaced by a new kind of worship that placed scripture at its centre rather than one person in the shape of the Pope.

This simple act proved a catalyst for what we call the Reformation, and the splitting of the church into Catholic and Protestant factions. The reformation was quickly championed by England's king, Henry VIII, who proclaimed himself head of the church in England, and took steps to remove much of the power, and especially the riches, that the Catholic church in England had amassed.

This English reformation was entrusted by Henry to one official in particular: Thomas Cromwell.

Cromwell was a power-hungry man, and one who did not baulk when it came to cruelty, setting a trend that would be followed later by Queen Elizabeth's chief courtiers such as Robert Cecil, who would become so important to Guy Fawkes' story. By 1535 Cromwell, already Lord Privy Seal, was also made Vicar General by King Henry, and given the important job of driving the reformation onwards.

To Cromwell this meant one thing above all else: crushing the Catholics. In 1536 he published 'An Act Extinguishing the Authority

2

of the Bishop of Rome', which was intended to end the 'pretended power and usurped authority of the Bishop of Rome, by some called the Pope'.[2] If Cromwell found the subjugation and conversion of Catholics in southern England easy, he encountered much greater resistance in northern England, a resistance that had its first outpouring in York in an event known as 'The Pilgrimage of Grace.'

While there were staunchly Catholic areas in East Anglia, Wales and the Midlands, it was Yorkshire and Lancashire that clung most ferociously onto their previous beliefs. By 1536 many of the people of these counties had a litany of complaints against the reformation, against the destruction of their churches and monasteries, against the fines being imposed upon them, and particularly against the increasingly violent edicts of Thomas Cromwell.

After an earlier revolt in Louth, Lincolnshire, a wealthy lawyer called Sir Robert Aske, originally of London, raised a band of around ten thousand men and occupied the city of York. Under Aske's rule, the Catholic way of life was restored, and priests, monks and nuns returned.

The Duke of Norfolk was sent by King Henry to meet and negotiate with the protesters, or pilgrims as they called themselves. Upon meeting them near Doncaster with his army of around five thousand, Norfolk was dismayed to find that Aske had around ten times that number of men, and that leading northern nobles including Sir Thomas Percy were backing the rebellion.

A peaceful settlement was made and the men were dispersed, but it's unclear whether Norfolk had the authority to make the concessions that he promised. What is clear is that within two years the deal and any amnesty that came with it was broken. Aske was executed in York, hung from gallows at the top of the castellated Clifford's tower before his lifeless body was suspended in chains from the wall.[3] By 1538, 216 people associated with the uprising had also been killed.

In the decades which followed the Pilgrimage of Grace's defeat, the new Protestant religion gained supremacy in York, officially at least. During the last years of Henry's reign, under the auspices of Cromwell, and in the later reign of Henry's daughter Elizabeth, acts of parliament encouraged their subjects to become good and loyal Protestants. Where the heart couldn't be won over voluntarily, financial punishments were invoked so that people who chose not to attend Protestant church services, those who became known as recusants, were often worn down by fines and the confiscation of their land and property. The 1552 Second Act of Uniformity[4] made it compulsory to attend official Church of England services, and from 1559 onwards a fine of twelve pence would be imposed on those who failed to attend. This fine would rise sharply in succeeding decades.

The reformation ensured that the Church of England became not only a spiritual movement, but also one that took an increasingly active role in legal administration, and therefore a money-making operation thanks to its system of fines and punishments. It was an ideal time to be an ecclesiastical lawyer, and one such man who served the city of York in the mid-sixteenth century was William Fawkes, a member of the Fawkes family of Farnley near Leeds.

William Fawkes had married well: his wife Ellen was from York's prestigious Harrington family, and her father had served as the Sheriff of York for five years before becoming Mayor in 1536. It is an irony, therefore, that it was Mayor Harrington, the great-grandfather of Guy Fawkes, who received Sir Robert Aske's demands at the start of the Pilgrimage of Grace, and who helped ensure its defeat.[5]

William Fawkes and other ecclesiastical lawyers were in even higher demand from 1561 onwards, as Queen Elizabeth I chose the city as headquarters for two major organisations: the Council of the North, and the Ecclesiastical Commission for the Northern Province.[6] This served two purposes for the Queen: firstly it would attract more people to the city that had been losing population thanks to increased competition in the wool trade, secondly it would help to prop up the authority of the Church of England in York, a city that she and her courtiers knew still housed a significant number of people sympathetic to the old Roman faith.

While the first child of William and Ellen Fawkes, Thomas, became a wool trader, their second son Edward followed in his father's footsteps by becoming a lawyer in York's ecclesiastical court.

Edward's talents were soon recognised, and he became a proctor of the Ecclesiastical Court,[7] and then an advocate in the Consistory Court of the Archbishop of York, based in Minster Yard next to the towering York Minster itself.

As an advocate in the Consistory Court, Edward Fawkes would play a major role in upholding church law, by which we mean the law of the Church of England. This would have involved him in civil matters, such as the settlement of debts or disputes between individuals, but it also placed him at the forefront of the battle against Catholics, and especially against recusants.

While never a wealthy man, Edward Fawkes did own land in several locations across York, and his job and background would have given him the undoubted status of a gentleman. With this status to his name it would have been expected that he'd marry a woman from a similarly respectable background, but instead, in 1567 or 1568, he married Edith Blake. Little is known of Edith's early background, indeed some earlier commentators conjectured that her surname may have been Jackson based upon one of Guy's confessions in the Tower of London.[8] Her family were merchants from the Scotton area, around twenty miles to the east of York, and it seems that she was less well educated than her husband, as recordings of her signature show a less than assured hand. This may have led to the Fawkes family looking down on the union, and it may also be pertinent that when her brother-in-law Thomas died in 1578, he made provisions for Guy and other relatives but made no mention at all of Edith in his will.

If the Fawkes family felt that Edward had married beneath him, there is no reason to think that they didn't enjoy a happy marriage. Indeed, it may have been a love marriage rather than one arranged for reasons of social standing as was common at the time. We know that Edith quickly became pregnant (and of course we could conjecture that this may have led to their marriage, rather than occurring afterwards). On 3 October 1568, Edith gave birth to a daughter who was named Anne. Unfortunately, tragedy soon struck and Anne was buried just seven weeks later.

As was traditional then, the name was passed on to their next daughter, who was born on 12 October 1572, and Anne Fawkes gained a sister Elizabeth on 27 May 1575. These were the younger sisters of the only son of Edward and Edith Fawkes: born on 13 April 1570, they named him Guy.

Guy's exact date of birth is unrecorded, but we can estimate it with confidence because we know that he was baptised on 16 April at St. Michael-le-Belfrey church in York, and baptisms usually took place three days after a child was born.[9]

St. Michael-le-Belfrey is a large and beautiful church in its own right, although it is towered over by York Minster lying adjacent to it. It was the parish church for much of the centre of York, and so would have been the regular place of worship for many of its citizens, rather than the grander cathedral alongside it. The church hasn't forgotten its infamous son, and a display on Guy's life is today situated at the rear of the building, along with a copy of his entry of baptism.

Directly across from St. Michael-le-Belfrey, on High Petergate, is the Guy Fawkes Inn. It's a charming place to eat and drink, and draws in many of York's tourists partly thanks to its blue plaques stating that this was the spot on which Guy Fawkes was born, and the magnificent gunpowder plot mural across an outside wall.

While the Guy Fawkes Inn of today dates from a period after Guy's life, it is a separate building to the rear of the inn that is of interest to Fawkes historians. This white coloured cottage bears the name of 'Guy Fawkes Cottage', and it has often been said that this was the building that saw him take his first breath on that April morning in 1570. The cottage is of the right age, and it seems likely that it's the building referred to in a document of 8 July 1579, when Edith Fawkes signed for the continuation of a lease for a High Petergate building from Matthew Hutton, Dean of York Minster.

Is this then the actual birthplace of Guy Fawkes? Like much in Guy's life, it is not certain, with two other spots in and around York claiming to be the place where he was born. The outlying district of Bishopthorpe has a long-standing tradition that Guy Fawkes was born there, in a house that no longer exists but which stood opposite St. Andrew's church. The question has to be asked why Guy was baptised in the centre of York if he was born in Bishopthorpe? Nevertheless, I firmly believe that oral traditions that have lasted for centuries have to be respected – and they often contain some element of the truth even if they aren't wholly truthful. Bishopthorpe was and is the traditional seat of the Archbishop of York, so it doesn't stretch the imagination to conjecture that the village may also have attracted lawyers from the Archbishop's court – such as Guy's father, Edward Fawkes.

My opinion is that Guy may well have lived for a while in Bishopthorpe during his childhood, and he probably also lived for a time on the site of what is now the Guy Fawkes Inn. Historian Katherine Longley, however, argues convincingly that the true birthplace of Guy Fawkes was a house on Stonegate in York, a short walk from High Petergate, the Minster, and St. Michael-le-Belfrey,[10] and that is what is now generally accepted.

Edward and Edith must have been overjoyed as they watched Guy grow up to be a strong and inquisitive boy, especially after the loss of their first child. Here was a boy who would grow into the man to carry the Fawkes name on into future generations. They might have dreamt that their son would follow his father and grandfather and become a lawyer. Unfortunately for them, the boy grew up to have other plans. The York that Guy came to know was very different to that of his parents' generation, and Guy's childhood and adolescence spent within its close, claustrophobic streets would change his life forever.

Guy's York was a city full of paranoia and treachery, a city where people kept a close watch on their neighbours, and where husbands would be forced to betray their wives; a city where justice was becoming increasingly violent, increasingly arbitrary. It was a city where, even as a young boy advancing in years, you felt that you were being spied upon. You were being watched not only by your neighbours and playmates, but by the all-seeing eye of Queen Elizabeth herself.

Chapter 2

The Glorious Queen

Her berth was of the wombe of morning dew,
And her conception of the joyous Prime
Edmund Spenser, *The Faerie Queene*

Guy Fawkes' life was full of turmoil and change, yet for all but his last two and a half years there was one constant: the rule of Queen Elizabeth, also known as the Virgin Queen, the Fairie Queen, or simply Gloriana – the glorious ruler – as long as you didn't find yourself on the wrong side of her.

During her forty-five-year reign, Elizabeth changed from a cautious, hesitant ruler easily swayed by her counsellors, to a dictator in all but name, a ruthless leader who would stop at nothing to preserve her power and promote her beliefs.

There were many contemporary portraits of the Queen, but one in particular, painted in her final years, shows what she had become. The 'Rainbow Portrait' was painted at the turn of the seventeenth century by Marcus Gheeraerts the Younger, the Flemish born artist who had become the most celebrated portraitist to Tudor society (although some claim it as the work of Gheeraerts' brother-in-law Isaac Oliver[1]). Whoever painted it, the overall effect is stunning. The Queen looks younger than her years, a timeless beauty who is at once both alluring and aloof. Her magnificent red hair is topped by an elaborate crown with a large ruby at its centre, and she is draped in a huge number of pearls. On her left arm is a serpent and in her right hand she holds a rainbow, above which is the inscription, *Non sine sole iris*, or 'no rainbow without the sun'.

THE GLORIOUS QUEEN

Elizabeth is proclaiming herself as the sun that nourishes everything good in her kingdom. But there is an odd and even more striking piece of symbolism in the portrait. She wears an orange cloak upon which are a succession of ears and eyes. Elizabeth is saying that she sees everything and hears everything, and by the time the portrait was commissioned by her chief courtier Sir Robert Cecil, he had made sure that it was a reality.

Copies of portraits like this would have been displayed in public and civic buildings, such as the Consistory Court in York where Guy's father Edward Fawkes worked, and their main purpose was to instil devotion and awe in those who saw them, and failing that, fear.

Life could be precarious for many of her subjects, but then from her earliest days, life for Elizabeth was fraught with threats and danger too. Elizabeth Tudor was born in 1533, the daughter of King Henry VIII and his second wife, Anne Boleyn. At the time of her birth she was second in line to the throne behind her older half sister Mary, the only one of six children of Henry and Catherine of Aragon to survive childhood. As the royal line of succession favoured males (as it continued to do until recently) Elizabeth was pushed down to third in line to the throne when her half-brother Edward was born in 1537. During her childhood, she may have set aside thoughts of the crown, and imagined a life as a princess married to some foreign prince, but she would also have known there were precedents for the throne being taken by those who weren't born as the natural heir.

Her father Henry only gained the crown because his older brother Arthur died of the 'sweating sickness' aged 15 (for diplomatic reasons Henry also inherited Arthur's wife, Catherine of Aragon). Indeed the founder of the ruling Tudor dynasty, Henry VII who snatched the crown from Richard III at the Battle of Bosworth Field, had only a tenuous claim to the throne via former royal servant Owen Tudor.

Elizabeth's half-brother duly ascended the throne as King Edward VI in 1547, and although just 9 years old he soon proved to be a strong-willed monarch, particularly on matters of religion. He was determined to see through the English reformation started by his father, becoming the first Protestant king of England (Henry had always considered

9

himself a Catholic, despite his reforms) and making it compulsory to attend Church of England services.

Six years into his reign, the teenage Edward was suddenly struck by a dreadful illness that left him wasted and bed-bound, and he died on 6 July 1553. While the cause of his death is today accepted as tuberculosis, rumours of poisoning spread across the court and the nation. Some said the Duke of Northumberland, who had acted as regent to Edward and held the real reins of power in the kingdom, had poisoned the young king, and others that Catholics from noble families were behind it, hoping to sweep away the monarch and his new religion with him.

To everyone's surprise, Edward had named not one of his half-sisters, but Lady Jane Grey, whose mother Frances was the Duchess of Suffolk and a niece of King Henry, as his legitimate heir. This was in opposition to a ruling made by his father King Henry, but in accordance with an earlier statement of Henry's that his two daughters, the ladies Mary and Elizabeth, were both illegitimate and therefore had no place in the line of succession. Northumberland's plotting was undoubtedly behind Edward's deathbed change to the line of succession, as he knew the more obvious successor Mary would remove him from power and likely return England to Catholicism.

Lady Jane Grey was pronounced Queen and taken to the Tower of London to await her coronation, as per the usual procedures of the time. The Tower was to become her prison, however, as Mary Tudor insisted that she was the rightful heir and gathered a large army behind her. Lady Jane Grey was to rule for just thirteen days before Mary took the throne[2] and, realising that while she lived she remained a threat to her authority, Queen Mary reluctantly had her rival, and cousin-once-removed, beheaded in February 1554.

Queen Mary was a devout Catholic, and set about reversing the reforms that Edward had brought in. She was also ruthless when it came to wiping out those who opposed her, especially those she thought were agitating against Catholicism. Bloody Mary, as she has become known to history, reigned for just over five years, but in that time she and the Bishop of London, Edward Bonner,[3] had 280 Protestants put to death, many of them burned alive.

Understandably, many Protestant nobles were greatly worried by the excesses and violence of Mary's rule, and their thoughts turned to her half-sister Elizabeth, a woman who professed the Protestant faith. This made Lady Elizabeth's position precarious, particularly when a rebellion organised by Sir Thomas Wyatt in 1554 aimed to prevent Mary from marrying King Philip II of Spain. Wyatt's unstated aim was to replace Mary with Elizabeth, and this led Mary to place her half-sister under house arrest for more than a year. Only Elizabeth's protestations of innocence saved her from being executed as a traitor.[4]

The half-sisters were eventually reconciled, and after two phantom pregnancies, Queen Mary was forced to concede that Elizabeth was her natural heir. Elizabeth ascended the throne on 17 November 1558 after Mary's death from uterine cancer, and soon, once again, the reforms of the previous monarch were themselves repealed and rescinded.

Queen Elizabeth I began her long reign at the age of 25. She had already survived being implicated in a plot against the previous monarch, seen her mother taken away from her to be executed when she was just 2 years old, and witnessed her half-sister die seemingly from failures in her attempts to secure a child and a successor. These events greatly shaped Elizabeth's character; she saw herself as a true successor to her father Henry – a monarch chosen by God against all odds, and she would exercise divine rule, believing herself to be God's representative in England. Seeing what effect marriage and the inevitably ensuing quest for children had had on Anne Boleyn and Mary Tudor, she declared that she would never marry. Her kingdom would be her husband.

At first, Elizabeth took a more relaxed view towards religion, but as the years progressed she grew more confident in her own authority, and as she became more aware of threats against it, she enacted a succession of laws against the Catholic religion and its adherents.

Being a ruler at that time was fraught with danger, from both within and without the court. Spain was the dark shadow hanging over

Elizabeth during her reign, particularly as Queen Mary's widow, King Philip II, did little to hide his desire to return England and Ireland to Catholicism.

In 1569 a group of Catholic nobles, led by the Earls of Northumberland and Westmorland, rose up in what was known as 'The Northern Rebellion' or 'The Rising of the North', in a similar way to the earlier Pilgrimage of Grace. Taking their lead from Robert Aske's example, they planned to besiege and conquer York, but they were soon chased into Scotland; the uprising failed and its leaders, including Thomas Percy the 7th Earl of Northumberland, were killed. Just a year before the birth of Guy Fawkes, York was once again the centre of a vanquished rebellion.

Tensions escalated further when Pope Pius V excommunicated Queen Elizabeth I in an official pronouncement (a Papal Bull) issued in 1570. This was partly in support of the Northern Rebellion, and a similar rebellion that had failed in Ireland, and partly a response to the 1559 Act of Supremacy which made the Church of England independent from the Pope's authority.

Pope Pius pulled no punches, referring to Elizabeth as a 'pretended Queen of England and the servant of crime'.[5] He also declared the Queen a heretic and freed Catholics from her authority.

Even before the Papal Bull, most Catholics of the time considered Elizabeth to be illegitimate as they didn't recognise Henry VIII's divorce and subsequent marriage to Anne Boleyn. An example of these attitudes can be found in the exiled Cardinal William Allen's 'Admonition to the Nobility and People of England and Ireland', in which he refers to Elizabeth as 'taken and known for an incestuous bastard, begotten and born in sin, of an infamous courtesan Anne Boleyn'[6] (one of the charges that led to Anne's beheading was that she'd consummated an affair with her own brother, George Boleyn, who was also executed).

The Papal Bull was issued just two months before Guy Fawkes' birth, and the fallout from it was to cast a shadow over his life and lead directly to the gunpowder plot of 1605. If Pope Pius had intended to improve the lot of Catholics in England, his plan went disastrously wrong. Already existing divisions were increased, as Queen Elizabeth and her courtiers now saw Catholics as the enemy within: a fifth column more willing to serve Spain than England.

The Pope's pronouncement enraged the Queen. A copy of the bull was pinned to the doors of the Bishop of London's Palace by John Felton, a Catholic lawyer, in mockery of Martin Luther's action at Wittenberg.[7] His execution was to be the first of many in the decades that followed.

Gone were the uneasy days of semi-toleration towards Catholics, and Elizabeth enacted a series of new laws directed against the religion and its followers. In 1581 the fine for being a recusant, that is a person who refused to attend Church of England services, was raised from its original twelve pence to an exorbitant twenty pounds. In 1587 this was made even more draconian, with twenty pounds being charged monthly, and two thirds of a nobleman's estate forfeited if he defaulted or refused to pay the fine.

The effect on the Catholic nobility was twofold. Many of them saw their fortunes decimated within a short space of time, with Lord Vaux of Harrowden for example having to pawn the robes that he wore in parliament. Other members of the gentry had to sell their land and stately homes, one such example being Sir William Catesby, who also spent time in prison accused of harbouring priests.[8] A ruling of 1585 banished all Catholic priests ordained after 1559, or ordained abroad, from the kingdom; if they were found they were to be adjudged a traitor and executed.

As the Catholic nobility became poorer and more oppressed they also became angrier, and the second half of Queen Elizabeth's reign was studded by a succession of plots against her life, many of them connected with Mary, Queen of Scots.

Just as Queen Mary of England had seen her relatives Lady Jane Grey and Elizabeth Tudor as potential rivals to her authority, so Elizabeth was to see a rival in Mary Stuart, her first cousin once removed. Mary Stuart became Queen of Scotland when she was just 6 years old, and she was also for a short time the Queen Consort of France, but many English Catholics championed her as the legitimate

Queen of England too. Mary had a turbulent life that saw her deposed as Scotland's Queen in 1567, with the crown handed to her 1-year-old son James. She fled to England asking for protection from Elizabeth, but instead found herself imprisoned in a succession of castles and manor houses. Quite simply, Mary was too much of a threat to be allowed to roam free, especially as she was a Catholic and had the potential to become a figurehead for those who wished to see the end of Elizabeth's increasingly authoritarian reign.

A reminder of this, not that the always-astute Queen needed one, came in 1571 in the shape of the Ridolfi Plot. The leader of the plot was Florentine banker Roberto Ridolfi, who had also been involved in the Northern Uprising two years before. Implicitly backed by Pope Pius V and King Philip II of Spain, Ridolfi planned to kill Queen Elizabeth and place Mary Stuart on the throne, who would then shore up her position by marrying Elizabeth's cousin Thomas Howard, the staunchly Catholic Duke of Norfolk. The plot was discovered and the Duke executed, although Ridolfi himself escaped punishment and lived out his days as a Florentine senator.

Other plots against Elizabeth followed in quick succession, including the Throckmorton Plot of 1583 that centred upon a proposed invasion by Mary's French relative the Duke of Guise. The 1586 Babington Plot was another attempt to assassinate Elizabeth and then replace her with Mary, who this time paid with her life. The Spanish Armada of 1588 was sent largely in response to Mary's execution, but it only served to strengthen Elizabeth's enmity against Catholics.

One particularly odd attempt on Elizabeth's life was the plot of the poisoned pommel, of 1598. A man named Edward Squires attempted to kill the Queen by rubbing poison onto the saddle she used for riding her horse, and her favourite courtier the Earl of Essex by rubbing the same poison onto the seat of his chair. The poisons failed, and only Squires lost his life.[9]

The precarious nature of life in Elizabethan England, and especially in the court, was demonstrated by no-one better than the Earl of Essex, Robert Devereux himself. Essex had become the undoubted favourite of the Queen, but in doing so he fatally angered another leading courtier Robert Cecil.[10] Cecil, like his father William Cecil before him, was a cunning master of machinations, and eventually turned the Queen's favour against Essex, so that he was placed firstly under house arrest and then banished from the court, after which he had his lucrative sweet wine licence taken away from him. A desperate Essex launched his own rebellion in 1601, but as with earlier plots it failed, and the Earl of Essex was beheaded.[10] Although not overtly Catholic himself, many Catholics had supported Essex in his rebellion, and young men including Robert Catesby and Francis Tresham found themselves with punitive fines and time in jail for their supporting roles in the plot.[11]

One thing that unified all these plots, in addition to their failure and the execution of their ringleaders, was that they were all foiled due to infiltration by government spies, or information passed on to spymasters. These masters of the dark arts of subterfuge, first Francis Walsingham, and then the Cecils, William and Robert, wielded great power in the Elizabethan court. They were the natural successors to Thomas Cromwell, men to be feared, men to be avoided whenever possible. It's often thought today that Robert Cecil not only foiled many of these plots, he also sowed the seeds of the plots as a way of furthering his own cause or harming the causes of others. Spies could be anywhere in Elizabeth's England, and the reward for being an informant was high. Plotters and dissenters never knew whether they were talking to a comrade in arms, or an agent provocateur who would at an opportune moment send them to their doom.

As Guy Fawkes grew up in York during this tumultuous and bloody period, he would see first-hand the result of being out of favour with Queen Elizabeth, whether that meant actively plotting against her or simply daring to practise a different faith.

Chapter 3

A School for Sedition

This age thinks better of a gilded fool
Than of a threadbare saint in wisdom's school
Thomas Dekker, *Old Fortunatus*

Edward and Edith Fawkes must have been relieved to see their young son Guy growing up strong and healthy, especially after the loss of his elder sister Anne. Nurtured by parental affection, he was crawling, toddling, and then striding through the childhood months that were typically the most dangerous in a person's life in the late sixteenth century.

Infectious diseases were rife in urban areas, from tuberculosis to typhoid, and children who had not yet built up any natural resistance to the pathogens were particularly vulnerable. Sweating sickness was a common killer of the young. Striking rich and poor, it had claimed Prince Arthur and almost accounted for his young bride Catherine of Aragon, who was lucky to survive both the sickness and a marriage to Arthur's brother Henry. What was then called sweating sickness may have been a variety of influenza, but without modern knowledge and medication it was frequently fatal.

Poor sanitation meant that dysentery and cholera were rife, and smallpox was another unseen killer that was ever present, and one which nearly claimed the life of Queen Elizabeth herself in 1562. A measure of the medical knowledge at that time is that the young Queen was wrapped in a red blanket throughout her illness as a potential cure.[1]

There was one disease that was even more rife, and it cast a shadow

16

over York throughout the sixteenth and seventeenth century: the plague. It struck York in 1550 and 1551, and again in 1604, greatly reducing the city's population on each occasion. Areas particularly affected by the plague were placed under a form of quarantine, and goods could only be bought using coins which had first been washed in vinegar – then seen as a plague-repelling disinfectant.[2]

One by-product of these epidemics was that the city guilds which controlled trade in York relaxed their erstwhile stringent regulations, inviting tradesmen from across the country to come and replace those who had been carried away by the plague and other diseases.

While Guy's parents were not wealthy or aristocratic, the Fawkes family of Stonegate were solidly middle class. They would have been able to afford to eat well, buying fresh produce from the butcher's shops that ran up and down the Shambles, such as that owned by John Clitherow, and that gave them some protection against illnesses that preyed upon the poorer members of York society.

Little is known of the house that Guy, his parents, and later his sisters Anne and Elizabeth, grew up in. Edith Fawkes may have had some assistance in running the household. The neighbour of the Fawkes', John Brocket,[3] is recorded as having had a servant,[4] so the same may also have been true of the Fawkes household.

John Brocket, like Guy's father Edward, was a public notary of the ecclesiastical court, a man who oversaw the swearing of oaths, and ruled upon the validity of wills and other important documents. As the two men not only worked together but lived side by side, it seems likely that they were friends, maybe on occasion sharing a drink at one of the many inns that were to be found on Stonegate and nearby Petergate. John Brockett and his wife Isabel had young children of their own, so it's easy to imagine the infant Guy playing with them.

One game Guy and his friends are certain to have played is Nine Men's Morris, a strategic board game that dates back to at least Roman times. It had become incredibly popular in the late sixteenth century and is even mentioned in one of Shakespeare's dramas.[5] It is played on a target-shaped grid containing twenty-four points. At the outset each player has nine pieces, and the aim is to create a horizontal or vertical line of three pieces which allows the player to remove one piece from his opponent. One advantage of Nine Men's Morris is that it could be played just about anywhere, with the game board being drawn on the street or in mud, and stones or other counters used as the pieces. While the rules are simple, the strategy can become complex, and subterfuge and forward thinking are essential; skills that Guy would put into practice in his later life.

We can assume that Edward and Edith Fawkes would have been highly protective of their son, striving to shield him from the lurking threat of disease and death that haunted the cobbled streets that had channels of effluent running down them. There was one other ever present threat to life in York however, and it was man-made rather than disease born.

On 22 August 1572, a large crowd gathered at a place known as The Pavement in York. The Pavement was so called because in the fourteenth century it became the first street in York to be paved, and that made it the focal point of one of the city's markets. On that August day in 1572, a different trade was being carried out.

A masked executioner stood in the centre of a crowd, a large axe in his hand, and beneath him, with his head on the block, was Sir Thomas Percy, the 7th Earl of Northumberland. Northumberland, along with his fellow ringleader of the Northern Rebellion the Earl of Westmorland, had escaped to Scotland, but he was betrayed by the Scottish government who handed him over to England in exchange for £2,000.

At his trial, Percy was sentenced to death, but given a chance to spare his life if he would denounce his Catholic faith and become a Protestant. He refused, unwilling to be used as a tool to persuade other recusants and dissenters to do the same. Before his public execution at The Pavement, the Chancellor of York Minster, William Palmer, asked him to recant his faith and pray with him. Percy refused again and made his final speech:

'I should have been content to meet my death in silence, were it not that I see it is the custom for those who undergo this kind of punishment to address some words to the bystanders as to the cause

18

of their being put to death. Know, therefore, that from my earliest years down to this present day, I have held the faith of that church which, throughout the whole Christian world, is knit and bound together; and in that same faith I am about to end this unhappy life. But as for this new English church, I do not acknowledge it.'[6]

His speech finished, the axe was brought swiftly down, and to a gasp from the crowd his severed head was held up before them. While the body was interred, the head was displayed on a large spike on Micklegate Bar. The 2-year-old Guy was too young to see the execution, but he would have heard the story many times as he grew up and would have seen the evidence with his own eyes – Percy's head remained on its spike for many years, until it was eventually stolen away by those sympathetic to his cause and buried. As for Percy, execution ran in the family – his father the sixth earl, also called Thomas Percy, had been executed on the orders of Henry VIII for his role in the Pilgrimage of Grace. Three decades later Guy Fawkes' fate would become entwined with yet another Thomas Percy who would be judged a traitor and lose his life.

While Guy's childhood included time for games such as Nine Men's Morris, and other activities based upon running and hiding from friends, his father Edward would have kept a strict household, and Guy would have been compelled to attend regular Church of England services at St. Michael-le-Belfrey church.

Some people find it surprising that Guy Fawkes, the man who played such a central role in a Catholic terror plot, was born and raised into a Protestant family, but as we shall see this is just one of the things that many of the gunpowder plotters had in common.

Guy was expected to follow his father and grandfather into the life of an ecclesiastical lawyer, a staunch upholder of the Protestant faith, and to do this he would need a solid educational background. While Guy's sisters were given rudimentary lessons at home, at the age of 8 he was sent to school.

Earlier in the century, chantry schools closely tied to churches and monasteries were the destination for boys from middle or upper class families, but the reformation saw these schools closed along with the monasteries in the 1540s. In their place came grammar schools, or free schools, and York's very own grammar school opened its doors in 1557.

St. Peter's School, York, is still in existence today, although it no longer stands outside the city as it did then, in a street known as the Horse Fayre. The free school can trace its ancestry back even further, to York's first St. Peter's School founded by St. Paulinus in the year 627, making it the fourth oldest school in the world.[7]

York was a city in turmoil during Guy's childhood, much of it hidden away, as Catholics sought to hide their true beliefs and activities to escape fines and worse, and the same could be said of St. Peter's School. When Guy arrived it was under the jurisdiction of a headmaster called John Pulleyn, but the previous headmaster was John Fletcher, a man relieved of his post in 1575 and then imprisoned for twenty years for the crime of being a Catholic.[8]

Guy would have found life at school harsh and regimented, but it was intended that way as an excellent training for the life that he and many of his fellow pupils would have in their adult lives. Early lessons focused on learning Latin by rote, an essential skill for someone hoping to be a lawyer or notary like Guy, as well as instruction in Hebrew and Greek. In later years, the boys (and of course it was an exclusively male school) were taught literature and composition, and mathematics. There were also music and drama lessons, as headmaster Pulleyn was known to like the arts, and indeed staged a play featuring his pupils in January 1584, for which the school received the sum of forty shillings.[9] It is also known that many of the pupils played at football, at that time a rough-and-tumble game that was strictly prohibited.[10]

The school had an excellent academic reputation, with pupils being attracted from far afield. In 1589, the Archbishop of York reported that St. Peter's had around two hundred pupils in attendance, and that it was 'the only good school in this great city'.[11] Lessons were taught six days a week, beginning at 6.30 or 7 in the morning and continuing until 5 or 6 at night (depending upon the time of year). There were only two masters, so senior pupils would have been expected to help with the discipline – discipline that was dispensed regularly and with the aid of a birch or switch.

Religion, too, played a large part in the repetitive routine of Guy's school. Daily Church of England services were compulsory, and after the embarrassment of John Fletcher, the school had taken no risks when it came to appointing John Pulleyn. The Archbishop of York had insisted that the new headmaster must be of good and sincere religion, and that he should use no vain or profane books or teach anything contrary to the teachings of the Church of England. Pulleyn passed this test, and seemed to be an exemplary Protestant, but all was not as it appeared.

Pulleyn was without doubt a learned man who had perfected his trade as a master of Mary Bishophill Junior School, and who helped the school flourish, but he was almost certainly a secret Catholic.

John Pulleyn was wise enough to know what would happen to him if he professed his Catholicism openly, after all he only had to look at the example of his predecessor John Fletcher. Rather than being openly recusant, with all the dangers that entailed, he was a Church Catholic – a person who attended Church of England services and was outwardly Protestant, and yet inwardly believed in the Catholic faith. Pulleyn retired in 1591, and it is believed he then joined a Catholic order, but even while headmaster he may have had the chance to disseminate some of his beliefs in the old religion. Certainly, a look at some of his pupils at St. Peter's School is very revealing.

Alongside Guy Fawkes himself, in his year was Christopher Wright, commonly called Kit. His brother John, known as Jack, was also at the school, two years above Guy and Kit. The Wrights were the sons of John and Ursula Wright of Plowland Hall, Holderness, and were born Protestants but in their 30s they, along with Guy, would find themselves plotters in the gunpowder treason.

Another pupil at the school was Robert Middleton, who converted to Catholicism and was executed for his faith in 1601. Edward Oldcorne was at the school too and later became a Catholic priest; although it is doubtful that he knew much if anything of the gunpowder plot, he was linked to it at the time and executed in 1606.

Yet another was Oswald Tesimond, who became a Jesuit priest and went under the alias of Father Greenway. He too was a wanted man after the discovery of Guy Fawkes and the unravelling of the plot in 1605, but he escaped to the haven of the continent by covering himself with a cargo of dead pigs that were being transported by boat to France.[12] From the safety of Italy, Oswald Tesimond later wrote an account of what he knew of the gunpowder plot (although he may have played down what he and some of his fellow Jesuit priests really knew). In his testimony he gives a glowing account of his old schoolmaster John Pulleyn and remembers Guy Fawkes as highly intelligent and well-read.

While at St. Peter's School, Guy was not only excelling at lessons, he was also learning about the Catholic religion from other boys and adolescents who were making a similar journey. These fellow pupils were by now like family to Guy, and it is possible that Guy looked up to John Pulleyn as a father figure, because by this time tragedy had struck at the heart of Guy's life.

Chapter 4

Changed Forever

Death hath a thousand doors to let out life
Philip Massinger, *A Very Woman*

We know of Guy Fawkes' attendance at St. Peter's School, and indeed it's still celebrated by the school, with the headmaster Leo Winkley having publicly stated that it is time to forgive Guy's role in the gunpowder plot: 'We like him as a former boy, but we don't regard him as a role model[1]... Time to move on and let the poor soul rest... You could argue that he's an icon of the complex and flawed nature of human beings.'[2] That's the official line taken by the historic school, with a bonfire being lit every fifth of November, but with no Guy placed upon it.

While we know some salient points of Guy's time at school, the curricular and extra-curricular activities that made up his school days, his academic qualities attested for by fellow pupils, and the somewhat controversial company he would have kept there, other details often remain tantalisingly out of reach.

Unfortunately, St. Peter's School has changed location more than once since the late sixteenth century, and the majority of its records dating back to this time have long since been lost or destroyed. One thing that we can't say for sure is when Guy started to attend the school, but it would have been usual for children of Guy's background to attend a grammar school at around the age of 6 or 7 when one was available.

So it seems reasonable to suggest that Guy entered St. Peter's

School some time between 1576 and 1578, and this latter year was a very important one in Guy's life as an event happened that would change his life forever – the sudden death of his father, Edward Fawkes.

Life was precarious for all classes in the Tudor and Stuart periods, thanks to the combination of rampant disease and medical ignorance. Injuries or ailments that would be nothing but an inconvenience in the reign of Queen Elizabeth II could prove fatal in the reign of Queen Elizabeth I. By the turn of the seventeenth century, the average life expectancy in England was around forty years, with approximately twenty per cent of children dying in their first year, as did Guy's older sister Anne, and a third of all deaths occurring to those under the age of twenty.[3]

These all-too-common early mortalities created a sense of fatalism in Guy and in many others of his generation: when death was so close at hand, holding onto life seemed less important. Was it better to fight to be a free man and die upon the gallows, or live a life of subservience and die of the plague or sleeping sickness? This conundrum must have crossed Guy's mind at many pivotal moments in his life, and he would always have the example of his father to look back upon.

Edward Fawkes was an educated and well respected man, with significant social and financial advantages over many other citizens of York, yet he was still struck down at the age of just 45, leaving a wife and three children behind him. He was buried on 17 January 1578,[4] bringing a devastating start to the year for the Fawkes household. Edith was left wondering how to provide for her young family, the youngest child Elizabeth being just 2 years old, and worrying over a less than certain future. From enjoying a life of relative comfort, was poverty now to be her lot? As the oldest surviving child, Guy was particularly hard hit; he was old enough to realise that although a young boy he was now the man of the house and expectations would have weighed upon his shoulders.

Just what was it that killed Edward Fawkes? There is no record to say whether he had suffered a long illness or whether he had been plucked from his family without warning, but the harsh winter days in the northern city could be particularly hazardous to health so it may be that a short illness had hastened his end.

Stress may also have contributed to his death. The role of an ecclesiastical advocate changed greatly in the years he spent in the job. While being a practising Catholic had in effect been illegal since the Act of Uniformity of May 1559,[5] it was initially lightly enforced in York, a city which was known to be largely sympathetic to the old faith. The Rebellion of the North had shown Elizabeth and her courtiers how dangerous this laissez-faire attitude could be; York's Catholics had been practising their faith with relative impunity, although by necessity in secret, and yet at the first opportunity they had gathered together to rebel against their Queen. It could not be allowed to continue.

Thomas Young took up his position as Archbishop of York in May 1561,[6] and as well as being the figurehead at the top of the consistory court for which Edward Fawkes worked, he also served for a time as Lord President of the Council of the North. While he was a committed Protestant, he showed little zeal for clamping down on the Catholics within the city, even though he was legally able, and indeed ordered, to do so. His successor as Lord President, the Earl of Sussex, also favoured a soft touch, but the next man to take the job was very different.

Henry Hastings, the Earl of Huntingdon, was appointed Lord President of the Council of the North, by then headquartered in York, in 1572. He was a Protestant of the puritan kind, and despised Catholicism, with all its ceremony and statues, saints and intercessions, more than anything else. To Hastings, Catholicism was based upon idolatry, it was a heresy that must be stamped out, and those who professed it must be brought back to Protestantism or pay a heavy price.

In this endeavour he was assisted by a new Archbishop of York, Edmund Grindal. Grindal had previously served as Bishop of London, where he too gained a reputation as a zealous Puritan. Within a month of taking over as London's Bishop he had ordered that all candlesticks and crosses be removed and destroyed, and the altar stones were taken away as well, to be replaced by a plain and simple table. He was later made Archbishop of Canterbury, but his excessive puritanism saw him suspended from his post before he was eventually reinstated.[7]

Archbishop Grindal was a man who liked to exercise supreme control, as shown by his appointment of William Palmer and Edmund Bunney to the role of preachers at York Minster. Palmer and Bunney were as puritanical as their master, and preached long sermons full of hellfire and damnation. Bunney was made Chancellor of the Minster, but he was far from popular with more conventional Protestants, who claimed that his fiery extempore preaching did more harm than good.[8] Taking into account Archbishop Grindal's zeal and temperament, it seems likely that he would have taken a keen interest in the proceedings of the consistory court, encouraging advocates to take a stronger line against Catholicism and other contraventions of church law.

With Grindal and Hastings occupying York's two positions of power, life for the city's Catholic population quickly became much harder. Fines were imposed without mercy, and those who could not or would not pay found themselves imprisoned at York Castle or at smaller prisons such as the Kidcote on Ouse Bridge. Around a third of those committed to York's prisons for prolonged periods of time would not leave alive.

Under these circumstances, one might expect that the Catholic population of the city would decline rapidly. That was the aim of the archbishop and the earl, but did that actually happen?

The number of Catholics in York in the latter decades of the seventeenth century is hard to estimate. Some commentators say it was as little as two per cent of the population, but that is highly unlikely given the popular support within the city for both the Pilgrimage of Grace and the Northern Uprising. One method that could be used to determine how many Catholics were in York at the time is to look at recusancy levels, with the names of recusants and the fines levelled against them being recorded, initially in what were called 'pipe rolls' and from 1592 onwards 'recusancy rolls'. These records show that far from diminishing, official levels of recusancy increased under the jurisdiction of Henry Hastings, and an exhaustive study made by Father Hugh Aveling in 1960 concluded that there were approximately 1,200 adult recusants in the West Riding of Yorkshire in the 1580s.[9]

Looking solely at the official recusancy statistics, however, can be misleading on two counts. Firstly, the rise when Hastings became Lord President could have simply been because he and his men were more zealous in rooting them out, recording them, and fining them. Secondly, the majority of Catholics in York and across the country as a whole were not recusants at all.

The Pope had decreed that Catholics could not take part in Church of England services, but many took a more pragmatic approach. The fines for recusancy could destroy a family, especially after the fines were raised and then levied on a recurring basis. In later years, being a recusant also meant that you were barred from taking any legal action or seeking legal redress of any kind whatsoever. Under these circumstances, it's little wonder that many Catholics followed the path of least resistance.[10]

Across the country, and especially in traditionally Catholic areas such as Yorkshire and Lancashire, many opted to become 'Church Papists'. These were adults who attended Church of England services and yet still saw themselves as Catholics in their hearts: Guy's headmaster John Pulleyn is one example.

It is impossible to estimate how many church Catholics there were, but it is likely that they were of a considerable number; this had been the faith of their parents and grandparents, and it may have been the one that they themselves were brought up in. It could even be that some of those in positions of power associated with the Church of England were church Catholics, as again exemplified by John Pulleyn, and also by William Hunt, an Anglican churchwarden in York who was later arrested after being caught during the raid of a Catholic mass.

As anti-Catholic legislation and brutality increased during the reign of Elizabeth I, many Catholic priests and scholars fled to mainland Europe. One such man, and a pivotal figure in the Catholic struggles that led to the gunpowder plot and similar plans, was William Allen.

William Allen was born near Fleetwood, on the Lancashire coast, in 1532, and soon showed himself to be a brilliant scholar. By 1556 he was Proctor of Saint Mary's Hall college at Oxford, and in 1558 he was a canon at York Minster[11] (then a Catholic church under the reign of Queen Mary). After Elizabeth's accession, he became one of many leading Catholics to leave the country, although he occasionally returned on clandestine missions designed to convert others to Catholicism.

Allen's defining moment came on 29 September 1568, when, with the encouragement of the Vatican, he founded his English College at Douai in north eastern France. This college was formed to welcome exiled English Catholics and train them to be priests who would then return to their native land in secret and spread their teachings.

The first wave of seminary priests, as those educated at Allen's seminary in Douai were called, arrived in England in 1574, and by 1580 another influx of priests, this time hard-line Jesuit priests, began to circulate across the country as well. Recusants were emboldened, and church Catholics found a new focal point for their beliefs, as well as opportunities to attend secret Catholic masses held by priests that were simply not available in previous years.

One result of this surreptitious Catholic invasion was a further crackdown on Catholics, and a vastly increased effort to find priests and those who were hiding them. This in turn put increased pressure on ecclesiastical lawyers such as Edward Fawkes. Could this stress have led to his early grave?

One sign that Edward's death may have been sudden is that he died intestate, without a will, which is a very strange outcome for a man who worked as an advocate and a proctor overseeing oaths and wills. It would take more than a decade for Guy's inheritance to be awarded to him, but as we shall see, when it came it completely changed the course of his life. (The loss of his father wasn't the only loss that Guy endured as a young boy. His grandmother Ellen Fawkes, who lived nearby on High Petergate, died when Guy was in his infancy, leaving him an angel of gold and her best whistle[12]).

At a time when life could be so precarious, Tudor life often revolved around the extended family, and so it's likely that Guy's

Uncle Thomas would have played a greater role in his life after the death of Edward. He would have provided much needed financial assistance to the family as well. But Thomas Fawkes himself died in 1581. In his will, he left his nephew Guy a gold ring, his bed and a set of bedsheets.[13] If the latter bequest seems a little odd to us today, it should be remembered that a bed was a symbol of prestige, and leaving it to someone in a will was a sign of affection; William Shakespeare famously left his 'second best bed' to his wife Anne in his will.[14]

With the death of his father and then uncle at an impressionable age, Guy turned to his masters and fellow pupils at St. Peter's School for company. They became more than friends and companions, they became role models. Role models like Jack and Kit Wright, who in 1586 saw their Uncle Francis Ingleby publicly executed for being a seminary priest.[15] Role models who would be further angered in the same year as they saw Margaret Clitherow imprisoned and then sentenced to a particularly horrific death in York, for refusing to renounce or implicate other Catholics. It was a moment that shook York to its roots, and one that changed Guy Fawkes forever.

Chapter 5

The Pearl of York

'Tis time to die, when 'tis a shame to live
Thomas Middleton and William Rowley, *The Changeling*

Shortly after the arrest of Guy Fawkes in 1605 his questioning in the Tower of London began. For as long as he could under the physical and mental strains of torture he resisted giving answers that could implicate others in the gunpowder plot, and which would send them to the fate he knew awaited him.

With some questions he was prepared to give honest answers from the start of his interrogation, whereas with others he changed his response as instruments of torture broke down his resistance and his ability to prevaricate. One such revised answer reveals Guy's state of mind as he progressed through his teenage years in York.

Guy was brought up a Protestant by his father Edward, so what made him become not only a Catholic, which brought with it financial and bodily dangers even for those who hid their faith, but a man prepared to kill and ready to die for the cause?

On 6 November, his interrogators asked Guy a question set down by King James himself: 'If he ever was a Papist, and, if so, who brought him up in it?'[1]

While originally stating that he had been raised a Catholic, a later statement from the Earls of Nottingham, Suffolk, Northampton and Salisbury (the King's chief minister Robert Cecil) reveals: 'He confesseth he hath been a Recusant about this twenty years'.[2]

This would date Guy's conversion to 1585 or 1586, when he was 15 or 16, a time when he would have been expected to leave his carefree childhood ways behind and make his own way in the world as a man.

Just what was it that made Guy convert to Catholicism in the mid-1580s, thus turning his back on a potential career as an ecclesiastical advocate and instead opening up an uncertain and challenging future? Rejecting the Church of England was a huge step away from a society that would have welcomed him with open arms. As a Protestant who had performed creditably at his grammar school he could have been expected to graduate from Oxford or Cambridge, find a job that would supply him with a steady income, and settle into a middle-class life with a suitable wife. Guy chose another path in life, and it's not one he would have taken lightly.

As his later actions show, Guy was a stubborn man who was prepared to stand by his beliefs whatever the consequences, and so it is likely that he'd been brooding on his conversion to Catholicism for some years. He had the examples of his fellow pupils like the Wright brothers to encourage him, and that of his head master John Pulleyn. He would also have heard of the execution of Sir Thomas Percy in York's marketplace, and as a young child would have seen the Earl's rotting head on a spike. As the years progressed he would hear more and more tales of aggressions carried out against the Catholics of York, of property being confiscated, women being jailed and separated from their families, and, after repressive acts of 1581 and 1585, when being a Catholic priest or harbouring one became punishable by death, an increasing number of executions.[3]

Henry Hastings, as ever, was keen to see the new anti-Catholic legislation enacted with its full ferocity, and five Catholic priests were captured and publicly executed at York Tyburn, a place of execution on the Knavesmire, in the first year. The priests were dressed in their vestments on their way to the gallows, made to carry their own coffins, and hung from a triangular gallows known as the 'three legged mare'. Crowds gathered to jeer and spit at those who had become thought of as the enemies of the people. Others watched and prayed with heavy hearts, and a growing thirst for revenge.

The Knavesmire executions of 1582, including the double

execution of Fathers William Lacey and Richard Kirkman on 22 August, would have been well known to Guy Fawkes and all the people of York. He may even have seen some of the executions carried out – it would have been considered fitting for pupils of the city's leading school to attend them.[4]

These horrific, bloody spectacles, combined with Guy's introspection and examination of the faith he was raised in, led to a growing sense of injustice within him: how could he reconcile these acts with the word of God that he read and listened to? One event above all others secured Guy's conversion and led to his future actions, and it involved a butcher's wife who was well known to Guy and his mother Edith.

Margaret Middleton was born in York in 1556 (the exact date is unknown) to parents Thomas and Jane. Thomas Middleton was a respectable gentleman, becoming Sheriff of York eight years after Margaret's birth.[5] He was a chandler by trade, however, which meant that his business was in decline. Chandlers were candle makers, and their products were in high demand for use as devotional tools during the reign of Queen Mary and prior to the reformation, but the changing face of churches during the time of Edward VI and Elizabeth meant that ornate and well made candles were now largely surplus to requirements.

Thomas died when Margaret was 14, and her mother Jane quickly remarried out of financial necessity. Her choice of husband was Henry May, a man who had been born in the south of England but had come to York because of its heightened economic prospects, thanks to its position at the heart of the Council of the North. Henry May was a vintner, or wine seller, an occupation that had been strictly controlled and licensed by the city's guilds in recent years, but which was now welcoming people like Henry from outside the city. He was an astute businessman and proved to be socially adept as well, being selected as one of the eight Chamberlains of York in 1568, not long after taking up residence in the city.[6]

Margaret was also looking to secure a better future for herself, which is why at the age of 15 she married John Clitherow, a man much older than her and already widowed with two sons. Such marriages were perfectly acceptable at the time, with John securing a mother for his children, and Margaret obtaining security and a position within York society at a young age.

John Clitherow was a sheep farmer of some standing, who had inherited land and a large house at Cornborough, ten miles to the north east of York. His main residence, which also doubled as a butcher's shop, was on the Shambles, and it was here that Margaret Clitherow started her new life in July 1571.

The Shambles is now one of the most popular tourist attractions in the city of York, with its ancient timber framed buildings still intact and leaning over until they almost touch in the middle of the street, but it was very different in the late sixteenth century. The Shambles takes its name from an old Saxon phrase meaning 'flesh shelves', a reference to the butchers' slabs running up and down the street. It was an established tradition in York that butcher's shops could only be situated on this street. With refrigeration still centuries away at the time that the Clitherows held court, animals had to be brought to the premises, slaughtered there, butchered, displayed and then sold as quickly as possible.

It is to the Shambles then that Edith Fawkes, sometimes with her daughters or her son Guy, would have come to buy her lamb and mutton. As John Clitherow was one of the wealthiest of the street's vendors, and therefore with a reputation for excellent produce, it's likely that families who could afford meat of good quality, such as the Fawkes family, would have gravitated towards his shop at number ten.

Both Margaret and John Clitherow would certainly have been known to the people who lived in the city of York, and the young mistress of the shop proved to be adept at running it and looking after both her staff and her two step-children. The Shambles was a close-knit community, with William and Millicent Calvert (née Clitherow, John's sister) at one side of the Clitherow shop, and Michael and Ellen Mudd (a relative of John's first wife) on the other.[7] It was another neighbour, however, that was to transform Margaret's life: Dorothy Vavasour.

The gunpowder plot of 1605 is a perfect example of how interconnected life at the turn of the seventeenth century was, particularly for the Catholic community of England. Many of the plotters knew each other beforehand, as with Guy Fawkes and the Wrights, and many were related to each other by marriage (for example Robert Catesby, Robert Wintour, Thomas Wintour and John Grant were all related in this way, and the plotter Thomas Percy married Martha Wright, sister of Jack and Kit[8]). Similarly if Margaret Clitherow had not grown to know Dorothy Vavasour, would she have been spared the dread fate that awaited her, and would that have prevented the Wrights and Guy Fawkes from embarking upon new courses in their lives?

Dorothy Vavasour was the wife of a man who had become the most famous Catholic in York: Dr Thomas Vavasour. The Vavasours were a well established family in Yorkshire, and Thomas studied first at Cambridge University and then in Venice before becoming a licensed physician. He was most known for being a vociferous Catholic who had spoken out against Elizabeth and her reforms. This made him a prime target for Henry Hastings, but Dr Vavasour eluded him time and time again, sometimes having fled from York and at other times hiding within his own house.

With her husband so often away, or at least appearing to be away, Dorothy Vavasour had to make her own way in the world, and she did this by becoming an unofficial midwife for the women of York. It was commonly whispered, however, that Dorothy was herself an ardent Catholic who not only helped women prepare for childbirth but also indoctrinated them in the Catholic faith.

It's intriguing to note that the infamous Vavasours of York whose fate became entwined with Margaret Clitherow may also have been related to Guy Fawkes, with an Anthony Fawkes of York marrying Frances Vavasour of Weston in the first half of the sixteenth century. After Anthony's death in 1551, Frances married Philip Bainbridge of Wheatley Hall.[9] Their son Denis would later become stepfather to Guy Fawkes.

It was to Dorothy Vavasour that Margaret Clitherow turned to as she prepared to give birth to her first two children, a son Henry named after his godfather Henry May, and a daughter Anne. It seems inconceivable that Margaret didn't know of Dorothy's reputation, so it could be assumed that she had already begun to think of converting to Catholicism, perhaps in response to the growing persecution of the faith.

The truth of the matter was that the Vavasour house was not simply one where pregnant women could find help, rest and advice, it was a clandestine centre for Catholic mass. Dorothy, and her husband Thomas when in residence, sheltered priests there and did all they could to spread their faith while at the same time avoiding capture. It was a dangerous tightrope to walk.

In 1574 the Vavasour house was raided, not for the first time, but on this occasion Dr Thomas Vavasour gave himself up for arrest. This resulted in imprisonment for both Thomas and Dorothy, with Thomas adjudged to be too dangerous to be kept in York and transferred to Hull Castle. He had influential connections, however, and was later released, only to be imprisoned twice more before eventually dying in Hull Castle in May 1585.

Dorothy's stay in the York Castle prison was a brief one on this occasion, but the raid, arrests and imprisonment of her friend stirred Margaret Clitherow's growing beliefs in Catholicism. Shortly before her death, Margaret avowed that she had 'been within the Catholic faith twelve years'. That is, her final conversion to Catholicism, the step that Guy Fawkes took in 1586, happened in 1574, after the arrest and imprisonment of Dorothy Vavasour.

As with converts to many different faiths throughout the centuries, Margaret's faith was unshakeable and stronger than many of those who had been born into Catholicism, and she refused to attend Church of England masses from that moment onwards. It was this act that would lead to Margaret's first, but not last, arrest.

Edwin Sandys had taken over as Archbishop of York in 1575, and if anything he was even more puritanical and authoritarian than his predecessor Archbishop Grindal. Within a year of taking his seat, he and the Lord President Henry Hastings demanded that a list of all the recusants in York be put together. There were 67 names on the list, 55 of them women: among them, the butcher's wife Margaret Clitherow.[10]

At the women's trial on 2 August 1577, the husbands were ordered to pay fines and told to ensure that they attended Church of England services in the future. The husbands however, including John Clitherow, refused to pay the fines levied by the court, and while they were taken to be imprisoned in the Kidcote on Ouse Bridge, the women were jailed in the city's main prison, York Castle.

While it's true that some prisoners died in York Castle throughout its use as a jail, conditions for the inmates were far less harsh than you might imagine. Inside the castle walls were a collection of dilapidated old buildings, and it is in these that the women were imprisoned, rather than in any kind of cell or dungeon.[11] The guards could easily be bribed, and as Catholic priests were also frequently interned there, Catholic prisoners could celebrate mass with more freedom and regularity than they could outside the castle's walls.[12]

John Clitherow was released from the Kidcote after three days, but his wife Margaret remained inside York Castle until February 1578 when she was released on bail. Her bail conditions stipulated that she could only leave the house to attend church, but as Margaret refused to enter a Church of England service she remained a prisoner in her own home. Even so, it meant that she was reunited with her young family, and could once more oversee the running of the family business.

If York's authorities, under constant pressure from Hastings and Sandys, thought this long incarceration would make Margaret Clitherow and others see the error of their ways, they were to be disappointed. If anything, it only served to make Margaret more devout and more rebellious, and the influx of Catholic priests into Yorkshire in the 1580s further fuelled their faith.

At some time in the 1570s, Margaret arranged for a secret room to be built on her Shambles premises above the normal living quarters. The carefully concealed entrance opened into a room containing an altar, books and everything needed for a Catholic mass. The room extended above a neighbour's house too, but by then Margaret had converted both Millicent and Ellen Calvert to Catholicism too.

In the following years, priests would hold regular Catholic masses above the butcher's shop on the Shambles. How did Margaret get away with this for so long, and how was the room kept secret, from customers of the shop like the Fawkes family, and possibly even from her own husband John?

John Clitherow was often away on business, or overseeing his farming operations near Cornborough, while others must have simply turned a blind eye to activities in the Shambles, but with agents of Hastings across the city, Margaret was treading a dangerous path.

In their efforts to clamp down on Catholicism in York, Hastings and Archbishop Sandys had adopted a two-pronged approach – people caught harbouring offenders or concealing what they knew could be punished, while rewards were offered to people who helped them catch Catholic priests and those supporting them.

There were plenty of warning signs for Margaret Clitherow to consider, if she chose to: Anne Foster who died in the Ouse Bridge jail, and whose body was then dumped on the bridge because she had refused a Protestant burial;[13] Robert Cripling, who was the city's Lord Mayor in 1579, but that didn't stop Hastings jailing him for not collecting enough fines from recusants;[14] William Hutton, the Protestant church warden, who was jailed with his pregnant wife Mary in April 1581, after being caught attending a Catholic mass at the Vavasour house.[15]

Rather than being deterred, the 1581 arrest of Dorothy Vavasour spurred Margaret on to open a second mass centre in York in addition to the one that already existed above her home and that of her neighbour. Oral tradition in York states that the new mass centre was at the Black Swan Inn at Peasholme Greene just outside the city centre; a strange choice as a place to harbour priests, as it was also frequently used as lodgings by agents of Queen Elizabeth.[16]

While these activities went undetected initially, her refusal to attend church could not be explained away, and on 8 March 1583 she was once more arrested. Margaret remained inside York Castle until May

1584, when her husband John was asked to post a bond of one hundred pounds. John was not the only family member who was being put under strain by Margaret's arrest and reputation, as her stepfather Henry May was rising through the ranks of York society. His concern that she would bring discredit or disgrace to his name, and derail his political career, would have dreadful consequences.

After her release from prison in 1584, Margaret took her subversive activities still further by opening a secret school in her home where local children could be taught the Catholic faith rather than having to be sent to France, as she had by then done for her own son Henry who was at the English college in Rheims (which had temporarily replaced the Douai college).

This greatly increased the risk that Margaret was taking, as it meant not only relying on her servants and neighbours to keep quiet, but also the pupils. Things came to a head on 9 March 1586. Margaret's mother Jane had died a year previously, leaving Henry May free to remarry, but it also removed any impediment to him taking action against his step-daughter. Henry was made Lord Mayor of York in January 1586, and one of his primary concerns was how to prevent Margaret from blackening his reputation. Whether he meant to simply frighten Margaret Clitherow into submission or to remove her threat completely we can't be sure, but it was Henry himself who ordered the March raid on Margaret's house.[17] The priests and the teacher Henry Stapleton escaped through a secret exit, but under pressure from the officials one of the children revealed the entrance to the hidden mass centre.

Margaret's arrest was the talk of York; surely even her husband's money couldn't save her this time?

Margaret was quickly brought to the court, before judges John Clench and Francis Rhodes, who asked her, 'how will you be tried?', to which the prisoner replied, 'I will be tried by none but God and your own consciences.'

Clench and Rhodes blanched at this answer; learned in the law they knew the implication of it much more than Margaret did. If she had pleaded guilty she would have faced a quick and simple execution, and there was always a remote possibility that clemency could be offered. But by refusing to enter a plea, Margaret would automatically be judged guilty, and sentenced to the worst death possible: 'peine forte et dure', death by being slowly crushed to death.

Clench especially seemed reluctant to pass this sentence on her and he sent her back to her prison cell, encouraging her to make a plea on the next day. The next day however found Margaret equally stubborn. After arguments in court, Margaret said, 'I think you have no witnesses against me but children, which with an apple and a rod you may make to say what you will.'

It was at this point that Judge Rhodes spoke out: 'Why stand we all this day about this naughty, wilful woman? Let us despatch her.' The terrible sentence of *peine forte et dure* was pronounced, to which Margaret responded, 'I thank God heartily for this.' On her way back to her cell, this time the New Counter prison hanging over the River Ouse, it is said that Margaret handed out money to crowds who had gathered.

Even now, many in authority were reluctant to pass the sentence, possibly through sympathy for the woman who was to die, maybe because of feelings of guilt, or possibly because they were afraid of her becoming a figurehead for the oppressed. It was for this reason that Margaret was questioned as to whether she was pregnant; if she was found to be with child the sentence would be delayed, and in time it may even have been rescinded. The examining midwives pronounced that they did believe Margaret to be pregnant, but Margaret herself said that she was unsure whether she was or wasn't, and the hope of clemency passed away.

The full sentence stated that the punishment would be as follows: 'You must return from whence you came, and there, in the lowest part of the prison, be stripped naked, laid down, your back upon the ground, and as much weight laid upon you as you are able to bear, and so continue three days without meat or drink, except a little barley bread and puddle water, and the third day to be pressed to death, your hands and feet tied to posts, and a sharp stone under your back'.[18]

Despite the wording, it was made clear to Margaret that only the

THE REAL GUY FAWKES

final part of the sentence would be carried out, and that she would not have to spend three days under stones. Nevertheless, the days leading up to the execution must have been ones of dreadful torment and anguish, even to one as sure in her faith as Margaret Clitherow. She spent the time creating a simple gown that she hoped to be allowed to wear, and onto the sleeves of which she helpfully sewed lengths of tape that they could use to tie her to posts.

The day of execution was Friday, 26 March 1586: the Feast of the Annunciation, or Lady Day, a feast day for Catholics who celebrated the Archangel Gabriel's visit to Mary, and in the Tudor calendar the official start of the new year. Margaret had a short distance to walk from her jail to the tollbooth at the end of the bridge, where she was to be killed, but the gathered crowd was so large that her guards had to push their way through it. En route, once again Margaret handed out money to those she passed.

There would have been no school on that day, so we can easily imagine that the headmaster of St. Peter's School John Pulleyn would have been among the onlookers. So too would have been Jack and Kit Wright, and with them their friend Guy Fawkes, silent, stern faced, angry, vengeful. This was the moment that twenty years later Guy Fawkes, then undergoing his own tortures, would tell his interrogators made him become a Catholic.

Once in the tollbooth, Margaret was ordered to strip naked, but she was then allowed to don her hand-sewn garment before being placed upon the sharp stone. A door was then lain on top of Margaret, ready for heavy stones to be loaded on top of it. The guards themselves could not bring themselves to carry out the task, and four beggars had to be paid and brought in to do it. One of the watching sheriffs, William Gibson, collapsed to his knees by the door in tears.[19]

Margaret's last anguished cry was, 'Jesu! Jesu! Jesu! Have mercy on me!' It took around fifteen minutes for her to die: fifteen minutes of agony, under eight hundred pounds of stone that somehow had to be borne, with a sharp stone digging into her back, all under the gaze of guards and vagrants.

What were the motivations behind Margaret's cruel execution? Did

Henry May hope that she would be given a minor sentence that would make her turn away from her brazen and unlawful activities. Did he hope to grab the property that she had inherited upon her mother's death?[20] We can be certain that the authorities, and in particular Henry Hastings, wanted her death to act as a deterrent to others who were actively Catholic or thinking of converting, but in this he was to be greatly disappointed.

Margaret Clitherow's death, and especially the manner of it, created outrage among the populace of York and beyond, even among those who had little personal sympathy for the Catholic cause. Queen Elizabeth herself condemned the action, and wrote to the citizens of York to say that she was horrified at the treatment of a fellow woman.

The stones remained on top of Margaret for six hours, and then, with the crowds dispersed, the body was taken away in a cart and hidden underneath a rubbish heap, lest Margaret in death should become even more of an inspiration to Catholics than she had been when she was alive. Under cover of darkness, a group of Margaret's friends, led by one of the priests she had often hidden away, Father Mush, began the search for her body. Eventually it was found and taken to be buried in a location that remains secret to this day.

One tangible reminder of Margaret Clitherow still remains, and I had the honour of seeing it in person while researching this book. Not far from York railway station is the Bar Convent. It is now not only a working convent, but an exhibition centre and a museum of the Catholic persecutions of the sixteenth century, as the convent itself was set up in secret in 1686 – a hundred years after Margaret's death. There, in the chapel, housed in a small and beautiful reliquary, is the preserved hand of Margaret Clitherow.

The convent was originally founded, at great danger to herself, by Frances Bedingfield. She was a follower of an order founded by Margaret Ward, niece of Jack and Kit Wright, Guy's school friends and later Guy's fellow conspirators. Margaret's story still resounds: in 1970 the woman who became known as 'the Pearl of York' was canonised by Pope Paul VI as Saint Margaret Clitherow, one of the forty martyrs of England and Wales. Her shrine stands today as a haven of peace amidst the tourist hurly burly of York's Shambles.

She had a more immediate impact upon one man, Guy Fawkes, who had watched with growing anger throughout his formative years as he saw Catholics bankrupted, imprisoned, tortured and executed. The stones that broke Margaret's back were the straw that broke the camel's back for Guy: this was the moment when he would turn against his father's example and the faith he was raised in, and take a new path as a Catholic, and one who was prepared to fight for his new beliefs. Guy had now become a man, and he would be driven by an increasing sense of fury and injustice. It would drive him on beyond hope and despair, beyond morality, and beyond the narrow streets and confines of York.

Chapter 6

A Picturesque Scene

I loved her whom all the world admired,
I was refused of her that can love none;
And my vain hope, which far too high aspired,
Is dead, and buried, and for ever gone
Robert Devereux, **Earl of Essex**, *To Plead My Faith*

The year 1586 had been a momentous one for the city of York in general, and for Guy Fawkes in particular. The horrific execution of Margaret Clitherow had galvanised the youthful Guy into taking a step that would change the whole course of his life. Scholarly pursuits were no longer of interest to him, thoughts of following the family traditions in the ecclesiastical courts were abandoned, there was only one thing that mattered to him now: his new faith of Catholicism, and with it a fight against the injustices that he saw being levied against it and its adherents.

For now the change would be an internal one, one that by necessity he would keep to himself, except perhaps for sharing it with fellow travellers, fellow converts like his schoolmates the Wright brothers. It can easily be imagined, however, that in common with many converts to a new faith, Guy became increasingly pious. In later life he was known for his quiet piety and steadfastness,[1] and this may have become apparent to his family and friends from this time on.

The child who had laughingly joined in the games of his playmates, the boy who was keen on books and learning, became a sober and thoughtful young man. This was not the only change happening to Guy as he left his youth behind and entered adulthood, as a family upheaval was taking place that would also have a huge impact on his life to come.

Married life was the way of things for most people in the late sixteenth century, as much for its social and economic benefits as for anything resembling our modern notions of love. For that reason most widows, of both sexes, would rapidly remarry after the death of their wife or husband. Some of her contemporaries may have thought it strange, therefore, that Edith Fawkes did not immediately seek to find a new husband after the death of Edward. His death would have had a great financial impact upon Edith and her children, but her fidelity to her late husband seems to indicate that she had a great affection for her spouse, something which was not always to be expected at the time.

By around 1587 however, nine years after Edward's death, Edith Fawkes had found a man who would become her second husband, and a stepfather to Guy, Anne and Elizabeth. The man was Denis Bainbridge, also referred to in documents of the time as Dionis Baynbrigge.

Little is known about Denis Bainbridge except that he was a 'gentleman' with some independent wealth, and so it may be that he was a farmer. It may also be that his wealth had come from an inheritance, or a series of inheritances, as he had a reputation for being unreliable and profligate with his money.[2]

Bainbridge lived in the rural village of Scotton near Knaresborough, around twenty miles to the north west of York, so how did he and Edith Fawkes meet? It seems likely that there was a familial connection between the two, but as often in these times the lines are tangled and confused because of the prevalence of remarriages and a lack of clear documentation of some births, weddings and baptisms.

We know with certainty that Denis had connections with the Pulleyn and Vavasour families, and that these families also had links with the Fawkes extended family (it should be noted, however, that the Pulleyn family of Scotton were not related to John Pulleyn, Guy's headmaster at St. Peter's School). Denis was the son of Philip

Bainbridge and Frances Vavasour of Weston, who had previously been married to Anthony Fawkes. Like Edith, Denis was a widow, having been married for three years to a Joanne Hopperton. After the death of Denis's father his mother Frances married for a third time, this time to Walter Pulleyn of Scotton.[3]

Denis's first wife was buried in April 1587, and we know that he had married Edith Fawkes by February 1588 as Edith is named as his wife in a deed granting rental of a property to his mother Frances for the sum of two pounds per year.[4]

In late 1587, or possibly early 1588, Guy Fawkes left York behind, and went to live with his mother, sister and new stepfather, initially at the Pulleyn house in Little Trimble, and then in a much larger property they acquired in Scotton. This was to be a pivotal moment in Guy's life, for while his father had been a lawyer acting in the cause of Protestantism, his new stepfather was a well-known Catholic recusant. Indeed, Scotton as a whole was a hotbed of Catholic recusancy, being home to leading Catholic families including the Pulleyns and the Percys.

Scotton was not a parish in its own right, but served as a sub-parish of nearby Farnham, and yet it had a centuries-old chapel that was dedicated to the Virgin Mary. The old faith remained strong in the area, not least in its two largest and most celebrated houses. The first of these, the Old Manor House, was later rechristened Guy Fawkes House, and is now commonly known as Percy House.

It was a traditional home of the Percy family in Scotton, but was bought by Denis Bainbridge for his new family in 1588, along with the extensive lands that came with it and which were spread around Scotton. Visitors to the Percy House today will see a building that dates mostly from the nineteenth and twentieth centuries, but inside and preserved from the many restorations it has endured are the timber-clad remains of the original sixteenth century manor house. One feature of particular interest is a sixteenth century plaster ceiling upon which can still be seen four shields: three of the Percy family and one of the Fawkes family of Farnley.

Denis Bainbridge added the Fawkes shield to the ceiling as a tribute to his wife and the family she had originally married into, showing that once again Edith's marriage may have been one of love rather than one of mere convenience. The presence of the Percy shields also show how proud the Scotton Percys were of their heritage. They were a distant branch of the Percy family that ruled as the Earls of Northumberland, and therefore distant relatives of Sir Thomas Percy who had been publicly executed in York in 1572 for his role in the Northern Rebellion.

It's also possible, perhaps even likely, that the Percy family of Scotton were related to another Thomas Percy who would play a key role in Guy's future: Thomas Percy the gunpowder conspirator. We will look at this Thomas Percy in greater detail later, for he is perhaps one of the most complex and controversial of the conspirators but his origins are shrouded in mystery. We know that he was a distant relation of the Earl of Northumberland, and that the patronage of the Earl helped him gain increasingly senior positions. It is often conjectured that he was the son of Edward Percy and Elizabeth Waterton of Beverley, making him a second cousin of the Earl of Northumberland. While this may be true, there are no hard records to support it, and he may alternatively have been a member of the Scotton branch of the Percy line. Certainly Thomas Percy knew the Wrights, and married their sister Martha, and his place in the conspiracy with Jack and Kit Wright and with Guy Fawkes may be at least partly because they all knew each other from York. Whether Percy hailed from Scotton or perhaps visited Scotton to see relatives, this could explain a close bond between Guy and Thomas Percy, with Guy later adopting the persona of John Johnson, servant to Thomas Percy.[5]

As one of the leading gentlemen of Scotton, and owner and resident of the Old Manor House, Denis Bainbridge would have been a frequent visitor to Scotton Old Hall, and his stepson Guy would often have accompanied him. While outwardly respectable, Scotton Hall had a secret life, one that would certainly appeal to Guy.

Scotton Old Hall was a traditional seat of the Pulleyn family of Scotton, who had family members scattered around the village. Head of the family at the time was Walter Pulleyn, the Steward of Fountains

Abbey and stepfather of Denis and step-grandfather of Guy, and like both Denis and Guy he was an avowed Catholic.

As the sixteenth century drew towards its conclusion, the dangers for Catholics, and especially for their clergy, were increasing, and one event in particular led to increased pressure being put upon them. In the summer of 1588 a large fleet sailed from Cordoba in Spain, on the orders of King Philip II. Its aim was to call at Flanders, then part of the Spanish Netherlands, and transport a large army across the channel to England. Once in England, the army would overthrow Queen Elizabeth and impose a Catholic ruler.

Thanks to a combination of poor planning, slow reactions, and bad weather, the Spanish Armada was defeated, but Queen Elizabeth was all too aware of the danger that had been averted, and she laid the blame at the feet of Catholic agitators. She wasn't wrong in this view, as exiled priests such as Cardinal William Allen had been exhorting King Philip to take such a course, and in later years other exiles, including Guy Fawkes himself, would urge the Spanish king to launch a new invasion.[6]

The failure of the Armada spurred Elizabeth on in her efforts to find and punish Catholic priests, and they had to take increasingly drastic action to avoid their hunters. Nevertheless some Catholics were prepared to risk all to harbour their clergy, and Scotton Hall was one of the places that was used as a shelter.[7]

Denis Bainbridge today is chiefly remembered for a comment from Father Robert Collinge that he was 'an unthrifty husband',[8] but without doubt he had an influence on his stepson. Guy had been without a father through his formative childhood years, with his only male companions being school friends such as Jack and Kit Wright, so he must have looked up to Denis Bainbridge with something approaching adulation. While Denis may not have been a role model in terms of his financial management, he was an inspiration in another aspect: his faith and courage.

Bainbridge not only knew what was happening at Scotton Old Hall, visiting priests and attending mass there, it is likely that he was also involved in the harbouring of priests. It is said that a tunnel was created

47

that ran from Scotton Hall to what is now Percy House, then the residence of Denis Bainbridge and his step-family. It could have been used to attend Catholic masses surreptitiously and, as he was now an avowed Catholic himself, there is little doubt that Guy Fawkes would have attended mass with him.

The tunnel also served another purpose: it could be used to transport priests from one building to the other if a search party sent by Hastings was in the area. Given Guy's militancy in the Catholic cause in the succeeding years, it seems more than plausible that he would have been one of the people helping to hide priests. This tunnel is not in evidence today, but in recent years local archaeologists believe they have found evidence of the line that this tunnel took.[9]

It seems that Denis also succeeded in converting his wife Edith to the Catholic cause, although she may have always harboured Catholic sympathies but suppressed them to protect her first husband Edward's position as an ecclesiastical lawyer. A list was made in 1604 of the known Catholics, i.e. the recusants, in Yorkshire – a list that features both Denis Bainbridge and his wife.[10] They are listed as 'Dynys Baynbrig gent. his wife: noncommunicants.'

The life that Denis, Guy and others had embarked upon became increasingly dangerous from 1591 onwards, when the first wave of Jesuit priests had arrived in England. First among them were the Jesuit Fathers Richard Holtby and Robert Curry,[11] and others soon followed. These Jesuits were often more radical than the seminary priests that had preceded them, by which we mean the priests who had been taught at seminaries such as Douai, and wanted nothing less than the overthrow of the Protestant system and the restoration of Catholicism. Often landing in darkness upon the long Yorkshire coastline, they would disperse across the county, finding refuge at places like Scotton Hall.

The Jesuits were seen as a greater threat even than the seminary priests had been, and punishments for the priests and those who facilitated their missions were cruel and swift. A Jesuit priest unfortunate enough to be caught, and those found to be sheltering him, could expect only one fate: to be condemned as a traitor and then hung, drawn and quartered.

While the years spent at Scotton were dangerous for Guy, something he would soon become accustomed to, they also brought love, or at least marriage to his family, with Guy's sisters both marrying local men. Elizabeth Fawkes married Will Dickenson in July 1594 and Anne Fawkes wed Henry Kelburn in October 1599.[12]

Guy himself had long left Scotton behind by the time these happy events occurred, but it is rumoured that Guy may have had a marriage of his own during his time in Scotton. There is only one piece of evidence for this: a record which says that Guy married a Maria Pulleyn in 1590 and that they had a son called Thomas a year later. This is contained on a genealogical record on the International Genealogy Index of the Church of Jesus Christ of Latter Day Saints, but unfortunately there is no information given on the source used for this claim.[13]

There are no church records of any marriage for Guy, as there are for his sisters Elizabeth and Anne, but this in itself isn't evidence that it didn't occur. Many Catholics who felt deeply about their faith refused to get married in Church of England ceremonies, or to have their children baptised by the church. It is for this reason that the baptismal records of the parish of Farnham at this time, which as we know incorporated Scotton within its boundary, contain no baptism records of any children in the Percy or Pulleyn families.

Weddings between Catholics were often conducted in secret in concealed rooms or passageways, in copses, or in open fields by the light of the moon. The list of Catholics in Yorkshire in 1604 contains a number of reports of such ceremonies. One such entry, pertaining to the village of Bransby in the North Riding of Yorkshire, reads:

> Secret marriage: Richard Cholmley esquire married with Mary Hungate in the presence of John Wilson, William Martin, Hugh Hope, and Christopher Danyell in a fell with a popish priest.[14]

A nineteenth century editor and transcriber of the 1604 list, Edward Peacock, has added the following note to this entry:

Here is the record of a picturesque scene. The lady and her lover dare not marry in her father's house for fear of spies, so an appointment is made to meet at some secluded nook on the wild moorlands; a priest is ready at the risk of his life to perform the rite, and the wedding party returns home without discovery. Such incidents must have been very frequent during the darker periods of the English persecution.[15]

The marriage of Richard Cholmley and Mary Hungate was not recognised by the authorities of the land, but these authorities in turn were not recognised by people like Richard Cholmley and Mary Hungate, or by people like Guy Fawkes. Their marriage was sanctified by a Catholic priest, deemed legitimate by the Catholic church, and witnessed as such by their friends, and that was all that mattered to those taking part in the ceremony.

This is why we cannot expect to find any formal recognition of a marriage between Guy Fawkes and Maria Pulleyn, and while it is impossible to prove that it did take place, the absence of an official record is certainly no indication that it didn't. Guy would have been around 19 or 20 at the time his marriage is alleged to have taken place, which would have been a perfectly acceptable age to marry in the late sixteenth century. Young men's minds then, as now, often turned to thoughts of love as the flush of youth began to mellow into manhood, and if he had fallen in love with the daughter of a neighbour, with one of the Pulleyns, then marriage would have been a natural step.

From the Pulleyn point of view, the marriage of a daughter of theirs, Maria, to a stepson of Denis Bainbridge would also have made sense. Denis today has the reputation of being frivolous with his money, but we don't know how accurate that description is. He must have been a man of some means, as his acquisition of the Percy family property in 1588 shows, and through his mother's marriage he himself had family connections to the Pulleyns. Guy was an educated man and above all an ardent Catholic, and these qualities would have made him a suitable choice for a Pulleyn daughter.

A PICTURESQUE SCENE

If Guy did marry Maria, and if they did have a son Thomas, why was Guy not with them later in his life, and why are Maria and Thomas not mentioned in any family wills? With childbirth such a dangerous event in this era, it is likely that both Maria and Thomas died during childbirth, or shortly afterwards.

Early death was something that people in the late sixteenth century had to face with much more regularity than we do today. We shouldn't think, however, that it had any less impact on those close to the deceased. Guy's grief at the loss of a young wife and child would have stayed with him throughout his life, and it could be this that led to his decision to start a new life on his own terms. Guy Fawkes was about to come into his inheritance, after which he would leave Scotton and Yorkshire far behind.

Chapter 7

By Fire and Water, Thy Line
Shall Come to an End

Now I'll tell you without asking. My master is the great rich
Capulet, and if you be not of the house of Montagues,
I pray come and crush a cup of wine
William Shakespeare, *Romeo and Juliet*

'By fire and water, thy line shall come to an end and it shall perish out
of this land!'[1]

A silence descended on those present as the friar uttered his curse,
arm outstretched, before turning on his heels and walking out of the
abbey forever. The man receiving the curse must have been shaken at
first – these were times when superstition and science existed side by
side – but after a momentary pause a smile returned to his face,
followed by an uneasy laugh from the company at large. He was Sir
Anthony Browne, one of the winners in the rapidly changing world of
Tudor politics, so what harm could an oath do him?

The English reformation had greatly enriched King Henry VIII,
especially after the dissolution of the monasteries in 1536, and these
rewards also fell upon nobles who were fortunate enough to have
abbeys and monasteries on their land. One such man was Sir William
Fitzwilliam, the Earl of Southampton.

Sir William had proved himself one of King Henry VIII's most
loyal courtiers and most reliable generals, helping to put down the
Pilgrimage of Grace, and playing a central role in the removal of
Queens Anne Boleyn and Catherine Howard. He was richly rewarded
for his service. In 1529 Sir William acquired land and property from

Sir Henry Owen, a distant relative of King Henry himself.[2] The star of the estate was the newly built Cowdray House, which had been created on the site of an earlier property, Coudreye,[3] a Norman word referring to the nearby woods of hazel trees.

When the monasteries were dissolved Fitzwilliam was awarded the nearby Easebourn Abbey.

By 1542 Sir William was dead, and with no heirs his estate passed to his half-brother Sir Anthony Browne. Sir Anthony was also a loyal servant to King Henry, and even though it was believed that he was not a supporter of the reformation he was given increasingly senior positions by the King. In 1538 he was awarded Battle Abbey, and one of his first acts was to pull down the Abbey church before converting the Abbey into a stately home for himself. It is this action that led to the famous Cowdray curse being levelled at the man who would become lord of Cowdray House four years later.

Sir Anthony died in 1548, and was succeeded by his son, another Sir Anthony, who was made the first Viscount Montague after the marriage of Queen Mary to King Philip of Spain in September 1554.[4] The new Viscount already had a stately home worthy of his title, for Cowdray House was a huge and magnificent building. It was, in fact, a building fit for royalty and was often graced with visits by kings and queens.[5]

Cowdray House is situated near Midhurst in West Sussex, and it still draws tourists today to gaze upon it with a mixture of awe and sadness. Cowdray House is not what it once was, not a large and lively hub, a courtly centre of Sussex culture and life; it is a ruin of a building, but a wonderful ruin.

In 1778, restoration was being undertaken on Cowdray House in preparation for the marriage of the 8th Viscount Montague, but a workman left a candle unextinguished at night. By the morning, much of the building was destroyed, including the north wing that had housed a horde of priceless paintings by Renaissance masters, as well as artefacts and relics from Battle Abbey. Within two weeks the 8th Viscount had died, drowned on the Rhine Falls, and the line and title of Viscount Montague came to an end. Whether by accident or design, the curse had been fulfilled.

There was little sign of the curse's efficacy during the time of Sir Anthony Browne, the first Viscount. The fact that Sir Anthony was so honoured by Queen Mary gives a clue to his character and beliefs, and they differed greatly from those of his father and half-uncle who had preceded him at Cowdray. From the man who had put down the Pilgrimage of Grace, Cowdray House had now passed into the hands of a man who was an ardent Catholic, and one who would surround himself with Catholic gentlemen and retainers – one of whom was Guy Fawkes.

In April 1591, Guy had turned 21 years of age, and had formally inherited his father's lands, even though he had died intestate thirteen years earlier. This represented a considerable elevation in the world for Guy, and an end to any immediate money worries, but it also brought with it questions and choices – just what was Guy going to do with his life? As a recusant he would be unable to enter the law, and so a career working his new lands as a farmer was a possibility, but there was a problem there too.

The anti-Catholic legislations of 1581 and 1585 stated that recusants like Guy now had to pay twenty pounds a month in fines, a vast sum of money. Those unwilling or unable to pay could have all their private property confiscated along with two thirds of their lands.[6] Guy must have realised that while he was now a landowner, unless he acted swiftly it would soon be snatched away from him.

Guy's course of action was one that many landowning recusants before him had chosen – he leased his land so that it could not be confiscated. The man who rented Guy's lands was a tailor from York called Christopher Lumley, and the lease between them was concluded in October 1591, and witnessed by Denis Bainbridge, George Hobson, John Jackson and Christopher Hodgson.[7] We can assume that Lumley must have been an acquaintance of Guy or his stepfather, or both, and with the lease he was given control of lands in York and Clifton.

Guy still had some lands left, and he spent the following months deciding what to do with them, and what to do with his life. In August 1592 we come across Christopher Lumley again, and this time he is witnessing a document in which Guy sells all of his remaining lands to a York spinster named Anna Skipsey for the sum of twenty-nine pounds thirteen shillings and four pence.[8] Comparing monetary values of the late sixteenth century with those of today is a difficult task; money went much further in those pre-consumerist days, but taking the bare inflationary rises this equates to a base figure of £7,377 in 2015 terms. Perhaps a more realistic way to measure modern worth would be to also take into consideration the income index of per-capita GDP in the intervening years, and this gives an equivalent value of £264,700.[9]

As Guy's father Edward had died intestate his wife Edith also had a claim to this land, but she and her husband Denis had signed away their right to it in what was called a quit deed.[10] This shows their affection for Guy: they were giving up their legal claim to a considerable sum, and it also demonstrates that they must have known of his decision to leave Yorkshire.

The selling of his estate severed all Guy's economic ties with the county of his birth, and it was also a sign that he had decided to start a new life, perhaps inspired by a recent traumatic event such as the death of a wife and child. Opportunities for a recusant like Guy would have been severely limited when compared to those of a Protestant with a similar social background, but he found employment and a home over 250 miles to the south of Scotton: in Cowdray House.

By 1572, Guy Fawkes had found service as a footman for Anthony Browne, Lord Montague, and his wife Magdalen. A job as a waiter upon tables was not below a lower middle-class man like Guy. It offered the possibility of rising through the household to a position of some power within the estate, for those who were interested in such advancement. But Guy had a different reason for working at Cowdray House.

There were many manors and stately homes across England at this time, so it seems reasonable to ask why Guy chose one almost as far from his Yorkshire roots as it was possible to get, when there were countless others that were much closer? The second Marquis, also called Anthony Browne, later claimed that Guy was given the job by a cousin of his called Spencer, who was Steward of Cowdray House.[11]

The steward was the most senior position within the household, so his recommendations would certainly have carried weight, but there is no direct record of a steward called Spencer at Cowdray House or of the Fawkes family having any connections to a family called Spencer. As many of the records of this time are now lost, and given that family ties could be so complex, this in itself doesn't prove that it wasn't the case, but there was another reason that Guy would be attracted to Cowdray – it was a well-known centre of Catholicism.

While ordinary Catholics had to be very careful about how they practised their religion in the late sixteenth century, much of the Catholic nobility was more upfront. There were stately houses across the country known for their Catholic sympathies – houses belonging to families like the Vaux family, the Throckmortons, the Dacres. While the Catholicism of these families was well known, as long as it was practised surreptitiously, and as long as the individuals concerned showed loyalty to Queen Elizabeth, then their activities were often turned a blind eye to. If, on the other hand, they became too militant in their Catholicism, or their activities threatened the state in any way, then the penalties would be severe and frequently deadly.

We have already seen a prime example of this in the case of the Earl of Essex, Robert Devereux. While possibly not a Catholic himself, it was known that he had Catholic sympathies and employed people of that religion. He rose to great power within Elizabeth's court, becoming the rival to Sir Robert Cecil as the true power behind the throne. It was a dangerous game, for while Essex had breeding, charm and good looks on his side, Cecil had the guile and intellect to crush him as he did so many others. By 1601 Essex, urged on by many leading Catholics, had decided to take control of the court and remove Cecil – it was even thought that he planned to make himself king. The rebellion failed and Essex lost his head, as did many of his co-conspirators.[12] Some on the fringes of the rebellion were imprisoned and then fined but had their lives spared; men like Robert Catesby, who lived to fight another day.[13]

The first Viscount Montague would have been all too aware of how precarious life could be for someone like him under the rule of Queen

Elizabeth, especially as he had risen to eminence under her predecessor and half-sister Queen Mary. As a sign of this favour, Mary had chosen Montague to act as her envoy and visit Pope Julius III in Rome in 1555 to begin negotiations aimed at returning the Church of England to Catholicism.[14]

Unfortunately for Montague, although it was a relief to the Protestant population, Queen Mary's reign was short,[15] and after her death Queen Elizabeth quickly dismantled her religious reforms and reversed the party being persecuted. Montague, who had become closely associated with Queen Mary, must have feared the worst, but more than most Catholic courtiers he displayed the ability to survive the dangerous balancing act that was Tudor politics.

While nobody, least of all Elizabeth, doubted his Catholicism, he did attend Protestant services on occasion and took every opportunity to display his fidelity to the Queen, to show that this loyalty to his monarch came before his loyalty to his faith. This was famously demonstrated in 1588 as the Spanish Armada neared. While many Catholics were quietly ready to support an invasion, the 60-year-old Viscount Montague raised troops and pledged to fight for Queen Elizabeth.[16]

Montague was passing the loyalty test, but the Queen was to challenge it again when she paid a personal visit to Cowdray House during her progression of 1591, just months before Guy Fawkes entered service there. Elizabeth made a number of such 'progressions' during her long reign; they were journeys across England that would allow her to meet her subjects, thus fuelling the hero worship, the cult of Gloriana, that was growing around her.

During these travels she would make extended stays at the homes of chosen courtiers and nobles. The Queen stayed at Cowdray House from 14 to 21 August 1591, a week that must have been telling on the Viscount. Not only because it would have involved vast expense on his part, thanks to the great feasts and revels that were organised in Elizabeth's honour,[17] but also because there was little doubt that she and her retinue would also have been looking for signs of Catholicism being practised within the house.

Montague and his staff would have been all too aware of what had happened thirteen years previously, when Queen Elizabeth had alighted at Euston Hall in Suffolk, home to the Rookwood family, during her 1578 progress. One of the Queen's retainers went to look for an item of plate that was missing, and while doing so found a hidden image of the Virgin Mary. This was brought into the presence of the Queen and 'treated with the greatest possible indignities'.[18] It was evidence that Euston Hall was being used for Catholic worship, and Edward Rookwood was arrested and imprisoned. He was incarcerated for ten years, and his family was almost bankrupted. This vindictive and humiliating act would not be forgotten by his young cousin Ambrose Rookwood, who would later be stirred into action[19].

Edward Rookwood had been used as an example, so that Montague and other Catholic members of the gentry and nobility knew that their freedom was always hanging by a slender thread. Montague had a lot to be worried about, for there were few homes in the whole of England that were more overtly Catholic than Cowdray House.

When Guy Fawkes arrived into service in the house in 1592, he would have found himself amidst a large and almost exclusively Catholic workforce. Montague's wife Magdalen was the driving force behind this, and she had a grand yet secret chapel built within Cowdray House that witnessed masses being held on at least a weekly basis. One contemporary, the chaplain Smith, recalled,

> Such was the number of Catholics resident in the house, and the multitude of note of such as repaired thither, that even the heretics, to the eternal glory of the name of Lady Magdalen, gave it the title of Little Rome.[20]

It is likely that Cowdray House was also home to many priests, all of whom would have faced certain death if captured. The celebrated Jesuit priest, and poet, Father Robert Southwell, used it as his regular base during the 1590s, and so it is possible that he, in the company of other priests, was secreted in the house throughout the visit of Queen Elizabeth. The house had at least one priest hole – an area in which priests could survive undetected for days at a time if necessary – and probably several had been created on the orders of Lady Magdalen.

Guy's time at Cowdray House would have given him a hitherto undreamed of freedom to practise his Catholic faith, and to attend mass in the company of some of the leading priests of the day, and yet his stay at Cowdray had a sudden interruption.

For some reason unknown, the first Viscount Montague was unhappy at Guy's conduct and sacked him after only four months of service. And there was another twist: the Viscount died just a few months later. The title passed to his grandson, an 18-year-old who also bore the name Anthony Browne, and who promptly hired Guy again.

After the arrest and interrogation of Guy Fawkes in 1605, any person known to have a connection to him soon found themselves arrested and questioned, and this is what happened to the second Viscount Montague. It was in anticipation of such questioning that the Viscount wrote to the Earl of Dorset,

> Yesternight, as I was going to bed, one of my folks told me, that he heard in the house that the miserable fellow, that should have been the bloody executioner of this woeful tragedy, was called Guy Faux; surely, if so were his name, he should seem to have been my servant once (though sorry I am to think it), for such a one I had for some four months, about the time of my marriage, but was dismissed from me by my lord upon some dislike he had of him; Some six months after my lord's death, at what time he coming to one Spencer, that was, as it were, my steward and his kinsman, the same Spencer entreated me, that for that instant (being some few days) he might wait at my table, which he did, and departed, and from that time I never had to do with him, nor scarcely thought of him.[21]

This testimony from the second Viscount is strange on many levels. He has obviously been warned that he is being linked with Fawkes, and it is this that has prompted his letter to the influential Earl of

Dorset, his father-in-law. Given this, we must base our interpretation of the letter upon the assumption that its sole purpose was to distance the Viscount from Guy Fawkes. Even so, it seems strange that he would have agreed to take in Guy as a table waiter for a few days, especially after his grandfather had earlier dismissed him from service at Cowdray. The term 'scarcely thought of him' also seems odd, if he truly was talking about someone he had only employed for a few days twelve years earlier.

We have some idea of what Guy's duties would have been as a table waiter for the second Viscount Montague. Montague was a stickler for things being done in exactly the correct way, and he wrote a book on this subject entitled *A Book of Orders and Rules*. In it he gives detailed accounts of the duties of his huge number of staff, including 'the yeoman of the cellar', 'the yeoman of the ewery', 'the yeoman of my buttery', 'the gentlemen of my horse', 'the brewer' and 'the granator'.

Guy served as a 'gentleman waiter', and his job was described thus by the Viscount:

> I will that some of my Gentlemen Waiters harken when I or my wife at any time do walk abroad, that they may be ready to give their attendance upon us, some at one time, and some at another as they shall agree amongst themselves; But when strangers are in place then I will that in any sort they be ready to do such service for them as the Gentleman Usher shall direct. I will further that they be daily present in the great chamber or other place of my diet about ten of the clock in the forenoon and five in the afternoon without fail for performance of my service, unless they have licence from my Steward or Gentleman Usher to the contrary, which if they exceed, I will that they make known the cause thereof to my Steward, who shall acquaint me therewithal. I will that they dine and sup at a table appointed for them, and there take place next after the Gentlemen of my Horse and Chamber, according to their seniorities in my service.[22]

BY FIRE AND WATER, THY LINE SHALL COME TO AN END

Given the fastidiousness of the Viscount in household matters, the haphazard way in which he hired Guy for a few days, as detailed in his letter to Dorset, seems unlikely. Perhaps there was another reason for Guy's service at Cowdray House, and for his dismissal? The house had a reputation for taking on Catholic staff, and this may have led to Guy being highly recommended to the first Viscount as a servant for his grandson. It could be however that Guy was already too militant, too rebellious a Catholic, for a man who was as careful in his dealings as the first Viscount Montague. Something in Guy's words or actions scared the first Viscount enough to dismiss him from his service before he could become an unhealthy influence on his grandson, but after the Viscount's death his grandson recalled Guy to Cowdray House as quickly as possible.

Guy learned to be subservient in his time at Cowdray House, and he learnt the art of etiquette, but it could also be where his Catholic militancy began to find its voice. We have already heard from Smith's report that many notable Catholics visited Cowdray House, not only priests but also a new angry generation of young Catholics. It is possible that it was in this East Sussex house that Guy Fawkes first met the charismatic and dangerous Robert Catesby.[23]

With Guy, once an idea found voice, it inevitably had to be put into practice. Guy had determined that action was needed, and he was now to sail away from England's shores and enter a world of warfare and intrigue, of espionage and betrayal, on the continent of Europe.

Chapter 8

Spies, Secrets and Sundry
other Places

Every ministering spy,
That will accuse, and swear, is lord of you,
Of me, of all, our fortunes, and our lives.
Our looks are called to question and our words,
How innocent soever, are made crimes;
We shall nor shortly dare to tell our dreams,
Or think, but 'twill be treason.
Ben Jonson, *Sejanus His Fall*

There are moments in the life of Guy Fawkes that remain a mystery to us. What, for example, was he doing during the year that elapsed between him being dismissed by the first Viscount Montague and being rehired by his grandson the second Viscount? The sale of Guy's property and his rental income would have given him some money to live on, but where did he stay? Presumably his whereabouts must have been known to the second Viscount, or to the mysterious steward Spencer who it was claimed obtained the job for Guy.

One possible location for Guy during these months of 1592 and 1593 was Cambridge University. This is given some credence by an answer given by Guy when he was under interrogation following his arrest in 1605. In answer to a question prepared by King James (the question being 'where hath he lived?'), Guy's reply was, 'He hath lived in Yorkshire, first at school there, and then to Cambridge, and after in sundry other places'.[1]

This confession is difficult to verify. Guy had not yet been subject to torture, and while he undoubtedly knew there was now no hope of his escape, he was determined to protect those who had been involved in the conspiracy with him, perhaps giving them time to make their escape or to enact a second part of their plan. He was also careful not to implicate others innocent of the plot but whom the government would have loved to see attached to it. This is why Guy's initial answers are comprised of truths, half-truths and untruths (for example he was at this time still successfully using his alias of John Johnson, as we shall later see, and he gave his father's name as Thomas Johnson and his mother's as Edith Johnson, née Jackson[2]). Questions that seemed to Guy relatively harmless, he did answer truthfully, as for example when he confessed that he had been to school in Yorkshire. But he didn't mention his time at Cowdray House, as he knew it would have brought danger upon his erstwhile employer Viscount Montague. This could add credence to his subsequent statement that he spent time at Cambridge.

The university system of England in Tudor times was very different to that of today: for starters, there were only two universities – Oxford and Cambridge. Attendance was possible from the age of 14 for those who could afford the fees, or who had a wealthy patron, and the only subjects taught were divinity and the classics.

Guy wouldn't have found his class or upbringing a bar to entry at Cambridge, but he would have found it impossible to graduate on grounds of religion. All students were required to swear an Oath of Supremacy pledging allegiance to Queen Elizabeth before they could receive their degree, and for that reason many Catholic scholars compromised by completing their course and then leaving without taking the oath and graduating. This was the path that Thomas Percy took at Cambridge University[3] and that Robert Catesby took at Oxford University[4] and it may be that Guy had planned to do the same before finding employment once more at Cowdray House.

Guy may also have spent time in London, a city that grew enormously during the latter half of the sixteenth century, and one that would have been an obvious port of call for a young man looking to progress in the world. King Henry VIII's dissolution of the monasteries had freed up land for housing,[5] and by 1600 the population of London was around a quarter of a million, a fivefold increase on what it had been just fifty years earlier.

London was a city Guy Fawkes would come to know well in 1605, in his guise as John Johnson, but it could be that he first encountered it in 1593 or 1594. He would have found it a city of contrasts, and one out of step with his increasingly pious nature. Scattered throughout the city, in areas like the Strand and along the north bank of the river Thames, were huge houses that served as the city residences of noble families, but nearby were cramped and crowded streets infested with rats, and where crime was common.

It was also a city with a growing number of inns to serve its thirsty and expanding population, and by the time that Guy was in the capital it was also home to a burgeoning new art form – the theatre. Playhouses could be found across London, offering entertainment to all social classes. A rather different form of entertainment was provided by the stews, the brothels and bawdy houses that were rife with customers and often rife with disease. These were primarily found in the growing borough of Southwark, on the south side of the Thames and therefore officially beyond the jurisdiction of the City of London authorities.[6]

Life in London could be dangerous for many reasons: there was always the risk of fire, or drowning with only one bridge across the Thames and small boats and barges used to ferry people across the river. Disease was rampant, with poor sanitation and densely packed streets creating a perfect breeding ground for cholera, tuberculosis, the plague, and the sweating sickness.

At dusk in the winter months, and at eight in the evening during the summer, bells such as the ones at St. Mary-le-Bow rang out across the city, signalling that the city gates were about to close, effectively creating a curfew.[7] Darkness was particularly dangerous in Elizabethan London, but even in daylight hours you never knew who was watching you or who was listening to your conversation.

As a Catholic, and one without the protection that a title could sometimes afford, Guy had to be wary wherever he went. Margaret Clitherow was just one example of how betrayal could bring about disaster, and death, without a moment's warning. In her case it was a

Flemish pupil who under pressure had betrayed her secret to the authorities,[8] but in others it could be a neighbour who had been suspicious of comings and goings from a house, or even a relative who wanted to gain revenge or an inheritance. The incentives for reporting a priest, or one of their enablers, could be great, and this created an atmosphere of danger and mistrust.

If the risks were high in York, they were far greater in London for it was the centre of a complex world of spies, double agents and subterfuge that grew up around Elizabeth's court. Given her family history it is hardly surprising that Queen Elizabeth was paranoid about plots and accusations. To counter this she oversaw the creation of a great network, a web that stretched to every corner of her realm and at whose centre sat the great spider Walsingham, spinning and spinning, forever spinning and forever feasting upon flies.

Sir Francis Walsingham was the most powerful spymaster of the Queen's reign. Fiercely loyal, he would ensure that he saw and heard everything, and then fed it all back to his mistress. Not for nothing was the Queen painted with ears decorating her voluminous royal dress, but it was Walsingham and his successors who whispered into those ears.

Walsingham occupied increasingly senior positions under the Queen, and by 1578 he had become Lord Privy Seal, Chancellor of the Order of the Garter, Chancellor of the Duchy of Lancaster, and Principal Secretary of State.[9] He was intelligent and ambitious, but most of all he was zealously anti-Catholic. Walsingham and his inner circle would hire promising graduates from Oxford and Cambridge who seemed ideologically sound, or recruit people from noble families. Using these agents he would spy upon people, predominantly Catholics, at home and abroad.

While there was a very real threat to the Queen and to Protestantism at home, there was danger from overseas as well. The wars of religion then raging across France and the Low Countries, what is now Belgium and the Netherlands, was a fight between Protestantism and Catholicism, and at the heart of it all was England's great rival Spain. Many English Catholics left for the continent to fight on the Spanish side, as indeed did Guy Fawkes, but even on the continent they were not safe from the spies of Walsingham and his successors.

Sir Francis Walsingham died in 1590, and his role as spymaster, not to mention chief courtier, was taken firstly by Sir William Cecil and then by his son Sir Robert Cecil, who maintained his power and position after Elizabeth's successor James had advanced to the throne.

These men did not hesitate to act unscrupulously to achieve what they felt was best for the Queen and for their country. One example of this was the eventual execution of Mary, Queen of Scots. Walsingham was more than aware of the support Mary held among the Catholic community, and yet despite his urgings Queen Elizabeth showed little inclination to execute her cousin-once-removed. Walsingham decided to take the matter into his own hands. There can be little doubt that his fingerprints were all over the Babington Plot of 1586,[10] and the letters that Mary thought she was sending in secret to conspirators planning to place her upon the throne, were actually being delivered directly to Walsingham. When presented with news that Mary was encouraging a plot to assassinate Elizabeth, the Queen had little choice but to finally order her execution. This use of agent provocateurs proved helpful to Walsingham and the Cecils on a number of occasions, and many scholars have pondered whether the gunpowder plot itself was provoked by agents of Sir Robert Cecil.[11]

Carrot and stick were both useful tools in the enlistment of spies. Those who were threatened with life-destroying fines, imprisonment, or worse, could sometimes be enticed into becoming a double agent, supposedly carrying out their activities as before but in reality feeding back information to their spymaster or acting to entrap those who had previously been their friends.

Even Catholic priests weren't immune to these enticements. Walsingham, and the Cecils after him, had a network of 'false priests'. Some of them were not priests at all, but men carefully trained in how to act as one. Others were Catholic priests who had fled England, or entered seminaries on the continent, but who had now agreed to forsake their religion and implicate others in return for a pardon and the opportunity to re-enter England. One such man was Father George Southwick. In the autumn of 1605 he and a group of other priests were making a surreptitious journey to England; upon landing they would disperse and then begin their preaching. The other priests were unaware that Southwick had already betrayed them to a certain death. All the men were arrested as soon as they arrived in England, and after a suitable length of time had passed to allay suspicion, Southwick was freed to continue spying for Cecil.[12]

Being denounced by a spy would frequently result in torture and then execution, but being a spy brought its own dangers too. Wary of threats from the other side, or perhaps aware of greater rewards, some Elizabethan and Jacobean spies switched to become double agents, before occasionally switching back again to confuse things even further. Others walked a dangerous tightrope by supplying information to both sides, the government and Catholics simultaneously.

Having access to the upper reaches of society made you a potential target for recruitment or monitoring. Leading playwrights such as Ben Jonson,[13] who fell foul of the authorities on more than one occasion, could have been linked to Catholic agents – we shall see how he met the gunpowder plotters as their plans neared fruition. William Shakespeare himself had connections to the Catholic community and would surely have known spies, even if he wasn't one himself, but he would also have had the example of Christopher Marlowe to remind him how dangerous life as a spy could be.

The late sixteenth century saw a brilliant flourishing of English drama, and at its zenith were Shakespeare, Jonson and Marlowe. Marlowe was the brilliant young man behind plays like *Doctor Faustus*, *Tamburlaine*, and *Edward II*, but he also had a complex personal life and was not a man who complied with the norms of his time. He was openly homosexual, and, more dangerously, openly atheist. Even more dangerously, he was working as a spy for Sir William Cecil.

Marlowe was to be found among the English garrison at Flushing, in Flanders, in the early 1590s, and it is believed that he was one of the chief intelligence gatherers there. Unfortunately, his volatile lifestyle created more headaches for his spymasters than his information was worth. He was back in London by May 1593, when a series of atheist tracts were posted across the city bearing the signature 'Tamburlaine'. This was obviously far too clumsy to be Marlowe's work, but he found a warrant issued for his arrest alongside his fellow playwright Thomas Kyd.[14]

Marlowe never came to trial, as he was killed on 30 May 1593 at or near an inn in Deptford in east London. It was believed for many centuries that he was killed as the result of a drunken brawl, possibly over a man, but that supposition and the findings of the official inquest[15] are now widely discredited. Some say that he was killed because he was a secret Catholic, some that he was assassinated because he had outlived his usefulness as a spy, and some that he was killed by a powerful man, possibly Sir Walter Ralegh, who was worried that Marlowe was going to implicate him in a plot. It has even been speculated that the death of Marlowe was faked and that he was sent abroad to protect him from those he had informed against (we shall see how this has an echo in rumours surrounding the plotter Francis Tresham), but this seems unlikely. While the exact cause of Christopher Marlowe's death may never be known, it seems highly likely that his former spymaster Cecil had some involvement in it.

The complex, confusing and dangerous world that Guy Fawkes was moving into saw ruthless spies and agents operating on both sides, but most of the Catholic espionage was being planned, by necessity, from across the sea. Chief among the Catholic agitators and spy chiefs were the militant Jesuit priest Father William Baldwin, the turncoat soldier Sir William Stanley, and the man who became known as the 'Welsh Intelligencer',[16] Hugh Owen. Born in the 1530s he had managed to escape England after being implicated in the Ridolfi plot of 1571, after which he spent more than three decades masterminding and encouraging Catholic plots, often with the support of the Spanish court who paid him a salary.

Hugh Owen was the number one target for Walsingham and the Cecils, and yet he always evaded their grasp. This triumvirate of Owen, Baldwin and Stanley would also become well known to Guy Fawkes as he made his way across the sea to Flanders to serve the Catholic cause from within the Spanish army.

Chapter 9

A Man Highly Skilled in Matters of War

So when thou hast, as I
Commanded thee, done blabbing –
Although to give the lie
Deserves no less than stabbing –
Stab at thee he that will,
No stab the soul can kill
Walter Ralegh, *The Lie*

In 1593, after leaving service at Cowdray House for a second time, Guy Fawkes set sail from England alongside his friend and distant cousin Richard Collinge, who was later ordained as a Jesuit priest.[1] Collinge was making the journey to further his spiritual education, Guy was going to wage war.

Guy Fawkes was now 23 years of age and his life was not turning out how his parents imagined it when they first looked down at the wailing face of their newborn child. Not for Guy was the life of an ecclesiastical lawyer, or even that of a gentleman farmer or respectable husband. Guy had turned his back on the faith he had been born into, and in doing so abandoned completely the path that had once stretched out before him.

Guy had loved and lost, he had found employment and been dismissed, and he had excelled at his studies without having any opportunity to use them for his advancement. Above all else, Guy had found a new faith which had become the cornerstone of everything he did in his life, and it was growing in strength day by day. It was this faith that made him sell his land and leave Yorkshire behind, probably it was his increased militancy that saw him adjudged as too dangerous to remain in service as a gentleman waiter, and it was his increasing anger at the injustices he saw all around him that made him take his fateful next step – Guy was never a man to lie down and submit, he was a man who preferred to risk all and charge in.

The late sixteenth century was a violent time, with civil unrest and uprisings occurring at frequent intervals. It is likely that Guy would have learned to fight while a schoolboy in York, both with his fists and with a sword. Carrying a sword was a sign of wealth, of position and prestige, but if you carried one, you had to know how to use it.

Guy's school friend Jack Wright certainly did, as did Thomas Percy who Guy may also have known in his youth. Wright and his brother-in-law Percy considered themselves among the best swordsmen of their generation, and when they heard of other acclaimed swordsmen they would travel to meet them and participate in pre-arranged duels. Wright and Percy fought across the country, always without protective equipment.

Jack Wright's prowess with a sword[2] is testimony not only to his ability and bravery, it also suggests that a fencing master was employed by St. Peter's School in York to teach their pupils the art of the rapier. As Guy progressed through his school days, his disaffection with life and society in general growing, he would have relished these sword-fighting classes, praying that one day he would be able to put his abilities to the test in a real arena. That opportunity presented itself to Guy in the middle of the 1590s.

We know that Guy eventually found his way to Flanders,[3] as did many English Catholics of the time, but it seems likely that he spent some time in France, and possibly Italy, first. One indication of this was that he was so proficient in French that his interrogators, on the orders of King James,[4] asked him where he learned to speak the language. Guy replied that he learned to speak French in England, and on his last journey beyond the seas,[5] but it is probable that he mastered the language during an initial sojourn in France in 1593 or 1594.

The last decades of the sixteenth century saw an escalation in the 'wars of religion' that had commenced as a result of Luther's reformation: it wasn't only in England that Catholics and Protestants found it impossible to live in peace with each other.

The dominant force in Europe at the time was the Habsburg Empire, led by the Holy Roman Emperor. Originating in Switzerland in the thirteenth century, the Habsburg dynasty soon ruled nations across Europe. In 1521, the empire effectively split itself in two, when Holy Roman Emperor Charles V[6] gave the Austrian lands of the Empire to his brother Ferdinand I. Even so, throughout the sixteenth century and beyond it remained essentially an empire controlled from Spain.

One hotly disputed region of the Empire was called the Spanish Netherlands, also known as the Low Countries, and an area that encompasses much of the Netherlands, Belgium and north eastern France using today's boundaries. In 1568 a conflict that became known as the Eighty Years War erupted, between the Calvinist Protestant forces of the north and Catholic forces loyal to Spanish rule in the south.

In the latter half of the sixteenth century, this conflict became particularly attractive to English Catholics. Not only would they have a chance to fight for a cause they believed in, they would also be free to pursue their religion openly and free of the persecutions of home. Fighting wars was a dangerous occupation, of course, but remaining in England could be equally dangerous, and expensive.

It was these attractions that brought Guy Fawkes to Flanders, the Catholic stronghold of the Spanish Netherlands, sometime in 1594. Guy is often referred to as a mercenary, but while it is true that he was being paid to fight for a foreign country, Spain, he was not a mercenary in the modern sense of the word: Guy did not switch his loyalties depending upon who offered him the greatest rewards, and he never fought against what he believed in. For Guy, the bloody and often chaotic battles he took part in during his years as a soldier were part of his duty to the Catholic church, and any killing his actions caused would be justified by the service he was performing for God: he later

71

used the same reasoning when preparing to light a fuse in a Westminster cellar in November 1605.

Guy would never have dreamed of changing sides, but he found himself fighting under a man who became infamous for doing just that: Sir William Stanley. Stanley was of a noble family, and related to the Earl of Derby, and while it was known that he held Catholic beliefs, he had gained renown fighting for Queen Elizabeth in Ireland against Catholic uprisings.

Stanley proved to be an effective soldier and leader, and on the surface a loyal one, gaining him a knighthood and increasingly senior positions, including being made the Sheriff of Cork[7] and de facto ruler of the Irish province of Munster.[8] He was as brave as he was fierce, once fighting without armour and refusing to surrender despite suffering multiple wounds.[9]

After more than a decade of fighting, and with the scars to show for it, Stanley had hoped to gain more favour from the Queen, but he was becoming increasingly despondent at being overlooked for positions he felt should be his, including that of Viceroy of Ireland. The first turning point in Stanley's career came in 1585 when he travelled to the Spanish Netherlands in the company of Robert Dudley, Earl of Leicester, to fight in support of the Protestants. Knowing his outstanding record in Ireland, Dudley sent Stanley back to Ireland to recruit men for the cause, but although he recruited over a thousand troops, he travelled to London first rather than immediately rejoining Dudley.[10]

It is believed that Stanley had in fact been talking to Jesuit priests and to the Spanish ambassador to England, Bernardino de Mendoza. In short, Stanley had decided to embrace his Catholic faith. It seems that he was also aware of the Babington plot to assassinate Queen Elizabeth, and may even have been involved in its planning.[11] He decided to remain in London in case the plot succeeded, so he could be ready to assist if the Spanish sent an invasion fleet.

When the Babington plot was foiled and the fleet failed to materialise, Stanley threw on the cloak of loyalty again and rejoined Robert Dudley. Playing a prominent part in the battles of Doesborg and Zutphen, where the Elizabethan courtier and poet Sir Philip Sidney picked up the injury that led to his terrible lingering death,[12] Stanley was once more back in favour. So impressed was Robert Dudley with Stanley's bravery that he stated he was 'worth his weight in pearl',[13] and he was made Governor of the city of Deventer, now in the Netherlands. It was here that his great act of treachery took place.

William Stanley was holding Deventer with his hand-picked troop of Irishmen, but conditions were hard and food was scarce, which made Stanley's dissatisfaction grow even stronger. In January 1587 he wrote to the Catholic governor of Zutphen, Juan de Tassis, and surrendered the city and its garrison to him. Stanley now changed allegiance formally, and he and around 600 of his men took up arms for the Spanish king, Philip II.[14]

Stanley embraced his new life as an officer in the Spanish army, and his growing unit became known as the 'English regiment', even though it also included Italians, Scots and Irish. His infamy in England, where he was seen as the ultimate traitor, made him an attractive figure to English Catholics looking to strike back against their own nation, and like a moth to a flame it was inevitable that Guy Fawkes would one day find himself among this band of outcasts.

Life in the English regiment was hard. The men were paid by the Spanish king, via his agents, but payment was not always fulsome or delivered on time. Winter especially could bring extreme hardship, and Ralph Sadler, a spy for Queen Elizabeth, reported that Stanley's men were surviving by eating handfuls of dry acorns.[15]

It may have been these hardships, rather than any fear of war or fighting, that led Guy to seek employment elsewhere. We get evidence of this in a letter from Father Richard Collinge, the cousin who had left England with Guy, to a Venetian called Giulio Piccioli. In it he writes,

> Good Sir,
> I pray you let me entreat your favour and friendship for my cousin germane Mr Guido Fawkes who serves Sir William Stanley as I understand he is in great want and a word on his behalf may stand him in great stead.[16]

This letter reveals that Guy had adopted the Spanish sounding Guido since joining the army of the Holy Roman Empire, and also shows that his funds and means of earning a living were depleted. By the time this letter was written however, 1599, the Spanish Netherlands had become less volatile under the new rule of Archduke Albert and Archduchess Isabella, who would become known as the Archdukes. Under these circumstances, Guy may simply have been seeking new adventures, or even have been looking to act upon a diplomatic mission in the Catholic cause; this is something that William Stanley himself embarked upon on a fairly frequent basis, so soldiers and officers were permitted time away from their military duties on occasion.

By this time Guy had become a great success as a soldier, and he was prized by Stanley and other military leaders such as Colonel Bostock. Guy would have taken part in many engagements with the English regiment and other units of the Spanish army, and we know that he was present at the Siege of Calais of 1596,[17] a victory for the Spanish forces.[18]

Warfare was going through a transformation in the Elizabethan age. While old weapons such as clubs, halberds and swords were still very much in use, gunpowder was creating a host of new weapons that would change the face of fighting for ever. The battles Guy took part in saw hand to hand combat using swords, as well as ranged attacks from crossbows and gunfire from weapons like the arquebus – slow to load and use, unreliable in its aim, and yet deadlier than anything that had been seen before.

Many of the battles of the Eighty Years War involved sieges of various duration, with defending troops taking up position in castles and fortified towers. Gunpowder transformed the art of the siege as well, as specialists in explosives would carefully position charges before firing them using a long train – a slow burning wick that would give the lighter time to reach safety before the huge explosions occurred. Given his later recruitment to the gunpowder plot, and his noted presence at sieges such as Calais, it is likely that Guy Fawkes had become an expert in the dark arts of gunpowder.[19]

A MAN HIGHLY SKILLED IN MATTERS OF WAR

Guy's prowess as a soldier is demonstrated by his rise through the ranks of the Spanish army's English Regiment, eventually reaching the rank of *alferez* which is similar to the English rank of ensign, just below that of a lieutenant. Military records at the Royal Archives in Brussels also show that by 1603 he was being considered for promotion to the rank of captain.

One of the deadliest battles Guy fought in was the Battle of Nieuwpoort, which took place on 2 July 1600. Maurice of Nassau and Sir Francis Vere were in charge of the Dutch Protestant army, and the Spanish troops were led by Archduke Albert himself, with Colonel Bostock in charge of the English regiment.[20] One of the factors that made it such a bloody and chaotic battle was that the Dutch ranged themselves along a bank of sand dunes, leading to the engagement becoming known as the Battle of the Dunes. Fighting in sand, weighed down with armour and weaponry, was an arduous and some might say idiotic task, and the golden dunes were soon stained red with the blood of both sides. Officially hailed as a Dutch victory, it was a pyrrhic one, with both sides losing more than 2,000 troops. Alferez Fawkes was forced to take a position of command during the battle – particularly after his regimental leader Colonel Bostock was slain, alongside thirty-six other high-ranking officers.[21] The retreat from the slaughter would have been difficult and terrifying, but although around 500 Spanish were captured Guy escaped to fight another day. To do so, he had to hack his way through one opponent after another, his legs sinking into the sand beneath him, and it is possible that this battle was the cause of the scars across Guy's chest that his interrogators noticed in November 1605.[22]

The Jesuit Father Tesimond, who narrowly escaped with his life after the gunpowder plot, described Guy in these glowing terms:

> He was a man of considerable experience as well as knowledge. Thanks to his prowess he had acquired considerable fame and name among the soldiers. He was also – something decidedly rare among soldiery, although it was immediately obvious to all – a very devout man, of

exemplary life and commendable reticence. He went often to the sacraments. He was pleasant of approach and cheerful of manner, opposed to quarrels and strife: a friend, at the same time, of all in the service with him who were men of honour and good life. In a word, he was a man liked by everyone and loyal to his friends.[23]

Tesimond also praised him as a 'man highly skilled in matters of war',[24] but he had seen more than simply war and killing during his time in Flanders. There is one strange and unaccounted-for reminder of his service that Guy carried with him. In 1605, during his interrogation and while under the guise of John Johnson, a letter was found in his pocket referring to him as Guido Fawkes:

> The letter that was found about him, was from a gentlewoman married to an English man named Bostock, in Flanders. The reason why she calls him by another name, was because he called himself Fawkes.[25]

It is one question that Guy will never yield an answer to and we will return to it in a later chapter.

As a soldier Guy Fawkes had looked death in the face, seen his colleagues fall by his side, gained scars and taken lives. He had also found respect and camaraderie, and although he'd faced physical hardship and want, he was fighting for a cause he truly believed in. As the sixteenth century turned into the seventeenth, however, events were happening in England that would change his destiny forever.

Guy was about to leave the sword and musket behind and become a diplomat on a top-secret mission. When that mission failed, he was to take a step that would condemn him to everlasting infamy.

Chapter 10

An Open Enemy, and an Enemy of their Beliefs

The fearful abounding at this time in this country, of these
detestable slaves of the Devil, the Witches or enchanters, hath
moved me (beloved reader) to dispatch in post, this following
treatise of mine to resolve the doubting both that such assaults
of Satan are most certainly practised, and that the
instrument thereof merits most severely to be punished
King James I, *Daemonologie*

Agnes Sampson was a midwife from the south east of Scotland. Known as 'The Wise Woman of Keith', she was also reputed to be a healer, and at this time when medical knowledge and assistance was scanty she was often called upon by locals. It was a dangerous reputation to have in Scotland in the late sixteenth century, for it led Agnes to become embroiled in one of the most shameful episodes in the country's history: the North Berwick witch trials.[1]

Agnes had to endure terrible tortures, from being deprived of sleep and food, to being imprisoned wearing a 'witches bridle' – a metal clamp with four spikes that stuck into the tongue and cheeks. Despite the physical pain inflicted upon her, from savage beatings to having her nails ripped out, she refused to confess to the charges conjured up against her. Her chief interrogator worked himself into a fury. It was commonly believed that witches would have a mark of Satan on their body, so Agnes' interrogator knew what to do, as a contemporary account reveals:

By special commandment this Agnes Sampson had all her hair shaven off, in each part of her body, and her head thrown with a rope according to the custom of that country, being a pain most grievous, which continued for almost an hour, during which time she would not confess anything until the Devils' mark was found upon her privates. Then she immediately confessed whatsoever was demanded of her, and justifying those persons aforesaid to be notorious witches.[2]

Throughout these tortured confessions, the interrogator laughed and berated the naked, broken wretch before him, but Agnes wasn't interrogated at home or in a prison cell, and the interrogator was no priest or witch finder. Agnes was in the grand hall of Holyrood Palace, and the pitiless man before her was none other than the King himself: James VI of Scotland. The woman's fate was sealed: Agnes was strangled and then burned to death on 28 January 1591.

James Stuart lived in an age of superstition, and he embraced it fulsomely. James had long held a belief that people were trying to do him harm, quite reasonably given the violent Stuart history; what seems more unusual to us at our distance of four centuries is that he believed that the danger came from supernatural as well as physical sources.

This belief was strengthened when in 1590 he sailed back from Oslo after marrying Anne, daughter of the King of Denmark and Norway.[3] A great storm put their life in peril, and a Danish Admiral informed King James that the storm was surely the result of witchcraft, caused by a woman he had insulted in port.[4] An investigation in Norway led to two women being burned at the stake, but James was now struck with the fear that home-grown witches were also behind the plot. It was this fear that lay behind the North Berwick witch trials. But there were many similar trials across Scotland. Throughout the sixteenth century, and in the decades on either side, around 4,000 were accused of being witches in Scotland with around 2,500 burned – approximately twice as many as in the much more populous realm of England.[5]

King James himself not only encouraged these witch hunts and executions, he was the driving force behind them thanks to his 1597 book entitled *Daemonologie*.[6] The book is full of rituals, and essays on the behaviour of witches and how to find them. It also touches on subjects as esoteric as werewolves and vampires. It is rather different to the other tome that famously bears his name, the King James Bible of 1611. *Daemonologie* is not a book that inspires confidence in the thought processes of a man who would come to rule not one kingdom but two.

As we see from the example of Agnes Sampson, King James sometimes delighted in being present at the inquisition of those who he thought had tried to claim his life – an irresistible opportunity to display his power and sate his sadistic streak. This was something that Guy Fawkes was to discover fifteen years later.

King James's other great terror was gunpowder and it is easy to explain why it held such a horror for him. James's childhood saw him placed on the Scottish throne aged just thirteen months, but it was a base tragedy rather than a regal fairytale.[7] James Stuart was the son of Mary, known today as Mary Queen of Scots, and Henry Stuart, Lord Darnley.

Mary was a controversial figure in Scotland, unpopular with many of the nobles and much of the populace. She had acceded to the Scottish throne even earlier than James did, at just six days old, and after her first husband, King Francis II of France, died she married Darnley, who was her cousin.

Darnley was a vain, often drunk, and frequently violent man, and these character faults put a strain upon his marriage to Mary. The Queen turned to her private secretary David Rizzio for solace, and perhaps more. It was widely rumoured that Rizzio was the father of the Queen's unborn child, and in a fury Darnley stabbed Rizzio to death in front of his pregnant wife on 9 March 1566.[8]

Not content with being the Queen's consort, Darnley wanted to take power himself. In doing so he estranged the Scottish nobles further, and it was this that sealed his fate. On 9 February 1567, Darnley was staying at Kirk o' Field, an Edinburgh church, while he recovered from a disease (probably syphilis[9]). Unknown to him two barrels of gunpowder had been placed beneath his bed chamber. Darnley survived the initial explosion but was caught by his assassins running from the church, and strangled to death wearing just his night shirt.[10]

Suspicion fell upon Queen Mary herself and upon the Earl of Bothwell, whom she married shortly afterwards. This led to Mary being confronted on the battlefield at Carberry Hill and forced to abdicate the throne, which in turn necessitated her flight to England, which led eventually to her execution by Queen Elizabeth, like a series of dominoes falling one against another.

Thus it was that James Stuart, son of Mary and Henry Stuart (unless the Rizzio rumours were true), acceded to the Scottish throne as a 1-year-old; he would hold onto it for nearly fifty-eight years. Gaining power at such an early age must have exerted a profound effect on his ego, but he would also have a lifelong fear of assassination, and especially of gunpowder: it was gunpowder and its aftermath that had swept his father and mother away from him while still a baby; although his mother Mary lived until her son James was 21 they would never see each other after her exile.

James was always born to be King of Scotland, but at the age of 35 he came into possession of a throne he could never have expected: the throne of England.

Queen Elizabeth of England's refusal to marry may have been based upon the example of what marriage had done to her mother, Anne Boleyn, or she may have taken the decision to ensure that she retained power for herself rather than being subjugated to a man. But as she grew older it created an ever increasing problem of the royal succession, until it became a shadow hanging over the land, seen by all but spoken of by nobody – at least not in public. One parliamentarian, Peter Wentworth, was imprisoned in the Tower of London in 1593 simply for raising a petition to discuss Elizabeth's successor, and he died a captive three years later.

There were a number of possible claimants considered throughout Elizabeth's reign. Some of these claims were based upon ancient history, including Henry Hastings, the Earl of Huntingdon, and later the scourge of York. He had Plantagenet blood, on the Yorkist side that had been defeated by Henry VII.

Mary Queen of Scots was the preferred choice of many Catholics, those remaining in England and those who had fled overseas, but the succession of plots revolving around her led, as we've seen, to her beheading. Catholics now found another champion in the form of the Spanish infanta Isabella, later Archduchess Isabella. Isabella's claim was an ancient one indeed, as she traced her direct lineage back to John of Gaunt, founder of the House of Lancaster and father of King Henry IV.[11]

Despite the distance of her claim, many Catholics supported Isabella as a way of returning England to its former faith. A tract written by the exiled Jesuit priest Father Robert Persons entitled *A Conference about the Next Succession to the Crown of England, Divided into Two Parts, where unto is Added a New & Perfect Arbour or Genealogy* promoted Isabella as the perfect and rightful Queen. It was smuggled into England and became as dangerous as dynamite.[12]

The succession had been complicated further when two obvious candidates, Lady Catherine Grey and Lady Mary Grey, died in 1568 and 1578 respectively. They were the granddaughters of Henry VIII's sister Mary Tudor, a bloodline which had earlier proved fatal for their elder sister Lady Jane Grey who as a teenager was placed on the throne against her will and then rapidly removed from it and executed. As Jane stood next to the executioner's block by the Tower of London she called out, 'Good people, I am come hither to die, and by a law I am condemned to the same'.[13] Jane was a chilling reminder to all who had a claim to the succession, however tenuous, of where it could lead.

The plots around Mary Queen of Scots, and the later promotion of the Spanish infanta Isabella, galvanised the leading Protestant courtiers into action. Seeing how precarious was their position, and that of English Protestantism, they had to find a suitable candidate of their own. There was only one man they could turn to: James VI of Scotland.

James was a great-grandchild of Margaret Tudor,[14] sister to King Henry VIII, through his father Henry Stuart. James's succession was problematic not because of his bloodline, but because it appeared that he had been specifically prohibited from becoming king by the will of Henry VIII which declared that all descendants of his sister Margaret would be barred from the throne as they were of foreign (Scottish) birth.[15] There was also the problem that Elizabeth detested James, calling him a 'false Scots urchin',[16] but as Elizabeth's own succession from Mary had shown, personal feelings could easily be ignored when required.

As the seventeenth century dawned, Elizabeth's chief courtier Robert Cecil knew that the succession could not be far away. Always both a pragmatist and a survivor, he started to correspond secretly with James VI of Scotland from 1601, ensuring that he would retain his favour once he ascended to the English throne.[17] Cecil wasn't the only one to embark upon diplomacy with James, as the Earl of Northumberland was also in correspondence with Scotland's king.

Northumberland hoped to convince the man who would surely be the next English monarch to be more tolerant towards Catholics than Elizabeth had been, and for this purpose he sent an envoy to have three meetings with James at Holyrood. The man chosen was a distant relative who had become a trusted and useful aide to him: the future conspirator and possible Scotton acquaintance of Guy Fawkes, Thomas Percy.[18]

James's longevity as Scottish king is testament to his political astuteness if nothing else, at a time when one false move could see even kings or queens swiftly disposed of. Whatever his true feelings were, he showed great civility towards Thomas Percy, and while not being fully committed on any subject he did enough to convince Percy that he supported tolerance towards Catholics, even if he wouldn't legalise open Catholic worship.

Thomas Percy was elated at the conversations he had with the King, and the news spread throughout the Catholic community. Whether by 'Chinese whispers' or by Percy's own exuberance, the half promises and suggestions of the King became amplified. We have only to read the testimony of Father Tesimond to hear what English Catholics expected from the man who was to become their new ruler:

> He made Mr Thomas [Percy] very generous promises to favour Catholics actively, and not merely to free them from the bondage and persecution in which they were then living. Indeed, he would admit them to every kind of honour and office in the state without making any difference between them and the Protestants. At last he would take them under his complete protection. The King promised all this and much more than I write here. Not only that, but in order to make himself more acceptable to the Catholics, the King pledged his word as a prince; he took Percy by the hand when he swore to carry out all that he had promised.[19]

Whether he shook Percy's hand or not, James certainly didn't put anything in writing. Nevertheless, Catholics began to look forward to his presumed succession – particularly as it was popularly believed that his wife Anne of Denmark had secretly converted to Catholicism.[20] Senior figures at the Vatican even believed that James himself, following the example of his wife, might one day convert to the old faith, but in this they were to be sorely disappointed.

Queen Elizabeth I died on 24 March 1603 from blood poisoning. Cecil and the other courtiers were well prepared, and immediately sent envoys to Scotland to declare King James VI of Scotland also King James I of England.

James left Edinburgh on 5 April, and used his journey to London to visit English nobles and see important areas of his new country. One of his longest sojourns was in York, and the streets were filled with loyal subjects and the sound of celebrations. One of York's sons, however, was not there to witness the arrival of his new king, one with whom his story would become inextricably bound – Guy Fawkes was preparing for a journey to Spain,[21] but he would soon return to the land of his birth with his sense of injustice, and his anger, burning more fiercely than ever before.

Not all Catholics believed King James's supposed plans for tolerance, and although he did initially put an end to the fines for recusancy, friendly relations with Catholics did not last long. If anything, the persecutions soon grew in severity along with the fines. The new king also brought Scotland and England together in a new union, and sealed peace at last with Spain. This was the deadly combination that led directly to the events of November 1605.

The milk of human kindness towards the monarch had soured, Catholics now found their hopes crushed, and the minds of some began to turn to action – to treason. Father Tesimond, a witness to the later events and known to many of the people involved in them, saw the actions to come as inevitable:

> The Catholics of England had arrived at the nadir of their miseries. There was no more hope for them. Not from the King, who had forgotten his promises and changed his mind now he was secure in his new kingdom. He showed himself rather their open enemy, and the enemy of their beliefs... Finding the King so easily persuaded to harm Catholics, or more exactly, so ready to persecute them, his ministers made every effort to bring the persecution to perfection... Kindled within them [the Catholic plotters] was a just desire, as it seemed to them, of retribution. They burned to liberate themselves and their friends from this cruel servitude and oppression. But at last they found a remedy for these evils which was no less lacking in pity and humanity than the very authors of such evil. Led by anger and desperation, they decided to open a way to new and better hopes by the utter destruction of their enemies.[22]

Chapter 11

The Spanish Treason

O eyes! no eyes, but fountains fraught with tears;
O life! no life, but lively form of death
O world! no world, but mass of public wrongs,
Confus'd and fill'd with murder and misdeeds!
Thomas Kyd, *The Spanish Tragedy*

Guy Fawkes was a courageous and proficient soldier, but he also impressed his superiors with his intellect and intelligence, and in 1603, as the new king prepared to take his place on the English throne, he was sent away from the frontline of Flanders to the courts of the Spanish king. Guy's mission was to persuade King Philip III to support an invasion of England – it was to become known as 'the Spanish treason'.

The initial attitude of the Catholic community to James I was mixed. Optimists believed the stories that had circulated since his audiences with Thomas Percy – that he would be a tolerant king who would allow them to practise their faith unhindered, free of punitive fines and the threat of imprisonment.

Even some of England's Jesuit priests, living every day with the fear of capture and execution, looked ahead to a brighter future. Father Henry Garnet was Superior, or leader, of the Jesuits in England, and even though he was, as always, in hiding, he wrote to King James, via the intermediary of a courtier, to explain that he and other Catholics wished to be 'dear and not unnatural subjects of the Crown'.[1] The conciliatory approach that Garnet took did him little good, as he was executed in May 1606.[2]

Other Catholics however, particularly the more militant members of the faith who remained in self-imposed exile abroad, took a more pessimistic view. Time would prove them right, even though at first James did repeal fines for recusancy.[3]

Among the chief Catholic agitators on the continent was Guy's former commander Sir William Stanley. By the time of James's accession to the throne of England, Stanley had spent more than a decade alternating his time as a soldier with visits to the Spanish court. These visits always had but one aim – to encourage the raising of another Armada and the invasion of England; but while the Spanish made encouraging noises they stopped short of giving him financial or military backing. Eventually Stanley became a nuisance figure whose visits were far from welcome. In truth, Stanley had never been the most popular figure among the Spanish authorities, for even though he had surrendered Deventer to the Spanish forces in 1587, King Philip II later said that while he approved of the act he despised the traitor.

Chief plotters alongside Stanley at this time were Hugh Owen and Father William Baldwin,[4] and as it became apparent that Stanley was making little headway in persuading Spain to support an attack on England, they began to use other envoys instead. One such man was Thomas James. A successful merchant in England, he left his trade and wealth behind to help the Catholic cause overseas. A close ally of Father Robert Persons, the English Jesuit leader in Rome, he arrived at the Spanish court in early 1602 to plead unsuccessfully for an invasion of England. He then remained in Madrid as the English Secretary to King Philip III.[5]

Philip III succeeded his father as King of Spain in 1598, aged 20, and the likes of Stanley and Thomas James soon found that he was less warlike than his father had been. While Philip II launched the Armada against England and took Calais from the French, among many other exploits, Philip III would eventually seal peace deals with England and with the Protestants of the Netherlands.

Another man sent to speak to Philip III on behalf of the English Catholics, this time by the Flanders triumvirate of Stanley, Owen and

Baldwin with the collusion of leading Catholics in England, was Thomas Wintour, who would later become an integral part of the gunpowder plot alongside Guy Fawkes. Wintour shared the same desperation and anger that galvanised the other plotters, and like many of the plotters he shared family connections. In Wintour's case, his own brother Robert was another conspirator, as was his brother-in-law John Grant. He was also a cousin of Robert Catesby, and shared an uncle with Jack and Kit Wright in the form of the executed priest Francis Ingleby.

Thomas Wintour arrived in Spain in 1601, using the alias of Timothy Browne,[6] carrying a letter of introduction from Father Garnet in England to Father Joseph Creswell, who was Superior of the Jesuits in Spain. Creswell often acted as a facilitator for English Catholics wanting to see the Spanish king, and so it went on this occasion.

Wintour, while again pressing the case for an invasion of England, also sought financial help for English Catholics who had been involved in the Essex rebellion against Queen Elizabeth and had now been met with punitive fines (men like Robert Catesby who, along with Baron Monteagle and Francis Tresham, was one of the English contingent who sent Wintour on the mission to Spain[7]).

Wintour was granted meetings with some of Philip III's chief courtiers, including the Duke of Lerma and the Count of Miranda, who held the Spanish purse strings, and finally with the King himself at the grand San Lorenzo de El Escorial palace in Madrid. The meetings seemed to be an unqualified success, at first, as the men, on behalf of the King, promised to supply Wintour with 100,000 escudos, or approximately £25,000 – a huge sum. King Philip also seemed, for the first time, to indicate that he was prepared to launch an invasion of England, saying that he himself would set foot in England.[8] Wintour, as revealed in his post-gunpowder plot confession,[9] encouraged the King in this enterprise by saying he could supply the Spanish army with up to 1,500 horses should they land in England – the transporting of horses from Spain to England being seen as a major difficulty in the launching of a successful invasion.

By late 1602, Thomas Wintour was back in England having passed on the good news from Spain, but the money from Madrid was not forthcoming, and some militant Catholics in England and the Low Countries began to worry that Philip now had his heart set on a more peaceful resolution to the decades-long conflict with England.

With Thomas James still in Spain, another surreptitious envoy was sent to convince the Spanish king to honour his earlier pledges. This man is named in official Spanish documents as Anthony Dutton, but it seems that as with Wintour, who had travelled as Timothy Browne, an alias was being used. This was a necessary precaution for those who planned on returning to England after Spain, to avoid the scrutiny of Robert Cecil's spies.

It is thanks to Guy Fawkes that we know the real identity of Anthony Dutton, for in his confession of 25 November 1605 Guy revealed, 'Christopher Wright had been in Spain about two months before this examinant [Fawkes] arrived there, who was likewise employed by Baldwin, Owen and Sir William Stanley'.[10]

This ties in with the date of Dutton's listed arrival in Spain of 15 May 1603, so there can be little doubt that Dutton was an alias being used by Kit Wright, and he will be referred to by his real name henceforth. Wright's port of call was Valladolid in north west Spain, at this time the country's capital. After seeing Creswell, he wasted no time in arranging a meeting with King Philip and his counsellors.

Wright had brought with him more detailed plans for the invasion mooted by Thomas Wintour a year earlier, and he also made clear that he and many other English Catholics had now reached a state of desperation. Wright declared that this was the last embassy they could send to Spain, and they needed to know whether they would receive funds from King Philip, and how Spain planned to proceed. This information, Kit Wright explained, would tell them whether they could carry out important plans, or whether they would have to leave them undone for ever.[11]

Wright had thrown himself upon the mercy of the Spanish court, begging it to help him and the Catholics of England before their new king, James I, made conditions even worse. Like so many emissaries before him however, he was listened to respectfully and then largely ignored. During his negotiations, Kit had spoken of another man who was being sent and who would bring things that he couldn't – and in the summer of 1603 he too arrived at the Spanish court: Guy Fawkes.

Guy and Kit had first met at St. Peter's School in York, but now found themselves together again nearly one thousand miles to the south. The ruddy-cheeked son of the ecclesiastical lawyer had now become a battle-scarred veteran of the religious wars, and a man deemed worthy to speak to the world's most powerful secular leader, Philip, King of Spain and head of the Holy Roman Empire.

These meetings that took place between 1601 and 1603, the Spanish Treason involving Thomas James, Thomas Wintour, Kit Wright and Guy Fawkes, show the extent to which there was a joined up community of dissident English Catholics, stretching from England itself, passing through Flanders, and having its spiritual home in Rome. Kit Wright clearly knew of Thomas Wintour's earlier meeting with the King and his advisors, and he also knew that Guy was being sent after him from the Low Countries, demonstrating a Europe-wide Catholic intelligence network. While these four men were chosen to be representatives of the cause, it is clear that the strings were being pulled by others: Father Persons in Rome, Baldwin, Owen and Stanley in Flanders, and the likes of Catesby in England – often with the subtle encouragement of Catholic nobles such as the Lords Mordaunt, Montague, and Monteagle.

Just what was it that Guy was bringing to Spain that Kit Wright couldn't? Firstly, there was the prestige of having fought valiantly for the Spanish army. Far from being a money-oriented mercenary, he had wholly embraced the Spanish cause, even adopting the name of Guido rather than his given name Guy. Indeed, although Guy had been given leave from the army to make his diplomatic journey, he was being considered for further promotion at this time.

Guy also possessed a skill that Kit Wright didn't: he was an excellent linguist, speaking both French and Spanish fluently. It's easy to get the wrong impression of Guy: to think that he was little more than a soldier, a man to light the fuse. In reality, Guy was intellectually able, and a natural leader of men. It speaks volumes for his abilities that out of all the English Catholics serving in Flanders at the time, many of them from far more exalted backgrounds, it was Guy Fawkes that Baldwin, Owen and Stanley chose to send to the King of Spain.

While Kit had brought news from England, Guy brought intelligence and information from Flanders, and he also presented the King with two new documents: a petition on behalf of England's Catholics that had earlier been given to James I by Father Thomas Hill,[12] an act that saw him imprisoned, and a letter in Guy's own handwriting detailing what would happen to England's Catholics if no action were taken against James.[13]

Guy's statement was angry, vitriolic, and vehemently anti-Scottish, but it was also prescient given that James had only been on the throne for a matter of months. At the time Guy wrote his letter many were still hopeful that James would be tolerant towards Catholics, but Guy saw through the new king's façade. James was a man who desired, in Guy's words, 'in a short time to have all of the Papist sect driven out of England... Many have heard him say at table that the Pope is Anti-Christ which he wished to prove to anyone who believed the opposite'.[14]

Whereas Kit Wright had been diplomatic and almost pitiful in his requests to the Spanish court, Guy was driven, forceful, compelling. Unfortunately for both men, and for those who had sent them, they had arrived at completely the wrong time in history. The accession of James to the English throne, and the more peaceable nature of Philip III compared to his father, had seen a rapid outbreak of diplomacy. In Rome, Pope Clement VIII had decreed that English Catholics should seek a peaceful resolution to their grievances, and he also encouraged peace talks between Spain and England.

To this end, at the same time that Guy and Kit were in Spain, Philip III had already sent Juan de Tassis, the man who had taken Deventer from the surrendering Stanley six years earlier, to England. His mission was to act as his ambassador and to ascertain the true state of Catholics there, while also encouraging King James to make peace with Spain.[15] De Tassis' view was that English Catholics would be reluctant to take up arms against the kings, further damaging any hopes that Guy Fawkes, Wright and others had of persuading Spain to launch another Armada.

Guy's efforts at diplomacy had foundered before he even reached Spain. Once again King Philip III pledged that he would provide the funds he'd mentioned on the earlier visit by Thomas Wintour, but the talks between Guy and Kit Wright and the Spanish court went on, and on, almost interminably. They had reached the point that Stanley had in earlier years, becoming irritants, but at the same time they were deemed too dangerous to let go.

While Guy and Kit were ostensibly still guests of the Spanish court in Valladolid and were allowed to travel unhindered in their immediate surroundings, they were, in effect, prisoners. Father Creswell, now favouring the Pope's plans for peace rather than war, was concerned that the two Yorkshire men would launch some kind of assault against King James if they were allowed to return to England, and that this would damage the overtures of peace being made by Juan de Tassis. For this reason he encouraged the Spanish court to keep the men safely in Spain for the time being.

Making unheeded pleas and yet regarded as a threat to plans for peace, and without a passport that would allow him to leave Spain, this must have been a most frustrating time for Guy Fawkes. He had become a man of action, but was now forced into inertia. The months passed by, the hot humid summer turned to a chill winter, and still there was no sign of any of his demands being met, nor of him being allowed to return to England or to the men in Flanders who had sent him on his mission.

At last, around March 1604, Guy Fawkes and Kit Wright were given passports and allowed to leave. Creswell and prominent members of the court had become tired of them, and with formal peace talks now opened between Spain and England, it was thought safe to allow their travel.

Guy Fawkes had been in Spain for eight months, and events in the outside world had moved on apace in that time. The peace talks between England and Spain had made rapid progress, and on 18

August 1604 the Treaty of London was signed at Somerset House.[16] This brought to an end nineteen official years of the Anglo-Spanish war, a conflict that in reality had been raging since the death of Queen Mary decades earlier.

While Guy and Kit had been kept under virtual arrest for fear that they would launch a plot, two actual plots had already been attempted, and foiled, during their time in Spain. They were known as the Bye Plot and the Main Plot, as it was suspected that the same masterminds may have been behind both attempts on King James's life.

The Bye Plot was a plan to kidnap King James and force him to repeal anti-Catholic legislation. The plotters also wanted some anti-Catholic courtiers to be removed, notably Sir Robert Cecil. Unfortunately for them, and predictably, Cecil already knew of the plot before it had a chance to be enacted. Catholic priests William Watson and William Clarke were executed,[17] and Sir Walter Ralegh, thought to be involved with both the Bye and Main Plots, was imprisoned in the Tower of London.[18]

The Main Plot of July 1603 was thought to be the work of Ralegh and Henry Brooke, Lord Cobham, and its aim was to assassinate King James and replace him with his Catholic cousin Lady Arbella Stuart.[19] It was uncovered during investigations into the Bye Plot, and saw Cobham take his place alongside Ralegh in the Tower,[20] although he was released shortly before his death in 1618.

Within months of King James coming to the English throne, two attempts had been made against him: one that would have seen him killed. The more peace-minded Catholics were appalled, correctly foreseeing that James would use this as an excuse to turn against England's Catholic population. Initially however, James praised the Catholics who had helped to foil the plot, notably the Jesuit Father Henry Garnet who had informed the Privy Council of the Bye Plot when it came to his attention.[21] This toleration was not to last. With memories of his father's fate always in his mind, along with the numerous plots which had involved his Catholic mother Mary, King James desired to do just what Guy Fawkes had predicted – to 'drive the Papist sect out of England'.

THE SPANISH TREASON

Catholic plots had already ruined any goodwill James had towards the faith, and the peace with Spain meant there was no longer any hope of foreign action against the English king. It was a perfect storm for those Catholics who were already burning with anger and frustration. Kit Wright returned to England, Guy Fawkes was once more in Flanders – but they would soon be reunited, and the storm would reach its violent climax under the thunderous direction of Robert Catesby.

Chapter 12

A Gentleman of Good Family

Ambition, like a torrent, ne'er looks back;
And is a swelling, and the last affection
A high mind can put off; being both a rebel
Unto the soul and reason, and enforceth
All laws, all conscience, treads upon religion,
and offereth violence to nature's self.
Ben Jonson, *Catiline His Conspiracy*[1]

Guy Fawkes' role in the gunpowder plot is frequently misunderstood in one of two ways: his role is often downplayed, so that he becomes little more than the muscles of the operation, at the periphery of its planning – he was more than this; alternatively, some people think of him as the leader of the plot, but while he is certainly the most famous, or infamous, plotter, that position was held by Robert Catesby. Catesby was a complicated man, and a charismatic leader who could make people bend to his will. It was Robert Catesby who would seal Guy's fate, and who in 1605 came close to destroying the whole ruling class of England.

Catesby was known as Robin to his friends, of which he had many. He shared many traits in common with the other gunpowder conspirators of 1605, including friendly or familial bonds with the majority of them. He was of a similar age to most of the plotters, including Guy Fawkes, having been born in around 1572. Also, like many of the plotters including Guy Fawkes and Thomas Percy, his faith and Catholic militancy seems to have developed later in his life, as we can see by his marriage to a Protestant woman, Catherine Leigh, in 1593.

A GENTLEMAN OF GOOD FAMILY

If the young Robert was a pragmatist when it came to religion, the same couldn't be said of his parents who hailed from two of the most notable Catholic and recusant families in the north of England – the Catesbys and the Throckmortons.

Another trait that Robert Catesby shared with many of the plotters was that he was from a solidly upper middle class family, one which owned a number of properties and manor houses, and yet they were one step down from the nobility. This is one of the factors that fed their sense of injustice, as although they freely mixed with lords and ladies, and even royalty itself, they felt themselves cut off from the ruling classes, and unable to make a peaceful contribution to the governance of England.

The Catesby family had risen rapidly from relatively humble beginnings, and yet perhaps not so humble as the Tudor kings and queens who traced their lineage back to the chamber servant Owen Tudor.[2] The family were of Norman descent and took their name from their dwelling in Catesby, Northamptonshire. It was in this area that they built their ancestral home of Ashby St. Ledgers. Their rapid ascent began in the reign of the controversial King Richard III, when William Catesby became one of his most trusted advisors, acquiring land, wealth and a knighthood as a result.[3]

Sir William Catesby was commonly believed to be one of the powers behind Richard's throne, as shown when the Tudor supporter William Collingbourne nailed a poem to the walls of St. Paul's Cathedral in July 1484, beginning, 'The cat, the rat and Lovell our dog ruleth all England under a hog'.[4]

Sir William fought alongside Richard III at the Battle of Bosworth Field, the bloody climax of the Wars of the Roses. He was captured and executed in August 1485,[5] and was later immortalised as a character in Shakespeare's play about the last Yorkist King. Sir William had chosen the wrong side and paid with his life – a trait that seemed to pass through the male line of the Catesby family tree.

Despite the execution of Sir William, the Catesby family could have been expected to continue advancing were it not for the English reformation. Robert Catesby's father, another Sir William Catesby,

95

would not make the required transition to Protestantism, and would not even make an effort to hide his Catholicism. This was the start of the downfall of the Catesby family that his son Robert would take to its nadir.

Robert was the third and only surviving son of Sir William and Anne Catesby. It is likely that he was born at Lapworth Hall in Warwickshire, as this had been the main residence of the family for the previous two centuries. He also spent time at Ashby St. Ledgers during his childhood, and at the beautiful Chastleton House in Oxfordshire, owned by his maternal grandmother.

While the family's Catholicism may have been disastrous to any hopes of courtly advancement, it did little to prevent their success in Midland society. Many of the landowners and gentry of the area were also Catholic,[6] making it one of the leading centres of Catholic resistance in the country, along with Yorkshire, Lancashire, and the north east.

Robert Catesby's childhood was presumably a happy one; he was brought up in a wealthy family and wanted for little. From what we know of him in later life, it is probable that he excelled at school, as he was certainly a fluent and persuasive speaker. In his recollections on the gunpowder plot, Father Oswald Tesimond gave a glowing account of him:

> Mr Robert Catesby was a gentleman of good family, indeed, of a house ancient and illustrious, rich and influential. He was some thirty-four years old at the time of the plot,[7] and was loved and esteemed not only by Catholics but by the very Protestants for his many unusual qualities both physical and mental. This gentleman it was who decided after much reflection to gather together all the enemies of the Catholic religion in England and get rid of them in one single blow.[8]

As would have been expected of him, Catesby made his way to university in his mid-teens, becoming a scholar at Gloucester Hall

College, Oxford, in 1586. The influence of his parents was still strong upon him at this point, as he left before graduating to avoid swearing an oath of allegiance that gave precedence to Queen Elizabeth over the Pope. This would have pleased Sir William and Anne, and it was hardly an unusual action at Gloucester Hall which had gained a reputation as the Oxford College of choice for Catholics,[9] and where many students chose not to graduate.

It is believed that Catesby then made a journey to the continent, and spent some time at the Catholic seminary at Douai,[10] but his next move after returning to England appalled his parents, when in 1593 he married Catherine Leigh. Catherine was the daughter of Sir Thomas Leigh of nearby Stoneleigh Abbey in Warwickshire, and a child of a prominent Protestant family. Catherine's grandfather, another Sir Thomas Leigh, had served as Lord Mayor of London and had led Queen Elizabeth's coronation procession (incidentally, Sir Thomas had a more famous descendant five generations later, the writer Jane Austen, who was a visitor to Stoneleigh Abbey).

Robert and Catherine's betrothal must have been a love marriage, as the two sets of parents were diametrically opposed on matters of religion, which was the burning issue of the day. Perhaps Robert Catesby persuaded his in-laws that he had seen the error of his ways, and that he had become a loyal Protestant. He may also have promised to bring up his children as Protestants; if so, he initially stuck to this vow, as we can see from the baptism record of Robert and Catherine's son, also called Robert Catesby, at the Protestant church of Chastleton on 11 November 1595.[11]

Catesby had inherited Chastleton House upon the death of his grandmother in 1594, and he and his wife made their home there. His early days at Chastleton were spent as a church papist, hiding his real faith and thus avoiding recusancy fines. Despite his fidelity to Catholicism it was an easy decision to understand – after all, Robert had enough examples in his own family of what could happen if you stepped too visibly out of line.[12]

His father, Sir William, was a bold man who refused to be bowed, and he was also a man who became ever poorer thanks to the recusancy fines levied upon him. The low point for Sir William came when he was caught harbouring the Jesuit priest Edmund Campion, and this landed both he and his brother-in-law Sir Thomas Tresham, alongside William Vaux of Harrowden, in the Star Chamber in 1581. The Star Chamber was the Westminster court of law used to try prominent members of the gentry and the nobility, and a terrifying place for Catesby to find himself. The three accused were lucky to escape with their lives, although they all spent extended periods in prison throughout the rest of their lives. A worse fate was to befall his mother's relative Sir Francis Throckmorton: in 1584 he was convicted of being behind a plot (one of the many plots) to free Mary Queen of Scots and place her on the throne, and for this he was tortured on the rack and then hung, drawn and quartered.[13]

Catesby was, to all intents and purposes, a good and loyal English subject in his first years at Chastleton House – one who fitted in, and who didn't cause trouble. He had seen how Catholicism could make its followers poor, or leave them languishing in prison or sent to a gruesome execution, and had taken a more conciliatory route by marrying into a Protestant family and baptising his son into England's new faith. The marriage to Catherine also brought Robert an instant financial advantage, as he gained a substantial dowry of £2,000 from her parents.[14] As a Protestant, or at least one who was hiding his Catholicism, he could have expected a promising future, so what went wrong?

In one of the many strange coincidences linking the gunpowder conspirators, it seems that the same events that led to Guy Fawkes' adoption of a more militant Catholicism were also behind Robert Catesby's radicalisation: namely the loss of the woman he loved, and at the same time the opportunity that was presented by coming into his father's inheritance.

Sir William Catesby and his daughter-in-law Catherine Catesby, née Leigh, both died in 1598, sweeping away the two main influences in Robert's life within the space of a few months. It was a time for reflection, as similar events had been for Guy Fawkes, and a time for renewal. Sir William had stood up for what he believed in, and had been unflinching in the face of punishment. Comparing himself to his deceased father, Robert saw himself as an embarrassment to the legacy he had inherited – he had become an appeaser rather than a man of action, self-serving rather than faithful to his own beliefs. Now, with his Protestant wife dead, he could put away his Protestant mask.

The change in Catesby was dramatic, as he not only embraced his Catholicism once more, but determined to become what his father had been – one of the leaders of England's Catholic cause. There is evidence, however, that Robert had begun this journey back to his old faith even before the deaths of his father and wife. In 1597, the Jesuit priest Father John Gerard made an audacious escape from the Tower of London by inching along a rope that had been thrown from a boat in the River Thames.[15]

This made Gerard one of the most wanted men in England, and one of the homes that he found refuge in after his escape was Morecrofts in Uxbridge, one of the residences of Robert Catesby.[16] The fugitive priest remained there until he regained his strength and resumed his ministry. Already hiding at Morecrofts in 1597 was Father Garnet who had made his way there after entering the country, although he would soon find a more permanent home in White Webbs near Enfield, the property of devout Catholic Anne Vaux.[17]

Catesby's militant Catholicism grew stronger and stronger after the deaths of 1598, and he became well known among those of his faith for harbouring priests, among them Oswald Tesimond of York, who under the alias of Father Greenway became Catesby's confessor. Catesby's inheritance gave him an annual income of approximately £3,000,[18] a vast fortune, and he used this to further the cause of Catholicism – as if in penance for his days as a church papist. Converting others to Catholicism became his only joy in life. Father Tesimond gives the following account of Catesby, and his activities, at this time:

> Physically, Catesby was more than ordinarily well-proportioned, some six feet tall, of good carriage and handsome countenance. He was grave in manner, but

attractively so. He was also considered one of the most dashing and courageous horsemen in the country. Generous and affable, he was for that reason much loved by everyone. Catesby was much devoted of his religion, as one would expect of a man who made his communion every Sunday. Indeed, his zeal was so great that in his own opinion he was wasting time when he was not doing something to bring about the conversion of the country... In fact it became almost a proverb that Robert Catesby could be seen nowhere without his priest. He seemed to have much more success in converting Protestants than many of the priests now to be found in England.[19]

A further example of Catesby's new way of life came in 1601, and it almost cost him his life. Already with a reputation as a fearless man of action among the Catholic community, it was inevitable that he should become embroiled in the Essex rebellion of 1601 that led to the downfall of Queen Elizabeth's former favourite. Catesby may not have been involved in the planning of the plot, on this occasion, but he did march fully armed into London and was wounded in the fighting. He was arrested and imprisoned, and among those arrested with him were Jack and Kit Wright, Thomas Percy, Francis Tresham, Thomas Wintour and John Grant.[20] They all endured periods in prison, in the Fleet in Catesby's case, and were only released when large fines were paid.

Robert Catesby had to sell Chastleton House to pay his fine of £3,000,[21] after which he moved into his widowed mother's home at Ashby St. Ledgers. The wounding and imprisonment did Catesby's reputation no harm, and his charisma and piety soon earned him the love and respect of those who had been caught up in the Essex rebellion alongside him, and who would shortly join with him, Guy Fawkes and others in an even deadlier plot. With family ties already binding the men, Catesby created a further bond by betrothing his son to the daughter of Thomas Percy at the age of 8: an agreement that they would marry when they were legally able to. This also created a bond with the Wright brothers, as the mother of Percy's daughter was their sister Martha.[22]

Robert Catesby's activities before, during and after the Essex Rebellion had inevitably brought him to the attention of chief courtier and spymaster Sir Robert Cecil. The scrutiny that he was under, and the suspicion in which he was held, was shown by the fact that he was temporarily imprisoned, as a precautionary measure, when Queen Elizabeth was dying. This fate also befell other Catholics who were adjudged to pose a threat to a smooth, and Protestant, succession.[23]

Catesby's reputation continued to grow among those who knew him, as shown in a letter to Catesby from his cousin William Parker:

> If all creatures born under the moon's sphere cannot endure without the elements of air and fire, in what languishment have we led our life since we departed from the dear Robin whose conversation gave such warmth as we needed no other heat to maintain our healths... let no watery nymphs divert you, who can live better with the air, and better forebear the fire of your spirit and vigour than we, who account thy person the only sun that must ripen our harvest.[24]

This letter is even more remarkable when you consider that the man who wrote it was formally known by the name of Baron Monteagle, and two years later it was his actions that would condemn Robert Catesby, Guy Fawkes and others to their death.

By the early seventeenth century Robert Catesby was the sun that ripened the harvest, the tall and imposing gentleman, the brilliant horseman, the charismatic leader, the pious Catholic, the eloquent and learned speaker and the relentless converter; he was also a man capable of extreme violence, one who would do anything to achieve his aims with complete disregard to others, and a man who was now ready to bring a plan to fruition that would shake the country to its core.

Chapter 13

Six Men in the Duck and Drake

Drink today, and drown all sorrow;
You shall perhaps not do it tomorrow;
Best, while you have it, use your breath;
There is no drinking after death.
Fletcher, Jonson, Massinger and Chapman,
Rollo Duke of Normandy

*Confiteor Deo omnipotenti, beatae Mariae semper Virgini, beato
Michaeli Archangelo, beato Ioanni Baptistae, sanctis Apostolis Petro
et Paulo, et omnibus Sanctis, quia peccavi nimis cogitatione, verbo et
opere: mea culpa, mea culpa, mea maxima culpa.*

The Latin words being intoned were familiar to all six men in the
darkened side-room with its door firmly locked. In English they read,
'I confess to almighty God, to blessed Mary ever Virgin, to blessed
Michael the Archangel, to blessed John the Baptist, to the holy apostles
Peter and Paul, and to all the saints that I have sinned exceedingly in
thought, word, and deed, through my fault, through my fault, through
my most grievous fault.'

This formula known as the *confiteore* was an introductory part of
the Catholic mass, as it had been since the eleventh century, and
continues to be so in a slightly altered form to this day. It was being
spoken quietly, slowly, deliberately by Father John Gerard – the Jesuit
priest who was still evading capture after his escape from the Tower
more than six years earlier.

The date was Sunday, 20 May 1604. This was no church fit for a
mass, however. It was a back room of the Duck and Drake pub just

off The Strand in London. Five men knelt and listened to the priest in silent reverence: they were Robert Catesby, Thomas Wintour, Jack Wright, Thomas Percy, and with them a man who had just returned to England from a self-imposed exile lasting over a decade – Guy Fawkes.[1]

From outside their room came the everyday sounds of the inn: wine being served to men of position, ale to those of a lesser standing along with the hop-brewed beer which was a new introduction from continental Europe; horses being fed, mounted or dismounted in the central courtyard; arguments over games of dice, and the echoes of drunken singing. The men inside the room were taking their first steps to a far from everyday occurrence, they were embarking upon a plot to destroy the ruling establishment of England – King, Lords and Bishops.

The chief instigator was Robert Catesby, and the gathering in the Duck and Drake marked the continuation of a feverish idea which had been growing within him for years. He had tried the passive approach of a church papist, tried to live a quiet family life, but in that time he had watched the Catesby fortunes dwindle and seen his father and uncle face persecution and jail. Harbouring Jesuit priests such as Fathers Gerard, Garnet and Tesimond had only served to fire his zeal for action – he didn't have the temperament to be a priest, but he certainly had the temperament to be a fighter in the Catholic cause.

While others of his generation, such as Guy Fawkes, had journeyed to Flanders to fight against the Protestant religion, Catesby knew that if true change was to happen then the fight would need to be brought to England. It was this burning belief, a desire for revolution, that made him throw his lot in with the ill-starred Essex rebellion. It was also this rising despair and anger that led Catesby to send Thomas Wintour to Spain in 1602, hoping to gain the military backing he needed to be confident of success in his plans.[2]

The failure of Essex's uprising and the lack of support from Spain brought Catesby to the realisation that he would have to launch an uprising of his own; it became an obsession bordering on the pathological that grew by the day from 1603 onward. While some Catholics continued to hope for tolerance from the new king, Catesby knew that James could not be trusted; there was no time to waste, but for any plot to succeed he would need a close group of men around him: men who felt as he did; men who were not afraid to die, not afraid to kill; men who could be trusted.

One man fitted the bill thanks to a zeal that almost matched that of Catesby himself, Thomas Percy, and it may have been a visit from Percy to Catesby in the summer of 1603 that cemented his intentions. Percy and Catesby had become close friends over recent years, as shown by the betrothal of their children, and Catesby had also chosen Percy to oversee the sale of his Chastleton estate to pay off the fines he incurred after the Essex rebellion.[3]

Thomas Percy too had become increasingly frustrated with the new King's reign. He had taken James's hand in his, talked to him man to man, and then told his friends the news that James had promised tolerance towards Catholics in England. It quickly became apparent that James would not live up to these promises, if indeed he had ever made them in the unequivocal way that Percy described. This was not only an affront against his religion, but against Thomas Percy himself. He felt his honesty and integrity being questioned.

This wasn't the first time that Thomas Percy's honour had been called into question. His role as Constable of Alnwick saw Percy accused of bullying and embezzlement on many occasions. His long-standing reputation as a ready swordsman and fighter ensured that most of his tenants were too scared to raise concerns against him, and yet in 1602 he was proven to be dishonest in court – not on one or two counts, but on 34 counts.[4] Nevertheless, his master the Earl of Northumberland rewarded him with ever greater powers – after all, it didn't do to follow the law too strictly when collecting rents.

Percy had faced even greater trouble in 1596 when he was arrested and imprisoned for killing a Scotsman named James Burne, but the Earl of Essex used his influence, at the time, to have Percy released. Writing to the judge, John Beaumont, the Earl of Essex said:

> I understand by this bearer, my servant Meyricke, of your willing disposition to favour Thomas Percy, a near

kinsman to my brother of Northumberland, who is in trouble for some offence imputed unto him. I pray you to continue the same, that thereby his life may not be in hazard. He is a gentleman well descended and of good parts, and very able to do his country good service.[5]

There was yet another matter that threw doubt upon Thomas Percy's piety, and that could have been particularly prejudicial to his role in the gunpowder plot. As we've seen, he was married to Martha, the sister of Jack and Kit Wright, but it was also said that he kept a second spouse in the south of England. The rumour may not have been true, and he would not have been the only man of this time to commit bigamy, especially when many Catholic marriages were carried out secretly and unofficially, but it gave him a reputation for dissolution.

It was widely reported in his lifetime that Thomas Percy had two wives and that while one was kept in Warwickshire the other lived in abject poverty in London.[6] Many people have taken this to mean that Martha Percy, née Wright, was the abandoned and impoverished wife, but it would seem more logical to assume that it was the other wife who was living in poverty – after all Martha had the family to support her;[7] and would Jack and Kit Wright have so willingly worked alongside a man who had treated their sister so shabbily?

Father Gerard described Thomas Percy thus: 'For the most part of his youth he had been very wild more than ordinary, and much given to fighting'.[8] However it was also reported that he had calmed down greatly in later years, thanks to his conversion to a more open Catholicism (having probably been a church papist beforehand) and that he always kept a priest in his house for his own use and that of his friends.[9]

Any changes which had taken place in this tall, strong, imposing man with white hair and a white beard were merely superficial; inside he remained volatile, quick to anger and ready to strike – although loyal to his friends and those he served. It was these qualities that made him so useful to the Earl of Northumberland, and it was the same qualities that made him attractive to Robert Catesby.

Catesby would not have been surprised by Percy's outburst during a meeting they had at Ashby St. Legers in June 1603, indeed he had probably provoked Percy into it to test the strength of feelings. Catesby talked of how different the actions of King James were to the promises that Percy said he had given to him, and this was enough for the volcanic Percy to vow he would kill the King with his own hands. A smile crossed Catesby's lips as he answered sardonically, 'No, no, Tom, thou shalt not venture to small purpose, but if thou wilt be a traitor thou wilt be to some great advantage. I am thinking of a most sure way and I will soon let thee know what it is'.[10]

Thomas Percy the bigamist, Thomas Percy the killer, Thomas Percy the embezzler, Thomas Percy the ready swordsman, Thomas Percy the friend: as he shook hands and took leave of him, Robert Catesby knew he had found a man he could rely on for the murderous deeds he was planning.

He was now convinced that Percy had the mettle and desire to join his plot, but he did not reveal it to him yet. The first to be gathered into the epicentre of the plot was a man almost as volatile as Thomas Percy, his old sword fighting partner Jack Wright.

By October 1503 – Catesby had revealed his intentions to Jack, and it was a plot both carefully targeted and yet ridiculously broad and ambitious. Catesby had known for a long time that killing the King alone would not be enough, a view shared by Guy Fawkes as he spurned a golden opportunity to kill the King not long before the plot was due to be enacted.[11] No, to gain tolerance and equality for Catholics, not only the King but all his ruling lords and councillors must be destroyed completely. It must be a blow so complete and terrible that the function of government would be stopped altogether, leaving a void that Catesby could fill with a Catholic puppet of his choosing. Tesimond summed up Catesby's plot, as he revealed it to the men he recruited, thus:

> [Catesby] decided after much reflection to gather together all the enemies of the Catholic religion in England and get rid of them in one single blow. Liberty and religion would

be restored to Catholics with no resistance. To carry out this resolve, the best way seemed to him to await the reassembly of Parliament, when the three estates of the realm would be together with the King, councillors, puritans and bishops. These were all of them determined that in that time and place they would give the final death blow to the Catholic cause, as we have said. In that same moment of time, the plotters hoped to bring upon their heads the evil they had designed for others. They would blow them up with a mine, and the Parliament-house along with them. In this way, the authors of those most cruel laws would be removed along with the very place where they had been made. By this means he [Catesby] also thought that no leader would be left to oppose the papists.[12]

We know that Jack Wright was the first to be recruited to Catesby's plot from the testimony of the second recruit: Thomas Wintour.[13] The Wintours and Catesby were cousins, and Catesby's confidence in them was shown by letters that he sent to both Thomas Wintour and his brother Robert on 1 November 1603, a feast day known as All Saints' Day, referred to in Wintour's confession as 'All-hollantide'.[14] It was a day of solemnity when Catholics remembered their saints and especially their martyrs, a fitting day for Catesby to recruit people to what he fully envisaged could be a martyrdom of their own.

Probably to his surprise, Catesby initially found the Wintours less than willing to answer the nondescript letter calling them to his home: in fact, Robert Wintour sent a simple letter declining the invitation.[15] Thomas too replied that he could not visit his cousin as he was not very well disposed. This was the first time he had ever declined an invitation from Catesby,[16] and so it seems clear that both Thomas and Robert Wintour had a premonition of the danger the outwardly innocent letter contained. It is possible Catesby had already dropped hints to the brothers of a possible plot, as he had done to Thomas Percy, and that they'd decided to keep clear of it if possible, but Catesby was never one to be turned down that easily.

Upon receiving Thomas Wintour's message, Catesby sent his messenger straight back to him at Huddington Court in Worcestershire and insisted that he must meet him. Unable to resist Catesby a second time, Thomas Wintour travelled to Lambeth where he found Catesby in company with Jack Wright.

Catesby asked Wintour about his plans to leave England to fight for the Catholic cause in Flanders, something they must have discussed previously, and dissuaded him from pursuing those plans. Wintour was told that he must not 'forsake his country', but stay to free it from its current servitude. It was then that Catesby revealed his dread plan to Thomas Wintour:

> He said that he had bethought him of a way at one instant
> to deliver us from all our bonds, and without any foreign
> help to replant again the Catholic religion, and withal told
> me in a word it was to blow up the Parliament House with
> gunpowder; for, said he, in that place have they done us
> all the mischief, and perchance God hath designed that
> place for their punishment.[17]

Wintour was shocked at the scale of Catesby's plot and countered that if they failed in their task, they, their families, and Catholics in general would suffer, and that they would be condemned for their actions rather than praised. As always, the persuasive Catesby had an answer:

> He told me the nature of the disease required so sharp a
> remedy, and asked me if I would give my consent. I told
> him Yes, in this or what else so ever, if he resolved upon
> it, I would venture my life.[18]

Throughout all of this part of Thomas Wintour's confession, drawn out of the badly injured man at the Tower of London,[19] there is no mention of the action or words of Jack Wright. He may have been sitting there as a silent witness, nodding encouragement at the right moments, or simply have been intended as an intimidating presence, but it is likely that Wright was behind what happened next.

Although agreeing to participate in the plan, even to the point of giving up his life if necessary, Wintour had still expressed some concerns about its ferocity. Catesby placated him by saying that they must seek a meeting with the Constable of Castile[20] first, to see if a peaceful resolution could still be found. The Spanish constable had travelled to Belgium in January 1604 to begin peace negotiations with England. Catesby asked Wright to travel to the continent to meet the constable, inform him of the parlous state of England's Catholics, and ask the constable to intercede on their behalf in his negotiations with King James – if this led to James revoking anti-Catholic penal laws then the plot would be abandoned.

This was Catesby's way of soothing Wintour's objections, and a counter to objections from any conspirators who may be added to the group later. Now at least they could say they had given the peaceful path one final chance, even though Catesby knew as well as anybody that the Constable of Castile, who was set on achieving peace with England at all costs, would not get any such promise or action out of King James.

Wintour's proposed journey to Flanders had one further reason – the real reason for the journey, that was added on as if it was an afterthought to the earlier conversation. Wintour, in his confession, remembered Catesby's words:

> Withal, you may bring over some confidant gentleman
> such as you shall understand best able for this business,
> and named unto me Mr. Fawkes.[21]

It seems certain that Catesby had already heard of Fawkes' reputation as a man of courage, a man fully committed to their cause and one who was willing and able to fight for it. It could be that he had already met Guy years earlier at Cowdray House, but the Guy of 1604 was very different to the one of ten years before: he was now battle-hardened and a man of the world, one who had consorted with royalty and scythed his way through bloody battlefields.

He may also have heard glowing reports of Guy from his sources overseas, namely William Stanley and Hugh Owen, and there was one other man who would have spoken highly of his abilities: the man who sat alongside Robert Catesby, Jack Wright. Jack could have remembered Guy from their school days in York, or have heard a more recent report of him from his brother Kit who had been in Spain with Guy, but Jack left Catesby in little doubt that Guy was a man who could be brought into their little group.

So it was that Thomas Wintour left Lambeth and sailed for Belgium. His meeting with Guy Fawkes would result in Guy's return to London, to a conspiratorial meeting in the Duck and Drake, to cellars underneath the House of Lords, to the torture chambers of the Tower of London, and to the gallows and lasting infamy.

Chapter 14

This is the Gentleman

Speak, speak, let terror strike slaves mute,
Much danger makes great hearts most resolute
John Marston, *The Wonder of Women*

By 1604, Guy Fawkes had spent around a decade away from the country of his birth. In those years he had fought valiantly for the Catholic cause with the Spanish army, and gained promotion, esteem and the scars of battle. In that time, however, he had also seen men slaughtered on the unforgiving sands of Flanders, and witnessed appalling conditions among his fellow soldiers, with troops failing to be paid and having to subsist on a handful of bread or a portion of cheese every day.[1] Men who had given their all for a cause were left to scavenge acorns for food, while others resorted by necessity to looting and pillaging.

It was not only Guy's bravery that had brought him to the attention of his superiors but also his intelligence, and it was this that led Stanley and Owen to select him to meet King Philip III in a final attempt to persuade him to use force against England rather than seeking peace. This had resulted in frustration for Guy: he had found the King and his councillors paying lip service to his words, and for months was kept a virtual prisoner, too dangerous to be set free in case his actions impacted upon the fledgling peace talks between Spain and England.

After Guy's release, and the failure of his mission to Spain, Guy returned to the English regiment in Flanders,[2] but he now had a more jaundiced view of life and the fight he was involved in than when he'd first crossed the sea from England. Peace was breaking out across Europe, and Guy saw now that the real fight between Catholics and Protestants was continuing, as it always had, in England. A visit from an old acquaintance would provide the opportunity he was now looking for.

After landing at Dunkirk, Thomas Wintour had sought out Hugh Owen, knowing that the Welsh Intelligencer had the knowledge and influence to gain him an audience with the Constable of Castile. The meeting was arranged at Bergen, the Dutch name given to present day Mons in southern Belgium, and it says a lot for Hugh Owen's standing and reputation that he was able to broker a meeting between Wintour and the Spanish duke who must have been busily occupied in the early stages of peace negotiations.

As Catesby had no doubt foreseen when sending Wintour to Belgium, the Constable was not prepared to offer any support other than non-committal words of semi-encouragement. In Wintour's confession he states that Catesby later asked him what the Constable's response had been, to which Wintour replied 'good words',[3] but it was clear that these words would not be backed up by actions, at least not by the Spanish army.

Following the disappointing conclusion to the meeting, Wintour travelled back to Dunkirk in the company of Owen, and pressed him further on whether he thought Spain would offer English Catholics any assistance if there was an uprising of some kind. Owen could be blunt when he had to, and replied unequivocally that the Spanish court cared little for the Catholics of England now, being solely focused upon concluding an armistice with their old enemy.

His answer was received by Wintour with a heavy heart, for he knew now that there was nothing which could stop Robert Catesby pressing ahead with his murderous plan – a plan to which he had pledged his allegiance.

There was no going back, and so there was nothing to do but to act upon the secondary part of his overseas mission, an action that he still didn't realise was the sole reason he'd been sent to the Low Countries. Here is Wintour's account of his conversation with Hugh Owen:

> I told him that there were many gentlemen in England
> who would not forsake their country until they had tried

their uttermost, and rather venture their lives than forsake her in this misery; and to add one more to our number as a fit man, both for counsel and execution of whatsoever we should resolve, wished for Mr Fawkes who I had heard good commendation of. He told me the gentleman deserved no less, but was at Brussels, and that if he came not, as happily he might, before my departure, he would send him shortly after into England.[4]

This paragraph from Wintour's confession reveals much about the esteem in which Guy Fawkes was held in 1604. Hugh Owen is full of praise for Fawkes, and although he is able to command Fawkes at will (saying that he will send him on to England) it seems that Guy has some degree of autonomy. He is in Brussels, far from any fighting, but may or may not appear in Dunkirk in the next few days. This could be an indication that Guy has left the life of a soldier behind, and instead become someone like Hugh Owen himself – an intelligencer, a spy and agitator for the Catholic cause.

Taking his leave of Owen, Wintour next made his way to Ostend hoping to speak to another of the leading Catholic exiles – Sir William Stanley. Wintour was disappointed in this endeavour as well, as he discovered that Stanley was away in Spain on another of his secretive missions. After two days, however, Stanley arrived in Ostend, and spent a period of four days with Thomas Wintour.

All this information is known from Wintour's confession, but there is further information that is conspicuous by its absence. Wintour is careful not to implicate Owen or Stanley in the gunpowder plot. But it is highly unlikely that neither man knew about it or had a hand in it. Even though they had spent long years in exile from England, they had a network of connections within it, and their machinations were probably at the heart of many of the plots during the late sixteenth and early seventeenth centuries. It is difficult to believe that Stanley and Wintour spent four days in each other's company without talking about the specifics of Catesby's plan, but you won't find any mention of such a conversation in Wintour's confession. Wintour does admit to talking to Stanley about Guy Fawkes, and gets a similarly glowing report to the one given by Hugh Owen a week earlier:

> I came to speak of Mr. Fawkes whose company I wished over into England. I asked of his sufficiency in the wars, and told him we should need such as he, if occasion required. He gave very good commendations of him.[5]

After four days alongside Stanley there was still no sign of Guy, so Wintour announced that he was leaving for Nieuwpoort, but as he was saying his goodbyes a shadow fell across them and a tall man entered the room before saluting them both. He was not only tall in stature but broad and powerfully built as well; he had an abundance of reddish-brown hair, a bushy red beard and a long flowing moustache[6]. He had the tanned skin of a man who spent time in the field rather than in the halls of some stately home, and his unflinching gaze spoke of his confidence as well as hinting at an inner menace.

Stanley smiled at the puzzled expression on Wintour's face, before explaining, 'This is the gentleman that you wished for'.[7]

It was no coincidence that Guy Fawkes arrived just as Thomas Wintour was about to depart. It seems likely that he had been in Dunkirk during the days that Wintour spent with William Stanley, waiting for a pre-arranged signal and deliberately holding back his presence so that his master Stanley could get as much information as possible from Wintour about his plans, and Guy's potential role in them.

If Wintour's confession is to be believed, even at this point he didn't give Guy any details of what Catesby had planned, instead telling him obliquely,

> I told him some good friends of his wished his company in England; and that if it pleased him to come to Dunkirk, we would have further conference, whither I was then going: so taking my leave of both, I departed. About two days after came Mr Fawkes to Dunkirk, where I told him

that we were on a resolution to do somewhat in England
if the peace with Spain helped us not, but had as yet
resolved upon nothing.[8]

Once again, we can read between the lines and assume that Wintour
revealed a little bit more than he admitted in his confession, a
confession designed to remove suspicion from Hugh Owen and
William Stanley.

Would the merest hint of a plan, and an admission that they had so
far 'resolved upon nothing' be enough to bring Guy Fawkes back to
England? It is more likely that Guy spent two days being debriefed by
Sir William Stanley before journeying onto Dunkirk, where Wintour
gave more than a hint that they planned to take direct action against
King James. This was exactly the sort of plan Guy would have
supported; no more hot, humid months waiting within whitewashed
walls in Valladolid, he would breathe the fresh air of home again, and
he would be breathing it with a purpose he had long dreamed of:
revenge for Margaret Clitherow, revenge for Robert Middleton,
revenge for all those who had lost their property, liberty and lives.

However much was revealed to Guy, it was enough to convince
him where his duty lay, and in late April 1604 both he and Thomas
Wintour were on a ship to Greenwich. Guy was sailing to his place in
the plot and to his black place in history, but what exactly was he being
recruited for? Primarily he was recruited because of his experience in
mining and the use of explosives, gained in encounters such as the
Siege of Calais. It's all too easy, however, to dismiss this as Guy's only
role, for as Thomas Wintour said in his meeting with Hugh Owen, he
was wanted not only to oversee the execution of the plot, but for his
counsel and help in organising it.

Another reason behind his recruitment was that Catesby prized Guy
not merely as a practical and courageous man, but for his strong links
to Hugh Owen and William Stanley. These links could be used if
necessary, Catesby reasoned, to bring armed men to England in
support of an uprising, or to gain extra supplies of weaponry or
gunpowder.

Guy stepped out of the boat at Greenwich a very different man to the one who had stepped into a boat alongside his cousin Robert Collinge a decade earlier. He knew that an uprising or rebellion was being planned, even if he didn't as yet know all the details, and that inevitably this meant his own life would be in grave danger. So be it, he had faced death many times in the Low Countries, and his homeland would be as good a place to die as any other if that was what God had ordained for him. Until that moment came, whenever and however it came, he would continue to do what he had always done: he would serve, and he would fight.

Guy and Thomas Wintour rowed up the Thames from the docks at Greenwich to Catesby's riverside residence at Lambeth, a distance of eight miles, a gruelling journey which took the men about an hour.

Catesby was impressed at his first sight of Guy Fawkes (or at least his first sight of him since he left Cowdray House): here was a man who was fitted to hard work, and one who would not shirk in the face of danger. Guy is likely to have been impressed with Robert Catesby too. He was imposing not just because his remarkable self-confidence and the force of his character, but by his physical stature too,[9] with his six foot plus frame being at least half a foot taller than the average man of this time.

Guy, although used to being among strangers, was pleased to see a familiar face in the Lambeth dwelling, even if both he and Jack Wright had changed physically from their school days together. It was further confirmation that he had made the right decision, and that fate was now showing him the path to take. Guy and Thomas were given food and wine to replenish their energy, and it is likely that Guy would then have met another old boy of St. Peter's school in Oswald Tesimond, under the name of Father Greenway, who was never far from Catesby when he was at home.

Guy stayed in Lambeth for several days, during which Catesby and Wright explained the state of England as they saw it – how hopes of tolerance for their religion under King James were gone, and how they could expect a persecution in excess even of that driven by Queen Elizabeth and her courtiers. As yet, however, there was no disclosure of the plot itself; that had to wait until another man arrived at the house.

Thomas Percy received the curt summons from Catesby, presumably similar to the one he had earlier sent to the Wintours, with glee. The scantness of information was itself a sign that things were to be discussed that couldn't be safely committed to paper, and his mind travelled back to that day a year earlier when Catesby had promised to tell him later of a plan he was formulating; this would be Catesby's 'most sure way' revealed at last.

Percy strode into the house with his characteristic confidence and loudness. Surveying the scene before him he gained further encouragement at the men seated around the room, particularly the sight of his old fighting partner Jack Wright. Here indeed were Thomas Percy's kind of plotters, and before uttering another word he famously cried out, 'Shall we always, gentlemen, talk and never do anything?'[10]

These words would have brought a smile to the men's lips, for after the failure of Thomas Wintour's talks with the Constable of Castile there was little doubt that this time they would turn their rhetoric into action. It is also telling that Percy didn't seem at all surprised to see Guy Fawkes among the gathering, and was prepared to speak openly with him present at a time when unknown people could easily be Cecil's spies or men who would sell you to the devil and the gallows for the right reward. This could be taken as an indication that Percy and Guy were known to each other, presumably from Scotton.

The five men were now gathered, but Catesby still remained silent on the details of his plan; all would be revealed in the proper time and place – that time and place being the Duck and Drake on 20 May 1604. The choice of a public inn for such a private, and potentially deadly, conversation may seem strange, but Elizabethan and Jacobean inns were different to today's public houses. They typically had many rooms that could be hired for a fee, and there was always background noise to stop prying ears hearing what they shouldn't.

Among those in the know, there were inns that specifically, if secretly, catered for the Catholic community, and where priests could often be found; the Duck and Drake was just such a place. Another example of the use of inns for this purpose was in 1586 when Anthony

Babington, who came from a wealthy Derbyshire family who owned large properties of their own in the county and beyond,[11] instead chose to plot the assassination of Queen Elizabeth in London inns.[12]

We have seen how an integral part of the gunpowder conspirator's meeting was the mass said by Father Gerard, but while this was all the incriminating evidence the government would need, the Jesuit priest remained unaware of what the men were gathering for.[13] Before mass was said, the five conspirators had gathered in another room for an essential part of the proceedings: it was there that Guy Fawkes and Thomas Percy placed their hand upon a primer, a book of prayers and devotions to be said at certain times of the day, and repeated what Catesby, Jack Wright and Thomas Wintour had already done – an oath of fellowship and an oath of secrecy. They swore before the others present, but more importantly before God himself, that they would keep secret whatever they were about to hear, on pain of death and eternal damnation. Swords were unsheathed before them as a symbol of what anyone who broke the oath could expect, but it was the thought of punishment after death that carried the most weight.

The oath was taken without any hesitation. Without yet being told the plan, Guy had pledged his silence and his life. From that room the five entered mass with Father Gerard, the communion bread and wine further sealing the new bond between them. With the mass over Gerard left the room, ignorant of their plans but undoubtedly able to feel the tension in the air. The men were alone, and it was now that Robert Catesby finally revealed the plan in its minutiae.[14] They would find a suitable property near to the House of Lords, and from there tunnel under the building before planting enough gunpowder to completely destroy it and anyone within. At the same time, a group of men would seize the Lady Elizabeth, daughter of King James, with a view to installing her as the puppet queen to a new Catholic regime.[15]

Guy wholeheartedly approved of the plan.[16] Any qualms he had about killing had been lost on the battlefields of Flanders, and he had no doubt that he and the men around him were fighting for a just cause. Guy was prepared to offer his all for his faith, for his country, and for the new brotherhood he had indissolubly entered into.

118

The Gunpowder Conspirators by Crispijn van de Passe the Elder.

The Discovery of the Gunpowder Plot and the Taking of Guy Fawkes by Henry Perronet Briggs.

The Execution of Guy Fawkes by Claes Jansz Visscher.

The Tower of London (note Traitor's Gate below).

Guy Fawkes laying
the gunpowder by
George Cruikshank.

Queen Elizabeth's
'rainbow portrait'.

Baron Monteagle by John de Critz the Elder.

James I (artist unknown).

Lady Elizabeth Stuart, aged 7,
by Robert Peake the Elder.
The plotters planned to make
her Queen.

Thomas Percy (artist
unknown).

The Somerset House
Conference, by Juan
Pantoja de la Cruz. The
conference sealed peace
between Spain and
England, fuelling the
gunpowder plot.

The Death Of
Catesby by George
Cruikshank.

Saint Margaret
Clitherow.

St Michael-le-Belfrey church, York,
where Guy Fawkes was baptised in
1570.

A Plot With Powder, seventeenth centrury illustration.

Sir Robert Cecil by
John de Critz the Elder.

Chapter 15

The Unknown Servant

I will do such things—
What they are yet I know not, but they shall be
The terrors of the earth. You think I'll weep?
No, I'll not weep.
William Shakespeare, *King Lear*[1]

The act the five conspirators had just committed themselves to carrying out was horrific on a human scale, and yet we can imagine the elation they felt as Catesby's plans were revealed. At this point in time the terrible outcome of the plot, the scores of dead, the limbless and wounded, were inconsequential when compared to the thought of the blow they were about to strike for the Catholic cause in which they so fervently believed.

As he returned to his lodgings, Guy, who may at this point have been taking a room at Catesby's residence or at the London properties of Thomas Wintour or Thomas Percy, would have felt a calmness that eluded the others. He had seen the dread and deadly outcome of gunpowder explosions, but his time as a soldier had taught him that the end justifies the means. Guy was not lacking in compassion for those he loved and valued, but the ending of his enemies lives, even on a grand scale, was an act akin to the snuffing out of a candle.

Before taking their leave of each other from the Duck and Drake, the five had discussions as to their individual roles within the plot. Guy was understandably given the vital task of organising the mining of the tunnel and the dynamite. One of the first tasks was to find a suitable property near to the House of Lords. This search occupied the

119

first few weeks following their meeting, until fate intervened in their favour.

The Earl of Northumberland was in charge of the King's Gentleman Pensioners. It was a title which belied their actual duties, for in fact they were the King's personal bodyguards. Northumberland had the authority to recruit suitable men for this prestigious role; whoever was chosen would have to be of noble stock and character, devoted to the King, trustworthy, honest and reliable, brave and willing to fight when necessary. These last two qualities were perhaps the only ones possessed by the man Northumberland appointed to the Gentleman Pensioners on 9 June 1604: his perennial favourite, Thomas Percy.

Percy's Catholicism should have made him ineligible for the Gentleman Pensioners as all members had to swear an oath of allegiance to the King, acknowledging that James had supremacy over religious leaders including the Pope. Knowing how strong Thomas Percy's faith had become, Northumberland didn't ask him to take the oath but made him a Gentleman Pensioner anyway. It was a gesture made in friendship, and it was one that would later come close to costing the Earl of Northumberland his life.[2]

As a Gentleman Pensioner, Thomas Percy would be expected to spend certain times of each year in proximity to Parliament, and this gave the conspirators the perfect cover to buy a property close to the House of Lords without arousing too much suspicion.

A suitable property was soon found in Westminster, owned by John Whynniard who was Yeoman of his Majesty's Wardrobe of the Beds. Once again the rather archaic title belies the importance of this position, as it gave the holder privileged access to the King. Whynniard, however, was not living in the property himself but had sub-let it to a man named Henry Ferrers. For that reason Whynniard and Guy Fawkes were destined not to see each other until the fateful night of 4 November 1605.[3]

Percy opened negotiations with Ferrers, but found them more difficult than he might have expected. In his capacity as rent collector for the Earl of Northumberland he normally found it easy to make people comply with his wishes, not always by lawful means, but he was under strict orders not to use his normal negotiating style with Ferrers, as the last thing the conspirators wanted to do was to draw too much attention to themselves at these early stages of the plot.

In some ways it's surprising that Ferrers was not more easily swayed, as he too was a Catholic recusant and the owner of Baddesley Clinton. Baddesley Clinton had been rented by Anne Vaux and her sister Eleanor between 1586 and 1591.[4] The Vaux sisters dedicated their lives to helping and sheltering Catholic priests, and it was probably at their behest that the manor house had three hidden priest holes constructed within it by Nicholas Owen.

Owen was known as Little John because he was very small, and he walked with a limp as the result of a riding accident. Despite his physical frailties, he was a man of great courage and the undisputed master of the construction of complex priest holes. Owen's hidden chambers were almost impossible to discover and they afforded their occupants vital shelter when searches were being made by the authorities. After a long career designing these holes he was captured in 1606, taken to the Tower of London and tortured to death, with his stomach bursting open and his intestines pouring out.[5] He was canonised by the Catholic Church in 1970, and it is believed that many of his priest holes remain hidden and undiscovered in houses across England to this day.

The effectiveness of Owen's priest holes at Baddesley Clinton were put to the test in 1591, when they successfully concealed nine Jesuits for four hours during a search, including Fathers Southwell and Gerard, who described the ordeal:

> Outside the ruffians were bawling and yelling, but the servants held the door fast. They said the mistress of the house, a widow [Eleanor Brooksby née Vaux], was not yet up, but was coming down at once to answer them. This gave us enough time to stow ourselves and all our belongings into a very cleverly built sort of cave. At last these leopards [the searchers] were let in. They tore madly through the whole house, searched everywhere, pried with

candles into the darkest corners. They took four hours over the work but fortunately they chanced on nothing. All they did was to show how dogged and spiteful they could be.[6]

With such excellent Catholic credentials, it seems surprising that Henry Ferrers was not more immediately compliant to Percy's wishes, especially as Catesby, who he must have known, and Anne Vaux of White Webbs could also have pleaded their cause. Eventually negotiations for the house were finalised and Thomas Percy took possession of the property, and with it the neighbouring house belonging to a man named Gideon Gibbons. To sweeten the deal Percy gave Henry Ferrers, a man always short of money, the substantial sum of twenty pounds, or, as Ferrers says at the end of his document granting the lease to Thomas Percy, 'And the said Thomas hath lent unto me the said Henry twenty pounds, to be allowed upon reckoning or to be re-paid again at the will of the said Thomas'.[7]

At last Guy Fawkes could begin the construction of the tunnel, but as soon as the ink on Percy's lease had dried they found themselves frustrated again. King James, holding the throne of both England and Scotland, had decided to unify the two nations, and this resulted in official meetings between councillors from both sides of the border. To the dismay of the plotters, the government commandeered Whynniard's house for this purpose. While the talks continued, plans for the tunnel would have to be put on hold indefinitely.

Guy Fawkes was a man of action, yet he now found himself facing a delay that might prove as frustrating and fruitless as that he had endured in Spain. His distress was heightened at the thought that the house they had planned to use as a base from which to destroy the persecutors of England's Catholics was instead being used to negotiate a union with the Scottish, a people despised by Guy.

Anti-Scottish sentiment was widespread across England, but Guy's hatred of Scotland and its inhabitants was extreme. This may have had its origins in Guy's York roots, as the people of York still passed on tales of the city's suffering during the Scottish siege of the city in

1297.[8] Guy also saw Scotland as the seat of Puritanism, and the followers of the Scot John Calvin were among the most vigorous persecutors of Catholicism. The depth of Guy's anti-Scottish feeling was shown in the letter he had carried to King Philip III of Spain, in which he wrote,

> There is a natural hostility between the English and the Scots. There has always been one, and at present it keeps increasing. Even were there but one religion in England, nevertheless it will not be possible to reconcile these two nations, as they are, for very long.[9]

Even when presented before King James himself, after being arrested and with torture and death inevitably to follow, he looked the King in the eye and declared that his intention had been 'to blow the Scottish beggars back to their native mountains'.[10]

With no likelihood of commencing work on the tunnel for some months, the conspirators dispersed to their homes around the country. It may be that Guy lodged with Thomas Percy at this time, for he had now adopted another guise – that of John Johnson, servant to Thomas Percy.[11]

One of Guy's great advantages compared to his fellow plotters was that he had been out of England for a decade. This meant he could go where he wanted, and do what he wanted to a certain degree, without arousing the suspicion of Robert Cecil's spies who had a heavy, if shadowy, presence in London. People like Catesby and Jack Wright were well known for their Catholic sympathies, and for their part in the Essex rebellion, and so they remained constantly under suspicion, and were treated accordingly. It is possible that the name of Guido Fawkes was known to the London spymasters because of his career in the Spanish army and his mission to Spain, but even if his name was vaguely familiar there would be no way of linking it with his face. As John Johnson, Guy could become the unknown servant, free to bring about the destruction of those oblivious to his real background.

By October 1604 the plotters had returned to London, Catesby having discovered that the initial talks on union would soon be drawing to a close. It was now that they began to gather some of the materials they would need for their plot, primarily gunpowder and timber, which were at this point stored in the house that Catesby had rented on the south side of the Thames, across the river from the property Percy had rented.

By the time of the planned explosion, the plotters had gathered a huge amount of gunpowder – it is estimated that they had around two and a half tonnes, contained in 36 barrels, and that this was more than 25 times the amount needed to bring down the House of Lords.[12] It would also have devastated the surrounding area to a radius of around 500 metres, taking in buildings as far away as Westminster Abbey. Guy Fawkes, in charge of the munitions and with a good knowledge of their efficacy, could have ordered this extra gunpowder to make allowance for the effect that damp conditions could have on its effectiveness, but it could have been another sign of his contempt for those he was targeting. As he stared at the pile of barrels hidden by timber on that fateful night in November 1605 a faint smile may have crossed his lips: this indeed would blow them back to their Scottish mountains.

Some have questioned how the plotters could have obtained such large amounts of gunpowder, as it was only officially available in the south of England from George Evelyn and his family who since 1590 had held a government sanctioned monopoly.[13] The increasingly peaceful situation in Europe, however, meant that the gunpowder suppliers may have been less stringent than usual about who they supplied it to, and in what quality. It is also possible that extra supplies were obtained by way of Guy Fawkes' ongoing connection to William Stanley and Hugh Owen in Flanders.

Gathering in Lambeth, the plotters decided to take on another man whose job it would be to hold the keys to the Lambeth dwelling and look after its stock while the others were away on their preordained business. The man chosen to hold the keys was Robert Keyes, who perhaps in part due to his surname was made the sixth member of the gunpowder plot. Robert Keyes was not a wealthy man, his wife worked as governess to the children of the Catholic peer Lord Mordaunt, but he must have been known to Catesby, who assured all that Keyes was 'a trusty honest man'.[14]

At last the news came that the men, and most of all Guy Fawkes, had been waiting for. On 6 December 1604 the Commission on Union between England and Scotland reached its initial agreement, freeing the house and returning it to its lawful inhabitant, the King's Gentleman Pensioner Thomas Percy.[15] Now Guy could put his expertise to good use. This was the moment he had been waiting for all his life; he would not fail now.

Less than a week after the building was vacated by the commissioners, the plotters had moved in, with Guy taking charge of the excavations. It was back-breaking work, particularly for the likes of Catesby who although strong had no experience of manual labour. The men worked long gruelling shifts, starting their work at night and subsisting on large supplies of dried and cured meats that they brought with them[16] and drinking ale (a common practice when water was often unsafe to drink).

Guy was the most experienced at tunnelling, and the most suited to the work, but his supervisory role entailed directing the others rather than wielding a tool himself. His soldierly instincts also meant that he acted as a lookout, looking and listening for anything that might signify danger. With each blow from a pickaxe and each sweep of a spade, Guy could feel his dreams approaching reality.

Guy knew how to dig tunnels as quietly as possible, and may have used materials to baffle the noise of excavations; as they worked primarily at night the plotters were in constant dread of being discovered. Working after dusk was essential: if figures as notorious as Catesby and Jack Wright were seen entering the house every day and leaving it hours later dirty and fatigued, it wouldn't take long for suspicions to grow.

The men made steady if unspectacular process, going through the laborious process of clearing space, propping it up with wood, and then passing the rubble and soil back down the tunnel to be disposed of into the Thames by moonlight. By Christmas Eve 1604 they had reached the outer wall of the Parliament House,[17] but there was much more work to be done if they were to have their task completed by 7 February, the date that King James was due to open Parliament.

On the night before Christmas they received unwelcome news: in light of the threat of plague, the opening of Parliament had been prorogued, the official term for being moved back, from February to 3 October 1605. This gave them more time to finish their work, which was a relief, but it also created more months of uncertainty and time in which their plot could be discovered and foiled.

The plotters were all men of action. Once they had formulated an idea, they wanted to carry it through there and then, so the announcement of the prorogue represented a low point for them, especially as some were already suffering the physical effects of mining in a dark, dank, unhealthy environment. Oswald Tesimond commented,

> It was remarkable that they should have been able to last out so long in work to which they were not accustomed and which involved such effort. So much so that in a short time they did considerably more than men would have done who were used to earning their bread by using their hands and muscles. It must be admitted that some of them became seriously unwell. These had to stop work. The rest, however, carried on.[18]

It was clear that the men were in need of a rest, physically and mentally, so Catesby took the decision to send them all back to their homes over the Christmas period, to reconvene at the Lambeth house in January.[19]

The conspirators, Catesby, Fawkes, Wintour, Percy, Wright and Keyes, were given strict instructions not to communicate with each other about the plot in any way during this time, and Father Tesimond describes how they gave themselves up to recreation: 'some engaged in sports and pastimes, others to seasonal devotions'.[20]

Guy's lodgings at this time are unknown, but as Catesby had

ordered them to leave London and to keep away from each other he could have returned to York. Visiting the one place where his face could have been known, however, would bring unnecessary danger, so he may instead have stayed just outside London at the White Webbs home of Anne Vaux, a woman always ready to give refuge to Catholics and who, when interrogated after the gunpowder plot, admitted that Guy had spent time under her roof on occasion.[21]

Guy Fawkes was no longer a man for recreations, the boy who played Nine Men's Morris was gone, and hunting and duelling had lost their appeal. It was a brooding Christmas for Guy, one spent largely on his knees praying for a speedy and successful resolution to the plot, and an end to the delays. There would be two more months in the mine, but at last in March 1605 it looked as if the unknown servant's heartfelt prayers had been answered.

Chapter 16

An End to Tunnelling

But screw your courage to the sticking-place,
And we'll not fail.
William Shakespeare, *Macbeth*

At Candlemas in 1605,[1] the six men who had sworn their oath of fidelity to the gunpowder plot gathered together once more.

In the meantime, the Christmas sojourn had given Guy Fawkes a perfect opportunity to achieve one of the aims of their plan – the death of King James.

On 28 December Guy was present at a wedding in Whitehall. This was no ordinary wedding, but that of Sir Philip Herbert to Susan de Vere. Herbert was a favourite of the King, who made him Earl of Montgomery a year after the wedding, and Susan was the daughter of Anne de Vere, the sister of the Earl of Salisbury, Sir Robert Cecil. Prince Henry, heir to the throne, led the bride to the church and King James gave her away.[2]

It was an occasion full of pomp, one with no expense spared. Somehow, whether by accident or design, during the gathering Guy found himself standing next to a very important guest, the King himself. Guy had his sword by his side, and in a second could have dispatched James without any difficulty, but when later questioned about his presence at the wedding, Guy stated that 'he went with no evil intent'.[3]

It seems hard to believe that Guy had indeed gone with no ill intentions, and it is also surprising that he, a stranger to all present, had been allowed to gain such close access to the King while wearing a sword. It was reckless of Guy: he was sure to have been noticed by

Cecil, even at the wedding of his niece. We must assume that Guy had gone there either to get a close look at the enemies he knew he was going to destroy, or that he had, on an impulse, decided to assassinate the King and then changed his mind at the last minute. Guy's hand would have trembled upon the hilt of his blade, heart racing, before he turned round and left the wedding party. His soldierly discipline had won through at the last, there was a bigger target than merely the King alone.

Guy kept this meeting to himself when he arrived at Catesby's Lambeth dwelling. Catesby looked into the eyes of the five men before him, assessing whether they were having doubts, whether they now regretted taking the oath that bound them in death and destruction, of themselves and others. His gaze was returned confidently by them; he had nothing to fear from his recruits.

One of the subjects discussed by the six was what to do after the explosion had taken place, and specifically how they would be able to get their hands on a member of the royal family that they could then use to further their means. At this point it was suggested that Percy, who as a Gentleman Pensioner had easy access to the palace, would enter it and snatch the 6-year-old Duke Charles (later to be King Charles I) under the guise of taking him into protective custody against any potential threat to his life.[4] Others would be gathered in the Midlands near to Coombe Abbey under the pretext of a hunt, where they could take Lady Elizabeth from her protector Lord Harrington, by force if necessary.[5]

It was time to return to the mine, but after two weeks further digging it became clear that the stone wall they had reached was proving too difficult for them to penetrate. The solution was to move the gunpowder from the Lambeth house to the house that Percy had rented on the opposite side of the Thames.[6] It was a mission fraught with danger and so was undertaken at night, using a boat to carry the barrels from one side of the river to the other. This made the logistics of the operation even harder, but it was an operation that would have to be undertaken at some point, and it meant that Robert Keyes could now be freed up to work on the mine with the others.

Even with Keyes' assistance, the task seemed almost insurmountable. The wall was made of stone around ten feet thick[7] and difficult to breach. Moreover the conditions in which the men worked were becoming increasingly difficult as the proximity of the Thames led to water flooding the tunnel periodically, which then had to be emptied by barrels passed from man to man in a chain.[8]

Guy made it clear to Catesby that further help was needed if they were to progress, and so Catesby made an obvious choice for the seventh man to join the conspiracy: Jack's brother, friend of Catesby, brother-in-law of Percy, and school friend of Guy Fawkes, Kit Wright.[9] Tall and strong, Kit was noted for his piety and for having a ruddy tan,[10] perhaps a legacy of his time spent alongside Guy under the blazing sun of Valladolid.

It is probable that another of the thirteen conspirators was enlisted as a miner too: Thomas Bates. Bates was of lowly birth, even compared to Guy Fawkes and Robert Keyes who were from less exalted backgrounds than the others, but for many years he had proved a loyal servant to Robert Catesby at Ashby St. Ledgers. Bates was no menial, however, but more of a trusted right-hand man of Catesby, with his own lodgings, his own suit of armour, and his own servant. Catesby knew that Bates would die for him if asked to, and so he too seemed an obvious addition to the group. Bates's loyalty to his master never wavered, and in choosing to follow Catesby he would leave behind a widow and children. Although Bates was a committed Catholic he was not as militant as many of the others in his beliefs, and Father Gerard states that just before his death Bates claimed that it was 'only for his love to his master that he was drawn to forget his duty to God, his King, and country'.[11]

Bates was also valuable to the plot because he would not look out of place doing menial tasks, making him perfect to drive deliveries of armaments around the country.

There were two further important considerations: money and horses. It was these that led to a meeting at the Catherine Wheel Inn[12] in Oxford in early 1605. The Catherine Wheel Inn was one of the network of inns throughout the country known for its Catholic sympathies. In May 1589, two Jesuit priests, Richard Yaxley and George Nichols, had been saying mass in the inn. That night they were arrested along with two laymen, Thomas Belson and Humphrey Prichard who was a barman at the inn. All four were tortured and then hung, drawn and quartered.[13]

Sixteen years later, the four people gathered in a room at the inn were Robert Catesby and Thomas Wintour and the men they had summoned, John Grant and Tom's brother Robert. Robert Wintour was reticent at first, saying that it seemed impossible for the plan to succeed without either 'foreign aid or some great men at home to join therein'.[14] Catesby's counter-argument was that there was no hope of foreign aid, and no great men that he would trust. Catesby's natural powers of persuasion, and the desire not to lose face in front of his brother, saw Robert Wintour take the oath and join the plot.

John Grant was easier to convince. A wealthy landowner, and importantly for the plot's chances of success the owner of a stable of horses, he was known not only for his devotion but for the ferocity with which he met the searches that all Catholic landowners had to put up with. Most of the Catholic gentry had grudgingly learnt to accept regular raids on their property that would inevitably leave them lighter in goods and money. John Grant however was known for meeting them head on:

> His [Grant's] courage was inferior to none in that company. This he had demonstrated often in facing up to the King's pursuivants when they came to search his house, a process which brought with it the danger of losing not only everything else he possessed but even life itself, thanks to the violence and insulting behaviour which those kind of people commonly use. On a number of occasions, he sent them packing after the kind of reception which made sure they did not trouble him again thanks to the experience they already had of him.[15]

Such was the reputation Grant had gained that he was seldom raided, and when the pursuivants, as the search parties were known, did arrive they came in large numbers and in fear of being thrown into the moat surrounding his home at Norbrook House in Warwickshire. This location was crucial to the plotters, as it was near Coombe Abbey where Princess Elizabeth lived, and its reputation and natural protections also made it an ideal place to store firearms and other weapons for the Midland uprising that Catesby had planned.

Once again there were family ties linking John Grant to others involved in the plot, for he was the brother-in-law of two of the men sitting with him at the Catherine Wheel Inn, having married Dorothy Wintour in 1602.[16] Marriage played an important role in Robert Wintour's reception into the plot too, for his union had made him far richer than the likes of Catesby could ever dream of.

Robert Wintour married Gertrude Talbot, daughter of John Talbot of Grafton. John Talbot was heir to the Earldom of Shrewsbury, but was one of the wealthiest landowners of England in his own right. Talbot was seen as a leader of England's Catholics, and he would spend over twenty years in prison for his beliefs. The marriage brought him further riches, but Robert Wintour was a wealthy man before his wedding. As the eldest son of George Wintour he inherited Huddington Court in Worcestershire along with the family's salt making business, a very lucrative enterprise.[17]

Catesby's plot was taking shape: he had men under Guy Fawkes' command digging the tunnel, he had amassed a supply of gunpowder ready for the opening of Parliament in October, he had a man in the Midlands who could ready horses and take charge of the abduction of Lady Elizabeth, and another who could help bankroll the operation in Robert Wintour.

In Guy's tunnel, however, a sudden omen of bad fortune shook their confidence. One day a ringing noise was heard, seemingly out of nowhere. After consulting with each other, the men gained a supply of holy water (probably from Father Tesimond who was constantly in touch with Catesby) and sprinkled it on the wall. The ringing returned, louder and stronger, and so the tunnellers resorted to covering a whole section of wall with holy water before they would proceed.[18] The sound of bells continued for several days, and must have been greatly disconcerting to the men in the mine. It was certainly a sign from Heaven, they would have conjectured, but was it a sign of God's favour or displeasure?

Not long after this disquieting incident, the ever wary Guy heard another faint noise coming from above. Holding out his hand to silence the digging operation, Guy could clearly discern a sweeping or dragging noise. The only thing to do was to investigate where the noise was coming from and what was causing it – after all it could have been government spies who were aware of their presence or it could be a structural problem that would render their tunnel unstable.

Guy took charge of proceedings, as he'd done as an officer on the killing beaches at Nieuwpoort, and volunteered to make the investigation himself. Back above ground, he calculated where the noise must have been coming from and upon entering found a group of grime-faced porters removing heavy sacks of coal. It was these bags dragging upon the ground that had caused the faint sweeping noises in the tunnel directly below. But, taking a look around his blackened surroundings, Guy realised that they represented a wonderful opportunity.

After consulting with the porters, Guy was conveyed to the owner of the cellar, Ellen Bright. She was the widow of a coal merchant, and leased the cellar from a Mr Skinner.[20] Guy introduced himself as John Johnson, servant to the Gentleman Pensioner Thomas Percy, and asked why the stocks of coal were being removed? Mrs Bright explained that she was selling all of her coal, and vacating the cellar. We can conjecture that this was due to a change of circumstances brought on by the death of her husband, or that she simply had no desire to run the business on her own and wanted the money for her retirement, but whatever the reason, it was the answer Guy had been hoping for. Taking leave of the widow, Guy promised to return to speak to her again after talking to his master.

All eyes were on Guy at his reappearance in the tunnel: would they be able to continue as before or was he bringing news that would halt their enterprise? Wearing his customary calm exterior, Guy called for Catesby and Thomas Wintour to join him before explaining what he had discovered. The cellar above them had previously been used as a kitchen area for the House of Lords, and was directly underneath the Parliament chamber. If they could take hold of the cellar, there would be no need for this tunnel beneath it, as they would have the perfect ready-made repository for their gunpowder.[20]

Thomas Percy was sent to negotiate the purchase, and Guy went with him[21] having presumably gained a rapport with Mrs Bright on their first conversation. The widow needed little persuading; the deeds were signed on 25 March 1605[22] and the destruction of King and Parliament moved a step closer.

The mining operation ceased immediately, to be replaced by night-time journeys between their old property and the new one. Once all the barrels of gunpowder had been placed into their cellar, Guy, and the plotters he engaged on the task, proceeded to cover the barrels with wood they had gathered for the purpose. Thomas Wintour stated in his confession that they used one thousand billets and five hundred faggots[23] – another indication of just how much gunpowder they had (as we shall see, Guy added more barrels of gunpowder later).

With the gunpowder now covered, they next brought in items of furniture, and mattresses, along with everyday objects such as cutlery. This provided a level of comfort should Guy or Percy have to spend time there, but it was done primarily to hide the true purpose of the cellar from anyone who should enter it.[24] They also stocked it with a year's supply of wine and cider.[25] While the room they rented is commonly referred to as a cellar, and I will refer to it as such simply because it was underneath the Parliament chamber of the House of Lords, it was not subterranean but a large ground-level property. It joined onto the 'Painted Chamber' at the north end of the parliament buildings and onto the 'Prince's Chamber' at the south[26].

The gunpowder was now in place, and all the men had to do was wait for Parliament to be opened. On that glorious day, Guy Fawkes, Catesby, and their companions would be ready.

Chapter 17

God's Lunatics

For God's sake, let us sit upon the ground
And tell sad stories of the death of kings;
How some have been deposed; some slain in war,
Some haunted by the ghosts they have deposed;
Some poison'd by their wives: some sleeping kill'd;
All murder'd: for within the hollow crown
That rounds the mortal temples of a king
Keeps Death his court.
William Shakespeare, *Richard II*

By good fortune Guy and his fellow conspirators had managed to place a vast supply of gunpowder directly underneath the House of Lords, but while the destruction of the House of Lords, and all within it, now looked within their grasp, there was more work to be done if their ultimate aim of returning England to Catholicism was to succeed.

During their conversations about the plot, the men had discussed what would happen in the aftermath of the explosion. They foresaw England being plunged into a chaos of confusion, and those who remained calm would have the upper hand. They would need a strong force with which to counter any anti-Catholic uprising that should occur, and this necessitated a journey overseas to try to rally troops and assistance. It was Guy Fawkes who was chosen for this important and sensitive task.[1]

One reason for Guy's journey to Flanders, and beyond, in the late spring of 1605 is that he was seeking expert advice on the building of fortifications in advance of an anticipated outbreak of unrest after the explosion. Once the gunpowder was in place in their new cellar, Catesby had sent Guy to reconnoitre potential sites for the building of such fortifications, along with 'two or three others',[2] but when Guy reported back, Catesby suggested to him that they should seek expert advice from people with long experience in this field. By this, he meant William Stanley and Hugh Owen. This was the other reason for Guy's journey.

One of Guy's most useful qualities, as far as Catesby was concerned, was that he still had links to the English Regiment in Flanders. While Catesby had given up hope of aid from Spain or France in the event of their uprising, he still felt it possible that the English Catholic exiles abroad could be persuaded to return and support their endeavours, and Guy's reputation within the English Regiment made him the perfect man to advance this cause.

Father Tesimond, in his narrative written in the years after the gunpowder plot, stated that Guy 'would be able to find out if it were possible, and by what means, to get a substantial quantity of gunpowder from those countries. This would be needed for the war which would probably break out as a result of the confusion and change of regime'.[3]

While gunpowder was still available via their old channel of the Evelyn family, Catesby had already spent a huge amount on the plot, and with a greater part of the expenditure still to come he was hoping to persuade William Stanley and the like to supply gunpowder, and guns along with it, for free. This was an important and sensitive task, and the fact that Guy was chosen for it says much for his character and intelligence as did his selection for the diplomatic mission that became known as 'The Spanish Treason'.

Guy Fawkes had a more senior role within the gunpowder conspiracy than he is often credited with. While Catesby was the founder and leader of the plot, and Thomas Wintour his trusted deputy, Guy seems to have been the next in command. He is entrusted with a succession of vital roles within the plot, and is also privy to information known only by Catesby and Thomas Wintour in addition to himself. Father Tesimond gives evidence of this when he refers to the induction of Sir Everard Digby into the plot: 'As far as I am able to find out, Sir Everard knew nothing of this plot until a month before it was due to be put into execution. The other plotters knew nothing about him, apart from the two mentioned above [Catesby and Wintour] and Mr Guy'.[4]

In his initial examination, Guy (then still posing as John Johnson) admitted leaving London around Easter, travelling to Dover, and sailing from there to Calais,[5] although he could not remember which boat he had sailed on, doubtless to protect the skipper of the boat from a future interrogation. After arriving in France, Guy made his way to the English seminary at Saint-Omer, founded by Father Persons eleven years earlier.[6] This may seem a strange move by Guy, delaying as it did his meeting with Owen and Stanley in Belgium, but doubtless Guy was hoping to recruit some people to their cause from the seminary.

Seminaries such as Saint-Omer were not only full of English Catholics training to be priests, they also contained English exiles of a more militant nature, and his visit to Saint-Omer, and later to the seminary at Douai, was a recruitment drive as much as a spiritual visit. Guy, acting on the instructions of Catesby, may even have had someone specific that he was seeking out, as Tesimond coyly notes: 'They commissioned Mr Guy with other particular negotiations, but I will say no more about them, either because they are uncertain, or else they could touch the reputation of English gentlemen still living in these parts'.[7]

It could be that Tesimond was here referring to William Stanley, for when Guy did finally talk to him he found Stanley less accommodating than he had expected. The reason, one that was kept from Guy and that he and the other conspirators would have found almost unbelievable, was that Stanley was contemplating abandoning his cause and petitioning Sir Robert Cecil for a pardon and permission to return to England.[8] William Stanley was never to gain this pardon, and died in Belgium in 1630 aged 80.[9]

It may be that Stanley's hopes of a return to England were not that he was seeking a peaceful old age in the country of his birth, however, but rather that he intended agitating against the King and his councillors from England instead of from overseas. When Guy arrived in Belgium after Easter 1605 he was greeted warmly by Hugh Owen, but informed that Stanley was away at the Spanish court again. This may have been on official duty, as William Stanley had been appointed Governor of Mechelen by the Spanish in 1600,[10] or he could even now have been trying to persuade the Spanish authorities to turn against the peace agreement with England.

With Stanley missing, Guy made his way to the camp of Ambrogio Spinola in Ostend. Spinola was born into an aristocratic family in Genoa, but had now become a general of the Spanish army in Flanders.[11] Once again Guy had found an ideal place to talk to potential recruits who could be used if war broke out in England as a result of the plot. Among the men Guy met in Ostend was Captain William Turner,[12] who had served as a soldier in Ireland; this was just the kind of man Guy and Catesby needed, and Guy passed on some, but not all, of the details of their planned action.

By July, word reached Guy that William Stanley had returned to Brussels, and Guy met him there in company with Hugh Owen and the Jesuit priests Fathers Baldwin and Tesimond.[13] As Owen had expected, Stanley was unwilling to commit any direct support for the English plan, although he may have agreed to provide some measure of financial or practical support in the form of gunpowder. The subject of fortifications would have been discussed at this meeting as well, and it is likely that there were subsequent meetings between the men as Guy spent a further month in their company.

It was dangerous for Stanley, Owen and Baldwin to spend so long in Brussels, but, unbeknownst to them all, the damage had already been done. Captain William Turner was a double agent working for Robert Cecil, and following his conversation with Guy, and further conversations with Hugh Owen, he sent a damning report to Sir Thomas Edmondes, the English ambassador in Brussels and a conduit to Sir Robert Cecil.

In this letter, Captain Turner claimed that Hugh Owen had recruited him for a pending invasion of England. Around 300 English cavalrymen, with infantry support, would join forces with 1,500 Spanish troops at Dover before capturing the English fleet at Rochester and then spreading across the country. Turner said that he had been told to wait in Dover for the coming of Father Tesimond and Guy Fawkes who would then take him to meet a Robert Catesby. After this meeting, they would be taken to meet friends of the nobility who would have arms and horses in readiness.[14]

This report could easily have resulted in the arrest of Catesby and caused the collapse of the plot, but it was too far-fetched to be believed. Turner, in his desire to prove his worth, had fabricated information and added it to the real information he did know, creating a mixture of truths, half-truths and damned lies. It was beyond comprehension that Spanish troops would attack England so shortly after their peace negotiations.

Sir Thomas Edmondes sent the letter on to Cecil in September 1605, with the caveat that Turner was an untrustworthy man who couldn't be believed.[15] Turner also passed his report onto England's ambassador in Paris, Sir William Parry, but Parry felt it to be of such little importance that he didn't forward it until 28 November,[16] long after the explosion and uprising would have taken place. Guy had narrowly escaped this time, but the report passed on by Edmondes may have brought his name to the attention of the ever vigilant Cecil.

Guy said his goodbyes to Owen, Baldwin and Stanley in August 1605, but he fully expected that he would see them again before the year was out. Guy's role within the plot had been further extended. A ship was to be held in readiness in London. After firing the slow match, Guy would make his way to this boat which would take him to the continent once more. It would then be his job to make contact with the Pope in Rome, presumably through the auspices of the Jesuit superior in the city, Father Persons, and explain why they'd acted as they had. Guy would then rally the English exiles in Rome and Flanders ready to support Catesby and the others if required.[17]

Before returning to England, Guy had one more call to make – and it reveals a lot about his thoughts at this time. In August 1605, a matter of months before he intended to light the match that would leave hundreds dead and maimed, he made a pilgrimage to the revered shrine of Our Lady of Montague in Brabant, southern Belgium.[18]

The shrine was centred upon a reputedly holy tree, on the site of which now stands the Basilica of Our Lady of Scherpenheuvel. Legend had it that the oak tree contained a statue of the Virgin Mary in its branches. One day a passing shepherd noticed that the statue had fallen from the branches, but clutching the statue he found himself unable to move. Once the Madonna had been taken from him and returned to the branches, the shepherd regained his mobility. The story had become widespread by the start of the seventeenth century, and Guy would have followed the pilgrim's tradition of walking three times round the tree while praying for what he most wanted. Guy's thrice-said prayers to Mary, his Queen of peace, were for the plot to proceed smoothly, and for the King, his heir, his lords and bishops, to be killed and wiped from the face of the earth. To Guy Fawkes there was no contradiction in a prayer for destruction.

Guy's clear conscience about taking life on a grand scale was shared by Robert Catesby, but he knew that others may be more troubled by the prospect, and so while Guy was in continental Europe, Catesby was busily trying to obtain the backing of the church, and specifically from the head of England's Jesuits, Father Henry Garnet.

Father Garnet and Robert Catesby were well known to each other; Catesby had provided the priest with shelter under his own roof on many occasions. Catesby reasoned that if he had Garnet's approval of his plot, he could use this to allay the fears and misgivings that anyone else recruited to the plot may have. He also knew, however, that Father Garnet was unusually peace loving and conciliatory for a Jesuit priest, so he would have to be approached carefully.

A meeting was arranged between the two men on 8 June 1605, probably in a room within an inn. After copious amounts of wine, Catesby dropped a question into the conversation: whether the church thought it was lawful to kill an innocent man, or men, for the greater good?[19] Catesby produced an example based upon the wars in Flanders, one that he had probably heard from Guy: sometimes in a siege the Protestant forces would put Catholic prisoners along the ramparts to prevent them being fired upon by those who shared their faith. To fire upon the ramparts would cost innocent lives, but to fail to do so would prevent the success of the siege, and prevent the final good from being achieved. Father Garnet was immediately worried by this line of questioning, but responded with what he understood church doctrine to be: the principle of double-effect.[20] That it is only legitimate to do bad when it is essential for the achievement of a proportionate good, when the bad effect has not been wished for or sought after, and when the two events happen simultaneously and unavoidably. Catesby smiled and said he would speak to him again on this subject in greater length.

Throughout the summer Catesby travelled across the country telling people that he was to be made a colonel in the Spanish army, and recruiting people to fight alongside him. The recent peace treaty with Spain made this an entirely legal thing to do, and Catesby even talked to Sir Robert Cecil personally on this matter to gain the King's permission and to obtain a passport.[21] There is no record of such a passport being issued to Catesby at this time, as there is to others including Lord Vaux and Francis Tresham, but interestingly the book that records these issues, the Docquet Book of the Signet Office, is missing two pages that have been ripped from it. We can conclude that these pages were expunged from the records after the gunpowder plot's discovery to cover up the fact that Cecil had indeed given Catesby a passport.[22]

Garnet knew Catesby too well, far better than Robert Cecil or any of the gentry that had agreed to join his regiment when it formed; he was deeply troubled by Catesby's line of questioning, and understood immediately that there was an underlying motive unrelated to talk of Flanders. At future meetings, Catesby would ask Garnet to hear his confession, but guessing something of its content and realising the danger it would put him in Father Garnet refused.

Father Garnet was bound by the seal of the confessional. He had gathered that Catesby had a plan that would risk innocent lives, but if he heard his confession he too could be held complicit, and his sacred code would not allow him to inform the authorities. Garnet took to trying to put Catesby off his plans, whatever they were, by referring repeatedly to the Pope's instruction to England's Catholics to seek peaceful remedies, and to leave their fate in the hands of God.

Father Tesimond recalls one such occasion that summer, when

141

many Jesuit priests and lay people were gathered around a table. Father Garnet repeated his familiar sermon of patience and forbearing, and reminded them of the injunction they had received from the Holy Father. Catesby was furious, and stood up to address those present:

> Mr Catesby said, as if speaking for the others, that some were not lacking who had grown tired of putting up with ill fortune and did not give willing ear to that teaching. They were asking if there was any authority on earth that could take away from them the right given by nature to defend their own lives from the violence of others. They were saying openly that the doctrine took away from Catholics spirit and energy, leaving them flaccid and poor-spirited. It put them in a worse position than slaves. Indeed, for that very reason they were called by their enemies out of contempt, 'God's lunatics'.[23]

Former friends, Catesby and Father Garnet now tried to avoid each other's company whenever possible, but Father Tesimond, who as Catesby's confessor already knew about the plot, engineered further meetings. Tesimond also asked his superior to hear his own confession, but mindful of what it would contain Father Garnet again refused, saying that he could not allow Father Tesimond to break the confessional seal.[24]

The decisive moment came on 24 July at White Webbs, the home of Anne Vaux. Garnet once more refused to hear Catesby's secret but said that whatever plan he had, he should seek papal permission before proceeding. Catesby agreed on condition that Garnet sent a letter along with his, and that his choice of envoy should carry them to Rome. The envoy chosen was Sir Edward Baynham, a Catholic of good pedigree who was renowned as a drunken brawler and had spent time in prison for it.[25] He was also a firm friend of Catesby, who secretly told him not to travel to Rome at all, knowing that the Pope would refuse to approve his plan, but to instead wait in France for news from England, and then return.[26]

The die was now cast for Father Garnet, and he knew it. Whatever plan Catesby had, and he had surely guessed the target of it, there was now evidence linking his name to it. Catesby would happily tell his conspirators and potential recruits that he had sought permission from the Jesuits and they had not ruled against his plan. Garnet, however, tried to distance himself from the plot, literally.

On 28 August, Father Garnet set out from White Webbs in Enfield with a large contingent: his destination was St. Winifred's shrine at Holywell in North Wales. Around thirty people took part in the pilgrimage, including Anne Vaux and her sister Eleanor, Fathers John Gerard, Oswald Tesimond, and Edward Oldcorne, and Sir Everard Digby and his wife Mary.[27]

They walked over 200 miles, with the last section undertaken barefooted. As Catholics they were used to practising in secret, but were now professing their faith openly in public. It was a bold and reckless act, it was a provocative act, but that was exactly what Father Garnet intended.

Garnet was a highly intelligent man, and understood perfectly how perilous his situation was. He reasoned that this public pilgrimage would give the authorities no option but to arrest him, and that this meant he would be in prison whenever Catesby's plot was enacted, giving him an alibi of sorts. Unfortunately for Father Garnet he was not arrested and, amazingly, the pilgrimage was completed peacefully and unmolested. Garnet was right to have been worried, for in the aftermath of the plot he and Father Oldcorne were arrested, charged with complicity (which was far from the truth), and then hung, drawn and quartered.[28]

Guy Fawkes arrived back in England in September 1605, and found that, for tactical and financial reasons, Robert Catesby had inducted two more into their brethren: Ambrose Rookwood and, fresh from his pilgrimage to Holywell, Sir Everard Digby. He was also to recruit one further man to bring the total members of the plot's inner circle to thirteen: Francis Tresham. Tresham was an old friend of Catesby, and a much-loved cousin, but his admission to their circle would have caused consternation among some of the conspirators. Their concerns would be proved correct.

Chapter 18

A Terrible Blow

Though those that are betray'd
Do feel the treason sharply, yet the traitor
Stands in worse case of woe
William Shakespeare, *Cymbeline*

It had been obvious to the conspirators for some time that extra recruits would be needed if their plot was to succeed in both London and the Midlands, and from there spread over the country as a whole. One pressing concern was the need to raise extra finances, as Robert Catesby himself had been bearing the bulk of this burden and was now finding it a severe strain.

The costs already incurred included the buying of gunpowder and arms, the renting of several houses across London and beyond, and the ship that was now in constant readiness for use by Guy Fawkes after he had lit the slow fuse leading to the gunpowder barrels.[1] Thomas Percy had initially said he would supplement Catesby's funds by giving him the cream from the rent he was collecting for the Earl of Northumberland, a practice he was well used to, but if he did do this it didn't make as significant a contribution as hoped for. At a meeting in Bath, a rump of the conspirators gave Catesby permission to recruit whomsoever he thought best.[2]

This presented the opportunity to gain new sources of funds, but it also presented more dangers: it would only take one misplaced word or one untrustworthy recruit to send them all to the gallows. There were no such worries about Catesby's first recruit in the autumn of 1605. Ambrose Rookwood was in his mid-twenties, making him younger than his fellow conspirators, but he was also full of youthful confidence and enthusiasm.

Rookwood was born into a wealthy Catholic family, and both his education at the Saint-Omer seminary and the fines and imprisonment of family members fired his zeal for Catholic action against the Protestant ruling elite. His wife, Elizabeth, was a cousin of Robert Keyes, creating yet another family connection within the conspiracy, and more importantly for his recruitment he was not only rich in his own right, he was also a breeder of horses. Under the instructions of Catesby, who had known him since he was a child, he rented Clopton Hall near Stratford-upon-Avon and stabled a string of horses there ready to be called upon at a moment's notice.[3]

Once again, Rookwood would leave a young family to mourn him, so he was sure that the plot would succeed, or perhaps beguiled by the charismatic Catesby:

> He left behind him at his death a wife who was beautiful and of gentle birth, together with two or three small children, and with them everything else he had on this earth. He preferred the companionship of this most wretched and foolhardy plot. In my opinion, one can tell from this how deep was the conviction which they cherished that the business would succeed.[4]

The hold that Catesby had over his fellow plotters was so strong that, as we shall see, most didn't flinch or flee in the face of terrible danger – even though that danger would fall not only upon themselves but upon all who they loved and held dear. Catesby had become a messianic figure to them, taking on the commands of Jesus who told his disciples that 'anyone who loves his father or mother more than Me is not worthy of Me; anyone who loves his son or daughter more than Me is not worthy of Me; and anyone who does not take up his cross and follow Me is not worthy of Me'.[5]

Horses would be essential for the success of the plot and the uprising to follow, and it was imperative to have them strategically

THE REAL GUY FAWKES

positioned around the country. Rookwood's stable would supplement the horses that earlier recruit John Grant had in place at Warwick Castle,[6] a choice of location that would prove a fatal mistake.

Although Rookwood was among the last three people to be formally inducted into the plot, it seems that he had provided financial assistance half a year earlier, probably under the illusion that he was helping Catesby's plans for a new regiment in Flanders. In his confession of 30 November 1605, Robert Keyes stated that 'Ambrose Rookwood about half a year since bought four barrels of powder and he and Christopher Wright brought them to Lambeth and took them to this examinate's [Keyes's] lodging, whereafter they were conveyed into the cellar'.[7]

Next to be recruited into the conspiracy was Sir Everard Digby. He, like Ambrose Rookwood, was younger than the other members of the plot, and his Catholic credentials were unquestionable. Although he had been raised as a Protestant, despite being born to Catholic parents, he had converted to Catholicism under the auspices of Father Gerard and was noted for his piety, as shown by his place on the Holywell pilgrimage alongside his cousins Anne Vaux and Eleanor Brooksby.[8] He and his wife Mary now lived at Gayhurst House in Buckinghamshire, complete with priest holes designed by Nicholas Owen, where they housed their own priest and confessor, and former schoolmate of the Wrights and Guy Fawkes, the Jesuit Father Edward Oldcorne.[9]

There was one reason above all others that Sir Everard was recruited to the plot: he was wealthy. After hearing the plot's details, he promised Catesby that he would supply him with £1,500. Digby was also told to rent Coughton Court near Alcester in Warwickshire for a month,[10] and also to be prepared to rent it for longer if necessary, and was then given the vital task of bringing the Catholic gentry together for a hunt at the time that the explosion would be taking place in London. Digby was known for organising hunts, and so no difficulty was seen in him being able to attract a large number of followers who would, at first, have no idea that they were actually being recruited for a Catholic uprising across the Midlands.

Digby's role as head of the hunt, as head of the uprising that would capture the King's daughter Elizabeth, was a particularly dangerous one, but Digby had the courage and strength to succeed in it. He was another imposing figure who could strike fear into men or inspire them to follow him, as we can see from this description of him by Father Tesimond:

> He [Sir Everard Digby] was some six feet tall. Although this was less than Mr Catesby's height, he was rather more strongly built, and somewhat more vigorous. I do not think that in the whole of England there were two gentlemen who were their equals.[11]

Like the other members of the plot, Digby had to take the oath of secrecy, but it was telling of his reputation for honesty and trustworthiness, and possibly of his elevated social position compared to the others, that he was not asked to seal the vow with the sacrament of the Eucharist, as the others had been – thereby condemning their souls to damnation if they broke their promise. In Digby's case Catesby instead presented him with a dagger and asked him to swear an oath of secrecy upon it:[12] the message was clear, if Digby or anyone broke the oath they would pay with their life.

The days, weeks and months leading to the planned execution of the plot must have been torturous for those involved, especially when the official opening of Parliament was prorogued once more because of further worries about the plague. Such were the fears about this outbreak that on October 5 London's theatres were closed to the public.[13] The opening of Parliament was moved from October to 5 November 1605, and the official notice of this delay was read at Parliament on 28 July.[14] Present at the reading of this decree were the Lord Chancellor, members of the Privy Council and some lords. Also present, as a very interested bystander, was Thomas Wintour.[15] He was pleased with what he saw, reasoning that if there was any knowledge of the gunpowder stored under the chamber at the time then this gathering of England's leaders would not have taken place. Even so, the delay was not a welcome one, and even outwardly calm men such as Guy Fawkes must have been feeling tense and nervous, if a little excited, inside.

Around the time of Parliament's prorogation, Guy decided to make a further check on the cellar and the gunpowder within it. He had placed certain indicators, invisible to others, that would show whether anyone had entered the chamber, but was relieved to find that no-one had been inside during his months spent overseas.

Guy was also concerned at the effect that the damp conditions could have taken on the gunpowder, as although the cellar was not as wet as the tunnel they'd been working on, it was still affected by the proximity of the River Thames. Opening the barrels and testing the powder by rubbing it between his fingers, Guy realised that some of the powder had deteriorated to the state where it would be unreliable, and so, with the assistance of Thomas Wintour, he replenished his stock: 'Meanwhile, Mr. Fawkes and myself alone bought some new powder, as suspecting the first to be dank, and conveyed it into the cellar and set it in order as we resolved it should stand'.[16]

With the powder in place, Guy would have allowed himself a moment of reflection: it was on this spot that the course of his life would be shaped; he would either successfully fire the powder and escape via the nearby ship, or he would be captured in the act or caught up in the aftermath.

He was a man who was used to danger, a man who had faced death before, but this was the greatest peril he had faced in his life. Perhaps it is for this reason that he made one last journey to York, allowing him to walk the streets that he had run joyfully down as a child, and paying a visit to his mother for the first time in over ten years. Their embrace as they parted would be their final one, as both Guy and Edith must have suspected at the time.

Guy's journey to York was one he was powerless to resist, a vestige of the dutiful and family-loving boy he had once been, but it was also a potentially dangerous move for one who was supposed to be keeping his identity secret. He found York unchanged in one aspect at least: it was still a dangerous place for a Catholic to be, as the executions of lay Catholics Thomas Welbourne and John Fulthering in York in August 1604 had shown.[17]

Guy was not the only senior conspirator taking risks at the time. Motivated perhaps by a desire to while away the time until 5 November, or to take his mind away from what lay ahead, or possibly to garner further funds, Robert Catesby now began to dine with some of the leading men in London at the time.

One such dinner took place at the Irish Boy Inn not far from the Strand on 9 October. Catesby, as always, would have taken centre stage and dominated the conversation, but the exalted guests alongside him were Sir Josceline Percy (brother to the Earl of Northumberland), Lord Mordaunt, Francis Tresham, Thomas Wintour, John Ashfield (brother-in-law to Thomas and Robert Wintour through his marriage to their sister Anne) and the playwright Ben Jonson.[18]

The talk around the table may simply have been about the everyday subjects of the day, fashion or who was in and who was out at the court, or they could have been discussing Ben Jonson's new play, *Sejanus His Fall*, which had premièred in London on 6 August.[19] A controversial play, it examined the story of Sejanus who had been given authority by the cruel Roman emperor Tiberius, but whose own failings and lust for power saw him killed.

This was an obviously dangerous choice of subject for Jonson, who seemingly hadn't learnt his lesson from the Isle of Dogs debacle,[20] dealing as it did with the tyranny of rulers and the threat of assassination. Some said that it was an allusion to the plight of Catholics, and others that it was an allegory of the life of the Earl of Essex during Elizabeth's reign. Ben Jonson was also in dangerous company on The Strand, as simply having been seen in the presence of Catesby would later lead to the arrest and questioning of many of those present.

Could this meeting with Catholic, or Catholic leaning, men of power, influence and wealth have been a means of raising funds for the events to come? It's certainly possible, though if he did, Catesby most likely presented to the men his tried and trusted tale of trying to raise a regiment for Flanders.

A meeting that is less easy to explain, and which surely brought far greater danger for Catesby and the plotters, took place on 24 October at the Mitre Tavern in Bread Street, near Cheapside in East London. It was reported to the authorities that Catesby was seen dining with Lord Mordaunt and Sir Josceline Percy, but also present were William Monson, Sir Mark Ive, Dr Taylor, Mr Pickering of Northamptonshire, Mr Hakluyt and Spero Pettingar.[21]

This information was given to Robert Cecil – but by whom? Was there an agent of his at the inn, or possibly even at Catesby's table? Richard Hakluyt (pronounced 'Hackett') was a strange table fellow for a Catholic conspirator such as Catesby to choose. A vehement enemy of Spain, he is known today as one of the prime movers behind the English colonisation of North America. He was also undoubtedly a spy for Sir Robert Cecil, and for this reason had earlier been made chaplain to the English embassy in Paris by Cecil's predecessor Francis Walsingham. As well as being a writer, Hakluyt was a Church of England priest, and in fact was personal chaplain to Robert Cecil.

Catesby would have to be at his most discreet at table with Hakluyt, who acted as Cecil's earpiece, and it may be that Spero Pettingar was another government spy. Pettingar had been at Oxford with Hakluyt, and had been a servant to the Countess of Essex, Lettice Knollys, mother of the ill-fated second Earl of Essex. This connection meant that Pettingar was examined on 23 October 1601, in the fallout from the Essex rebellion.[22] After dinner, it is reported that Hakluyt and Pettingar left together to 'study some papers concerning Francis Drake's navigation'.[23] Their actual conversation may have been of an altogether different nature if they had actually been at the tavern on an espionage mission.

At the same time another group of conspirators had reassembled ready for their part in the plot. Their organiser was Guy Fawkes, who on his way back to London had summoned Thomas Wintour, Thomas Bates, Kit Wright and Jack Wright to meet him. The place was the Bell Inn, Daventry. The innkeeper Matthew Young later testified[24] that Guy arrived first and ordered meals for the other men.

Catesby's dining and drinking sessions may have been innocent, or they may have been a desperate and dangerous attempt to gain more money for his enterprise. Costs were building up, and Thomas Percy, a man more suited to collecting rents than paying them, had not yet paid for his property, leaving it to Guy, as the servant John Johnson, to pay Henry Ferrers in October.[25]

There was one man as yet that Catesby had not called upon, and that he knew was wealthier than anyone yet recruited, and so on 14 October at the Catholic Lord Stourton's house, Catesby recruited his cousin Francis Tresham. Tresham was not only rich, having married wisely as well as inheriting property from his father Sir Thomas Tresham, he had also proved his worth to the Catholic cause. He, alongside Catesby and others, had been involved in the Essex rebellion, and imprisoned for it, and he had also worked alongside Catesby in sending Thomas Wintour to Spain. Tresham was also from a well-connected family, with two of his sisters being married to the Catholic Lords Stourton and Monteagle respectively. Why then was Francis Tresham added to the plot as an afterthought, a last resort?

The truth is that Tresham could be unpredictable, and was not liked or trusted by his peers. As a young man he had spent time in prison for assaulting a man and his pregnant daughter, claiming that the family owed him money.[26] Perhaps the best indication of Tresham's character comes from Father Oswald Tesimond who praises the other conspirators fulsomely, but of Tresham says:

> He knew how to look after himself, but was not much to
> be trusted. This was the view even of those who were
> most familiar with him. For this reason, I am inclined to
> think it was none other than Divine Providence which
> made the conspirators share their plot with him.[27]

Tresham did not even prove helpful with the funding of the plot, as Catesby had hoped. After making him take the oath of secrecy and fraternity, and revealing his plans, he had asked his cousin for £2,000 and the use of Tresham's palatial Rushton Hall in Northamptonshire.

Tresham complied with neither of these requests, although he later admitted giving a little money to Thomas Wintour.

Tresham questioned the validity of the plot, asking if it was right that Catholic Lords who would be in Parliament that day would die along with the Protestant Lords?[28] It was a question that others in the plot had already raised with Catesby,[29] and while Tresham spoke up for his brothers-in-law, Stourton and Monteagle, other members of the plot championed Lords Vaux, Mordaunt and Montague, and Thomas Percy stood up for his long-time master the Earl of Northumberland.

Catesby responded that it was a shame if they were to die too, but that to warn them directly risked destroying their whole plot. Reluctantly, at least if his own confession is to be believed, Francis Tresham agreed to join the plot and be guided by his cousin.

Nevertheless, on one occasion it seemed that Catesby defied his own instructions. Lord Montague, the man who had employed Guy Fawkes at Cowdray House, testified that he chanced upon Catesby while walking in the Savoy, a Thames-side area off The Strand, on 15 October. Perhaps Tresham's pleas a day earlier were fresh in Catesby's mind, for he stopped Montague and said, 'The Parliament, I think, brings your Lordship up now? I think your Lordship takes no pleasure to be there'.[30] On one reading, an inconsequential chat, but on an another reading a thinly veiled warning for Lord Montague to stay away from the opening of Parliament. As it happens, Viscount Montague did not attend Parliament on 5 November. If it was a coincidence it was a costly one, for it placed him under suspicion and led to his arrest ten days later.[31]

If Montague had been given a warning, there could be no question of other Catholic peers being warned, or could there? On the night of 26 October, Baron Monteagle was dining with his wife Elizabeth, Francis Tresham's sister, at their town house in Hoxton, formerly a property of the Tresham family. His servant Thomas Ward was outside taking a stroll in the evening air, when a tall stranger called out to him and asked if the baron was at home? Ward replied that he was at dinner, at which the man handed him a sealed letter and told him to ensure that it was placed into Lord Monteagle's hands, as it contained matters that concerned him.[32] Ward did as he was asked, but Monteagle's hands were sticky with food and so he broke the seal and handed it back to the servant to read to him. We can imagine Ward pausing at points during the letter, and being waved impatiently along by his master, for the contents were as scandalous in 1605 as they are today. Known as the Monteagle letter, it is one of the most controversial documents in English history, and it was to lead directly to the deaths of Guy Fawkes, Robert Catesby, and all those involved in the plot, along with many others who were inadvertently caught in its web. The missive was undated and unsigned, and it read:

> My Lord, out of the love I bear to some of your friends, I have a care of your preservation, therefore I would advise you as you tender your life to devise some excuse to shift your attendance at this Parliament, for God and man have concurred to punish the wickedness of this time, and think not slightly of this advertisement, but retire yourself into your country, where you may expect the event in safety, for though there be no appearance of any stir, yet I say they shall receive a terrible blow this Parliament and yet they shall not see who hurts them. This counsel is not to be condemned because it may do you good and can do you no harm, for the danger is past as soon as you have burnt the letter and I hope God will give you the grace to make good use of it, to whose holy protection I commend you.[33]

Chapter 19

A Traitor in the Brotherhood

Open suspecting others comes of secret
condemning themselves
Philip Sidney, *Arcadia*

The whole history of England would change depending on how Baron Monteagle reacted to the letter delivered to him on that October night. If he ignored the letter, or failed to see the importance of it, then the likelihood is that Parliament would have been blown up by Guy Fawkes, destroying the Protestant ruling class and plunging England into a civil war. The action Monteagle did take set in motion a chain of events that prevented this from happening, but which brought along deadly consequences of their own.

Lord Monteagle's confusion upon hearing the letter is understandable, and it was explained in the *King's Book*, a brief and speedily published official account of the gunpowder plot written on behalf of King James and with an introduction by Thomas Lord, Bishop of London:

> No sooner did he conceive the strange contents thereof, although he was somewhat perplexed what construction to make of it, as whether a matter of consequence, as indeed it was, or whether some foolish devised pasquil [a piece of wit or satirical writing] by some of his enemies to scare him from his attendance at the Parliament, yet did he, as a most dutiful and loyal subject, conclude not to conceal it, whatever might come of it.[1]

A TRAITOR IN THE BROTHERHOOD

The exact meaning of the letter was far from certain to Monteagle, but the menace within it was obvious – even if it did state that it meant him no harm. It also, of course, stated that the danger was past as soon as the letter was burnt, meaning the danger to the sender as this would destroy any evidence, but unfortunately for the sender, whoever it may be, Monteagle kept a firm grip upon it rather than consigning it to the flames.

There was only one person that Monteagle could trust with a letter of this kind, and who would surely discern the hidden meaning within it – the Secretary of State, Sir Robert Cecil. It was around seven o'clock in the evening when the baron received the letter from his servant, and yet he wasted no time in calling upon Cecil, donning his spurs and riding through the dark the four miles from his property in Hoxton to Cecil's at Whitehall. When he arrived he was fortunate to find not only the Secretary of State at home, but also the Earls of Worcester, Northampton, Nottingham and Suffolk who were taking a late supper with Cecil, who had himself been created Earl of Salisbury earlier that year.[2] Once the formalities of greeting were over, Monteagle wasted no time in asking to speak to Cecil on a private matter of some concern. Excusing themselves from the guests, Cecil escorted Monteagle to a private office, and it was there that the letter was handed over.

Cecil betrayed little emotion while reading the letter – as England's long serving spymaster he had read many like it before, and was expert at reading hidden meanings and half-cyphers. It would tie in with reports of growing Catholic unrest that Cecil had been receiving throughout the year, including the letter forwarded to him by the Brussels ambassador Sir Thomas Edmondes warning of a planned uprising backed by Spain.[3]

Cecil next showed the letter to the Earls of Suffolk, Nottingham, Worcester, and Northampton (the latter two were themselves Catholics[4]), and asked for their opinion on the matter. This was, in effect, a meeting of the highest councillors in England, for while Cecil was Principal Secretary of State, the Earl of Suffolk was Lord Chamberlain and the Earl of Nottingham was the Lord High Admiral.

The earls seemed less concerned than either Monteagle or Cecil had been, and were of the opinion that the letter was of no real importance. It was simply the product of a fantasist or a lone man holding a grudge against the King or his Parliament.[5] Cecil, however, said to the earls that the letter 'put him in mind of diverse advertisements he had received from beyond the seas... concerning some business the Papists were in, both at home and abroad, making preparations for some combination amongst them against this Parliament-time'.[6]

As ever, Cecil's opinion held sway, but as the King himself was away at a hunt in Royston, Hertfordshire,[7] they agreed to show him the letter upon his return and seek his opinion. He was expected back at the end of October, and as the threat was seemingly related to the opening of Parliament five days after that it was decided that the delay wouldn't bring any further risks. Cecil also hoped that these extra days would give the plot more time to ripen and that this would make the perpetrators more evident and easier to bring to justice.[8]

King James was a keen huntsman who often went on extravagant hunts lasting days or weeks,[9] and his courtiers knew not to disturb him when he was in the pursuit of pleasure. It is said that Robert Catesby told Anne Vaux, in conversation at White Webbs, that he himself had been planning to join the King on this hunt.[10] If true, this shows the confidence and calmness he felt a week before his planned assassination of the King and his ministers, and not a little recklessness. If Catesby was free to join the Royston hunt then it is likely that he had been on such hunts before. Catesby was renowned as an expert and fearless horseman, and was therefore just the kind of man the King would have wanted alongside him. In these circumstances an unseen push would been enough to kill the King in what would have been taken as an accident, but Catesby resisted temptation just as Guy Fawkes had when next to the King at the London wedding.

Lord Monteagle wasn't the only one facing a dilemma on that October day, nor the only one who would receive a message that chilled his bones. Thomas Ward, Monteagle's servant who had received the letter from the unknown stranger, was also connected to the complex web joining the conspirators together. It is believed that Kit Wright's wife, Margaret Ward, was the sister of Thomas.[11] Ursula Wright, younger sister of Kit and Jack Wright, had also married a Ward, Marmaduke, who may have been related to Thomas (it was Ursula's daughter Mary Ward who founded the Institute of the Blessed Virgin Mary who in turn founded York's Bar Convent[12]). While it is probable that Thomas Ward had familial connections to the Wrights, it is certain that he knew Thomas Wintour, as Wintour had also been in the employ of Lord Monteagle for many years.[13]

The day after the delivery of the letter, 27 October, Ward happened upon Thomas Wintour and told him about the strange encounter he'd had the night before, and about the letter read to his master and the baron's reaction to it.[14] Like most aspects of the Monteagle letter story, this raises more questions than answers. Did Ward accidentally alight upon his former colleague Wintour, and in passing tell him the latest news from the Monteagle household, or was it something more sinister? Is the truth that Ward deliberately sought Thomas Wintour out, recognizing or guessing his connection to the events hinted at by the letter? We shall never know, although it has been suggested that Ward was a spy for the Catholic cause and may have known much about Catesby's plot.

If Thomas Wintour managed to keep a disinterested face during this conversation it was in stark contrast to his inner turmoil. Here was evidence against the plot, and it was now in the hands of Robert Cecil and the Privy Council: evidence that could bring destruction upon his head and the heads of all those he loved.

Taking his leave of Ward in as calm a manner as possible, Wintour thought the matter through overnight, a restless, sleepless night, before travelling to White Webbs to see Robert Catesby in the morning. Having thought long and hard, Wintour had come to the conclusion that the danger was too great, they must abandon the plot and flee the country while they still could.[15] Catesby, however, was not so easily deterred, and decided to first send a man to the cellar to check whether the gunpowder store had been discovered. This task would bring immediate danger to the person undertaking it, so there was only one man for the job: 'He [Catesby] told me [Thomas Wintour] that he would see further as yet and resolved to send Mr Fawkes to try the uttermost... On Wednesday Mr Fawkes went and returned at night, of which we were very glad'.[16]

Catesby hadn't informed Guy of the letter, and the extra danger he was placing himself in, until he returned from his reconnaissance, but Guy answered that even if he had been told of this danger beforehand, he would not have failed to do what had to be done.[17]

Even without knowledge of the letter, Guy realised the danger that such a visit after an absence could entail. He would have approached the cellar cautiously, stealthily, checking the door first of all and listening for signs from within. Entering the door was the moment of greatest risk, for armed guards sent by Cecil could have been waiting for just such a moment. The handle was turned carefully, with one hand resting upon the hilt of his sword, but once inside, much to Guy's relief, it was apparent he was alone. After a silent yet meticulous search, he also ascertained that none of the secret signs he had set up, the carefully positioned objects, had been disturbed: the cellar remained undiscovered.

Guy's news was greeted joyously by Thomas Wintour and Catesby, and prayers of thanks were offered by the three men bound so closely in death and danger. The question now turned to who was responsible for the letter that could have put an end to everything, and the immediate suspect was one who had recently and seemingly reluctantly joined their endeavours, one who had a reputation for being untrustworthy: their thirteenth man Francis Tresham.

Catesby and Wintour sent a message to Tresham, asking him to meet them at Barnet. It was now Friday, 1 November, just four days before they were due to put their plan into action.[18] After opening the conversation with their usual conviviality, Catesby suggested that they take a walk through the nearby Royal Forest of Epping Chase.[19] With each step forward, Tresham could feel the atmosphere growing poisonous. The conversation had stopped and he walked with one man in front of him and one man behind, until they reached a clearing and halted. It was now that the serious questioning started. Catesby relayed the story to him calmly but with an unmistakeable menace in his words. The question was simple: had Tresham sent the letter to Baron Monteagle, and in so doing broken his solemn oath and betrayed them all?

Tresham's life was in the balance, as he well knew, but he vehemently proclaimed his innocence, calling upon the men to remember his service during the Essex rebellion, and talking to Catesby of the bond they had shared since childhood. He fell to his knees and prayed to God, asking to be struck down if he was lying. This was the moment that would decide Francis Tresham's fate. Catesby looked Wintour in the eye, they were in silent agreement: reaching down they took Tresham's hand and raised him to his feet; they believed him. If they had harboured any doubt, they had resolved to hang him in the forest there and then.[20]

Tresham was absolved of suspicion by the leaders of the gunpowder plot, so who was the secret hand behind the Monteagle letter? It remains one of history's enigmas, and if it wasn't for the fact that it can be seen in the National Archives to this day, many would doubt its existence entirely. Throughout the centuries many theories have grown up around the story of the letter, some of them plausible, some of them ridiculous, but all of them interesting.

If the writer wasn't Francis Tresham, then could it be another plotter with links to the baron? Thomas Wintour perhaps, who had been a loyal servant to Monteagle? Thomas Ward's visit to Wintour could indicate either that he thought somebody else was trying to betray Wintour, or that Wintour had sent the letter himself, via a go-between, and Ward was warning him about Monteagle's actions after receiving it. On the whole, however, I find Thomas Wintour an unlikely culprit. His actions throughout the plot show a man fully committed to it, and when he later had a chance to flee he instead chose to join Catesby and his comrades.

Guy Fawkes can certainly be taken out of the line-up of suspects. He and Monteagle did not know each other, as shown by the reaction, or lack of it, when Monteagle later spotted Guy in the chamber beneath Parliament.

THE REAL GUY FAWKES

Could it have been Robert Catesby? It sounds incredible at first, but there is circumstantial evidence. We know, for instance, that Catesby gave a warning of sorts to Lord Montague when they met in the street, and Catesby was a great friend of Baron Monteagle, as shown in his glowing praise of Catesby as the only sun that ripens the harvest and akin to the very air he breathes.[21] There was also, yet again, a familial connection, as Lord Monteagle's wife was not only the sister of Francis Tresham but also, of course, the cousin of Robert Catesby.

Father Francis Edwards, the great gunpowder plot scholar of the twentieth century, is convinced that Catesby's plot was not genuine at all, and that he was in fact an agent provocateur working for Robert Cecil.[22] We know that one servant testified that Catesby had secret meetings with Robert Cecil. George Bartlet, on his deathbed, stated that his erstwhile master Robert Catesby had visited Cecil on three occasions in the weeks leading up to 5 November, and was always admitted via a back door.[23] Was this the last utterance of truth by one about to die, or the unreliable ramblings of a diseased body and mind?

While Father Edwards' views must always be considered carefully, he does tend to see spies and agent provocateurs everywhere – also attributing this role to Thomas Wintour, Thomas Percy, Francis Tresham, Guy Fawkes, and Lord Monteagle, so that there seem to be more false agents in the plot than actual plotters. If Catesby was an agent provocateur then he was a very bad one: committing himself to a certain death, rather than simply stirring the plot and then retreating to safety. We must also consider that although Catesby escaped the gallows by being killed in a shoot-out, as we shall see, his body was disinterred and disfigured – which seems hardly likely if he had been working for the government all along. Catesby was inside what he appeared to be on the surface, a fanatical Catholic who would kill for the cause. His fanaticism could lead him to be reckless at times, but he was not an agent provocateur, and nor was he the man who sent the Monteagle letter.

Perhaps the sender of the letter was a woman? Did the married plotters keep this secret from their wives, as their oath compelled them to, or were secrets hinted at in the marital chamber? Anne Vaux had at least some knowledge of what was happening, and had spoken to Father Garnet of her concerns,[24] so could other women connected to the plot and plotters have had knowledge too? Lady Antonia Fraser conjectured that the letter writer could have been Mary Habington, Lord Monteagle's sister, and that by sending the letter she hoped to see the gunpowder plot halted.[25]

Is it likely that Mary would have known more of the plot than her brother? Would she have known more than Anne Vaux, who although sheltering members of the plot including Catesby and Guy Fawkes in the weeks before November was still ignorant of the exact nature of their plans? Above all, it seems unlikely that Mary Habington wrote a letter that would have endangered her brother if he had not heeded its warning, and which would make him look complicit if he acted upon the warning without informing others.

A more likely suspect in the family is William Parker, the 4th Baron Monteagle himself. His fervent Catholicism had cost him money, property, and reputation, as well as brought him time in prison. There are hints that he may have turned his back on his old faith in an effort to show his loyalty to the new king, and he wrote to James in 1604 to say that he wished to become a Protestant.[26] If Monteagle had heard hints of the plot, and especially who was involved in it, he may reasonably have expected that his name would be linked to it by Robert Cecil, with potentially disastrous consequences.

By fabricating the letter he could present it to Cecil and thus show his loyalty and exonerate himself. That is the case for Monteagle being the writer of a false letter, but if he had done so then why did he wait until night-time to ride across London to Cecil to deliver it? And why would he hire someone to deliver the letter to him at Hoxton? We know from Ward's testimony that the letter was delivered to Thomas Wintour,[27] but this would have been a completely redundant act if Monteagle had written the letter himself, and it would bring with it the possibility that the letter would not be delivered at all.

Monteagle was less overtly Catholic by 1605, but this was a political move to protect his family and his property rather than any change in convictions. Even at this time, Monteagle was still helping the Catholic cause and individual Catholics, as we can see from the financial assistance he was providing to Martha Percy.[28]

In recent times it has increasingly been suspected that the letter was a fabrication of another kind; that it was created by none other than Sir Robert Cecil. This theory surmises that Cecil knew of a plot, which is certainly possible given his large coterie of spies and double agents, and that he determined that such a letter would flush the plotters out of hiding.

While Cecil was cunning and unscrupulous enough to try anything to bring plotters to justice, protect the King, and enhance his own reputation, there is a large problem with this theory. It is eminently possible that the letter may have induced desperation in whoever the plotters were, causing them not to reveal themselves, but to carry out their plans there and then. Alternatively, it is more likely to have driven them further underground rather than bringing them into the open where Cecil wanted them. If Cecil had known about the plot for a long time, being fed information by an insider, whether Catesby, Percy or someone else, then is it really likely that he would leave a cache of gunpowder under Parliament, and wait until almost the last moment to foil it? This seems ridiculous behaviour for a man as stringent and meticulous as the Secretary of State.

One piece of evidence that some have used against Cecil is that on 9 November 1605 he wrote to Sir Charles Cornwallis, England's ambassador to Spain, that the letter was 'in a hand disguised'.[29] How could Cecil have known that unless he himself had written it? This is simply a matter of semantics. Cecil had seen enough letters and ciphers to know when handwriting looked disguised or natural, and his words simply mean that he didn't recognise the writing. Father Francis Edwards, who was convinced that Cecil was the culprit, had a handwriting expert examine the Monteagle letter and one written by Robert Cecil, but the conclusion is far from satisfying.[30] To this untrained eye there is little or no similarity between the handwritings, and while the expert gets around this by saying it is because the hand is disguised, the same conclusion could therefore be applied to anybody.

A TRAITOR IN THE BROTHERHOOD

Who then was the writer of the Monteagle letter? The simple explanations are often the best, and the truth was staring everyone in the face in 1605 just as much as it is today. The letter writer was indeed Francis Tresham, trying to save his beloved brother-in-law, and hoping to prevent the plot, with its undoubted loss of life, from taking place.

To Catesby and Wintour, Tresham was the obvious perpetrator from the very first, but his pleading convinced them otherwise. Many a person can put on a convincing act when their life depends upon it, and Tresham's prayers and protestations were all a lie. It may be questioned why he would send a letter instead of talking to Monteagle in person, but he may have suspected there would be spies in the house, Thomas Ward perhaps, who would report his actions to Catesby or Thomas Wintour. A letter would also be much more useful as a deterrent to the plot going ahead, which was Francis Tresham's ultimate aim.

Some have asked why, if Tresham wrote to Baron Monteagle, he didn't also write to his other brother-in-law Lord Stourton? The answer is that Tresham may well have written to Stourton as well, but that Stourton then ignored the letter or destroyed it. It is noteworthy that Lord Stourton was absent from the opening of Parliament.

With Tresham believed by Catesby and Wintour, the traitor in their brotherhood had escaped (and we shall see later the unusual way in which Francis Tresham evaded justice of another kind too). They now had a momentous decision to make, and the leaders of the plot were called together. The days were passing with wicked speed, and it was a matter of hours until the opening of Parliament. King James was back at court now, and would have been informed of the letter. Did the men continue as planned, or abandon the plot while they could, and in so doing spare their own lives? Guy was as adamant on this point as Catesby was: there could be no backing down – they would risk their lives, risk everything. They would proceed.

Chapter 20

A Very Tall and Desperate Fellow

Good, happy, swift; there's gunpowder i'th' court,
Wildfire at midnight in this heedless fury.
Thomas Middleton, *The Revenger's Tragedy*

King James returned to the Palace of Whitehall from his Hertfordshire
hunting lodge on Thursday, 31 October 1605, in time to preside over
the opening of the new Parliament on the following week.[1] Robert
Cecil, having had experience of the King's condition upon returning
from such trips, judged it best to leave James until the morning, when
he was sure to find him in a more sober frame of mind. So it was that
on Friday morning, the first day of November, the mysterious letter to
Lord Monteagle was placed into the King's hands.

Cecil at first played down the significance of the letter, maybe even
handing it over after some trifling documents that needed royal
approval. Before James had a chance to read it, Cecil informed him
that it was nothing to worry about, that it was surely the work of a
lunatic or idiot.[2] This was characteristically duplicitous of the
Secretary of State, for with the other intelligence that Cecil had been
receiving, and other information which he had surely gathered since
receiving the letter himself, he knew it was a missive that deserved to
be taken seriously.

Cecil, in downplaying the importance of the letter, was not only
creating a reason for not having interrupted the King's hunting trip,
but also giving the King a chance to gain the glory by seeming to solve
the letter's riddle himself. That was exactly what happened. Although
the official record contained within the *King's Book* states that James

remained perfectly calm throughout, it seems more likely that he would have exploded with anger. His ministers had missed what was obvious to his eyes – the letter was evidence of an explosion that was to shatter the opening of Parliament in less than one week's time. The use of the words 'they shall receive a terrible blow this Parliament' was proof of this, and the King also seized upon the injunction to 'burn this letter' as evidence that the writer intended the Parliament building to burn.[3]

Keeping a smile from his face, a bowing Cecil complimented the King on his genius at breaking the code, his majesty had grasped the true meaning of the letter which had eluded their less noble and less able minds. While this was nothing more than an act from Cecil, the terror was all too real for the King – a plot was being hatched against him that mirrored the one which had killed his own father at Kirk o' Field thirty-eight years previously. There was no threat more sure to grab James's attention, and more sure to be taken seriously, than one involving gunpowder.

The King's instructions were that the Parliament building must be searched thoroughly, including the adjoining buildings that made up the sprawling Parliamentary complex of the day. This task was given to the Lord Chamberlain, the Earl of Suffolk, to organise, and the date he set for the search was the eve of the opening, 4 November. Also asked to join the search was Lord Monteagle, who was now praised for his presence of mind when bringing the letter directly to Cecil.

If Monteagle was informed of this honour in advance of the search he kept the secret zealously to himself: his staff were predominantly Catholic, and there were spies on both sides of the religious divide. Nevertheless, he must have mentioned that King James had now seen the letter and had taken it seriously, for this message was relayed, once again, by Thomas Ward to his former colleague Thomas Wintour.[4]

This caused even greater perturbation among some of the plotters than the original news of the letter. Catesby had reassured them of his belief that the letter was too vague to be taken seriously, and that it would have no impact upon their plans, but here was proof to the contrary. While Catesby and Guy Fawkes remained steadfast, others were filled with growing fears, doubts and even a growing sense of impending disaster.

While Guy's fearlessness showed itself in untroubled sleep, even when in the greatest danger,[5] others inside the plot found it impossible to sleep without the torment of nightmares. Father Tesimond reports how he heard that Thomas Wintour had dreamed the barrels of gunpowder exploded in a succession of less than impressive explosions, doing nothing other than causing an eruption of laughter from the Lords in Parliament. Another, unnamed, plotter dreamed that the minutiae of the plot had been discovered and they would all be captured.[6]

Francis Tresham in particular was showing signs of distress as the opening of Parliament grew nearer. Tresham was staying in rooms at Lincoln's Inn and was visited there by Thomas Wintour.[7] Wintour may not have been a welcome visitor after their recent journey together with Catesby into the Royal Forest, but whether it was the memory of this, or a guilty conscience, Tresham was found to be nervous and distracted. He told Wintour that without a doubt their plot had been discovered, and that they needed to abandon it immediately and fly from the scene while they could. So violent was Tresham in this assertion that Wintour adjudged him to be 'a man who had lost control of himself'.[8]

Another meeting of the most prominent London based plotters was convened, with the notable exception of Francis Tresham.[9] Sat around a table were Catesby, Guy Fawkes, Thomas Wintour, and the brothers Jack and Kit Wright, and a heated debate soon ensued. Thomas Wintour's opinion was that Tresham must have heard something directly from Lord Monteagle himself, and that a knock could come to their door at any moment that would signal their arrest, disgrace, and death.

Tresham's agitation could also have been because he was indeed the man who had sent the letter to his cousin Monteagle, but had now found that rather than halting the plot as he had wished, it instead endangered all their lives. This thought occurred as much to Thomas Wintour and Robert Catesby then as it does to us now, but there was no time to pursue the matter further and it was essential that they remained united, in appearance at least.

A VERY TALL AND DESPERATE FELLOW

It is once more testimony to the strength of his character, and the devotion that he could inspire in others, that the primary concern of the conspirators was to ensure the safety of their leader Catesby. Wintour urged him to sail to the continent immediately, and argued that Catesby could still direct an uprising from there while the others would stay behind and carry out his orders.

Guy Fawkes was in favour of this plan, as long as it didn't mean the cessation of their endeavours that had been so long in planning and which were now so close to fruition. As Father Tesimond recalled, he was ready to take all the risk upon himself if necessary:

> Some of them thought that Mr Catesby should leave then and there for Flanders, leaving Mr Guy to look after the house. Magnanimously enough, Fawkes was quite ready to do this. In this way, when the main deed was done Catesby could put in execution the rest of the plan.[10]

Catesby himself, however, would hear nothing of their protestations, and insisted on remaining in the country. It was also imperative, he said, to talk to Thomas Percy on this matter, and he had not yet arrived in London.[11] Percy's lateness must have increased the fears of his fellow conspirators, who would have wondered whether he had backed out of the affair, or even whether he had been captured. It was late on Sunday evening when he reached London, and after greeting the five men present he was told, for the first time, about the Monteagle letter.

There can be little doubt that Percy was furious about this act of betrayal, and given his proficiency with a sword and his famed willingness to use it, it was fortunate for Tresham that he was not present. Catesby soothed Percy by explaining that they had talked to Tresham and been convinced of his innocence in this affair, but Percy must still have harboured his suspicions. The matter was then put to Percy, as it had been to the others, whether they should abandon their plot and seek safety?

For Percy, like Catesby and Guy Fawkes, there could be no

question of turning their backs on their plans with less than forty-eight hours to go. He insisted that he would stay, whatever happened, and see what fate had ordained for them. Percy was ready to 'abide the uttermost trial'[12] and, as ever, would not go down without a fight.

The final decision had been reached: they would take on their allotted tasks as if the discovery of the letter had never happened. It was agreed that in the morning Guy would proceed to the house they had rented from John Whynniard and from there go to the cellar under Parliament, to guard the gunpowder in these vital last hours. Catesby would ride northwards with Jack Wright and Thomas Bates, where they would meet up with Everard Digby at the Red Lion Inn in Dunchurch, Warwickshire, as had been agreed. Upon hearing news of the explosion they would then launch the second phase of their plan, the capture of Princess Elizabeth and the orchestration of a Midlands uprising that would spread across the country.[13]

Tuesday morning came, and Thomas Percy, the last to arrive in London, had adopted the calm demeanour which made him such a difficult opponent in a duel. One task he carried out was the purchase of a pocket watch that was later carried by Robert Keyes to Guy Fawkes,[14] now in his station beneath Parliament.

Percy then went to Syon House, the grand Thames-side mansion belonging to his great friend and mentor the Earl of Northumberland, to discuss the latest news about the union of England and Scotland.[15] Also at lunch that day were Edmund Whitelocke and a servant named Fitzharbart,[16] and it was to prove an inauspicious event for all concerned. After Thomas Percy's later arrest, suspicion fell on everyone present at the meal, with particularly disastrous consequences for the Earl himself.[17]

Percy, and other members of the conspiracy with the possible exception of Francis Tresham, sought the solace and confidence of company as the hours ticked by, taking their minds off what was to come by indulging in mundane conversation and carrying out everyday tasks. One man, however, was completely alone on 4 November: Guy Fawkes.

Upon rising before dawn on the Tuesday morning Guy Fawkes

made his way towards the house rented from John Whynniard, which led to the cellar underneath the Parliament chamber. He was now John Johnson, the humble servant of the Gentleman Pensioner Thomas Percy, a mere shadow, someone unremarkable in every way.

Guy was wearing a dark stove-pipe hat so typical of the period, and a black cloak that he wrapped tightly around him against the chill air of the November dawn. He also wore spurs upon his boots,[18] and would have walked carefully to prevent their noise from alerting anyone to his presence.

The spurs are a clue to Guy's intended getaway. The ship that was waiting to take him to Flanders must have been docked at a broader point of the river to the east of Westminster, presumably at a location such as Greenwich. Once the gunpowder had been lit, time would become of critical importance to Guy, and so the wearing of spurs indicates that he had a horse in position near to Parliament that could carry him swiftly to the port.

In his confession of 16 November, Guy admitted that he had tested his slow fuses to see how much time he would have to make his escape after lighting them. The one that he chose and took with him on 4 November would have given him precisely fifteen minutes.[19] Guy had learned the importance of preparation during his decade as a soldier, which is why he made the journey many times in the days leading up to the opening of Parliament, judging to the second exactly how much time he would need. The planned flight was not only for reasons of self-preservation, although Guy fully expected the explosion to take place and the ship to carry him overseas; while remaining focused on the firing of the powder, Guy also had an eye on his mission afterwards, persuading the Catholic soldiers of the continent to join their cause and finally liberate England from Protestantism.

The hours alone in the chamber passed with a terrible slowness for Guy, who alternated sitting, standing, and lying, but kept awake and alert at all times. He was listening carefully for an unexpected sound or approaching footsteps, hoping and praying that he wouldn't be disturbed.

At some point in the afternoon, that is exactly what happened. Guy had heard the footsteps drawing nearer before a key turned in the lock, and had ascertained that there was more than one man. He had seconds to decide whether to draw his sword and prepare to fight, or to remain calm as if he was merely a servant at his duty. The door opened, and in stepped John Whynniard, who must have retained a key to the chamber. Alongside him were Lord Monteagle, and the Lord Chamberlain, the Earl of Suffolk. The men looked around the cellar and their eyes were drawn towards a large collection of wood in one corner, it was only then in the dim light of the room that they noticed the cloak-wearing man alongside it.

Suffolk addressed the man, asking to know who he was. The stranger returned his gaze without flinching, replying in a calm voice with northern tones that he was John Johnson, servant to Thomas Percy. His master had hired the cellar to store his firewood and provisions. Suffolk turned to Whynniard with a quizzical look, but the man explained that the story was true – that it had been rented by Thomas Percy and he had a servant named John Johnson. Turning on their heels the three men left the cellar, to resume their search of other buildings in and around Parliament. Guy Fawkes had passed the test, the secret remained safe – for now.

Once outside the cellar however, the three searchers aired their concerns. Whynniard said that he was surprised that Percy, who was rarely in London despite his role as a Gentleman Pensioner, should need so much firewood.[20] Monteagle revealed that the naming of Percy had worried him too, as Percy was a great friend of his, and he knew how ardent a Catholic he was, and these factors now made him suspect that Thomas Percy may have been behind the letter he'd received.[21] The Lord Chamberlain was also dissatisfied. There was something about the man John Johnson that was not quite right. He had an air of menace about him, he in fact looked 'a very tall and desperate fellow'.[22]

Having found little else of note in the rest of their search, the men decided to inform the King of their suspicions without delay, and see what course of action he wished to take next.

Guy Fawkes now had a choice to make. There were mere hours left until he could fire the gunpowder, and successfully conclude that part of the plot. On the other hand, if he had failed to convince them of his story the men could return at any time, at which point all would be lost.

One option was to flee at that very moment, boarding the waiting ship and sailing to the continent. It was never a choice that a man with Guy's reserves of courage, and with his overriding sense of loyalty, was going to take. He could also have remained in station where he was, but that could have exposed his brethren in the plot to risk. With little time to waste in deliberation, Guy chose a third way. Leaving the chamber temporarily he sought out Thomas Percy, now returned from Syon House and ready and waiting near to Parliament, as pre-arranged, should Guy need him. The conversation was hurried, but the two men were of one mind – they could not stop now, whatever the dangers. Percy informed Guy that he would send Robert Keyes to see him later in the evening, and with that Guy returned to his post and his duty.

At around ten o'clock in the evening a knock on the door, following a pattern that had surely been arranged between those in the conspiracy, announced that a friend had arrived. Nevertheless, Guy approached the door with caution and ready to take action if necessary. To his relief, Keyes was waiting for him and handed over a pocket watch from Thomas Percy before turning and walking away into the now black night.

Guy, during his interrogation, explained the watch by stating that it had been given to him 'because he should know how the time went away'.[23] Watches were rare and expensive items at the time, normally beyond the remit of a man such as Guy, but he needed to know the precise time so that he could set the explosion to occur at a moment when the King and his lords had gathered above him.

Guy watched the hand travelling oh-so-slowly around the face, counting down the hours that would lead to triumph or disaster. It is natural that his mind would have been troubled as well by the fact that he was about to send hundreds to their death in a crescendo of noise, blood and pain. Wives would be widowed, children orphaned, just as his mother had been widowed and just as the children of Margaret

Clitherow had been orphaned. Perhaps one day there would be peace, but that day was not now, and Guy knew that he was not the man for a time of peace.

Pushing his qualms aside, he knelt on the now cold and damp floor and uttered a prayer to Jesus, Mary and the saints and martyrs. He was asking for forgiveness for what he was about to do.

The boy of York was gone, no more was he the laughing untroubled child who had played freely with his sisters and friends. So too, the servant John Johnson was gone, he was now once more the soldier Guido Fawkes, as he would refer to himself in his confessions.

The slow fuse was inserted through the prepared spot in the wooden billets, and he stood still by the light cast by his lamp upon the floor. The hands on the watch continued to move, but Guy's mind was now emptying itself of everything except what he had to do next. Perhaps a last piece of scripture came into his head, such as St. Paul's profession: 'when I was a child, I spoke as a child, I thought as a child, I reasoned as a child. When I became a man, I gave up my childish ways'.[24] Guy was now more than a man, he was an angel of death who would at last bring justice and revenge upon the heads of those who had done so much to harm his faith and his people. The watch ticked closer towards twelve midnight, it was mere minutes before the fifth of November. Guy now knew that nobody would disturb him; that nine hours from now his hand would strike a flint and set a flame burning along the fifteen-minute fuse that led to thirty-six barrels of gunpowder and carnage. Guy was wrong.

As one day turned into the next, Guy heard a faint noise from outside the cellar. He opened the door to see what was amiss, but stepping forward into the darkness, he found himself blinded by the light of a lamp thrust into his face. A man was upon him, who knocked Guy off his feet and pinned him to the floor. Guy overcame his momentary confusion and a brief yet fierce struggle ensued in which Guy crushed the man's hand so fiercely that he considered drawing his dagger and stabbing him before thinking better of it.[25]

Armed men came to the guard's aid, dragging Guy to his feet and binding his hands behind his back.[26] Pushed into the cellar, Guy was powerless to resist as he watched the men tear away at the wood coverings, hearing their curses as the barrels of gunpowder were uncovered and then opened. Guy's pockets were searched next and within them were discovered touchwood and a match.[27]

The leader of the men approached Guy with a look of disgust on his face, but Guy returned it with something approaching a smirk.

'You were lucky to find me outside the cellar,' Guy said in a calm, confident manner belying the sickening feeling growing within him, 'otherwise none of you would be talking about it now, because you would all have been blown sky-high'.[28]

Chapter 21

The Devil of the Vault

Within the bowels of these elements,
Where we are tortured and remain forever.
Hell hath no limits, nor is circumscribed
In one self place, for where we are is hell,
And where hell is must we ever be.
Christopher Marlowe, *Doctor Faustus*

He who had grappled with Guy was one Edmund Doubleday,[1] one of a troop of armed men sent to search the cellar under the leadership of Sir Thomas Knyvett.[2] It was fortunate for Doubleday that he had, at the last moment, resisted his dagger, for they were under strict instructions to capture the mysterious John Johnson alive.

Doubleday received an injured hand during the struggle, but he was to receive much more in the years to come. Hailed as a hero, in 1609 he was made Warden of the Mint alongside Knyvett, and was then responsible for production of the nation's coins. Doubleday became very wealthy, and in 1614 was elected Member of Parliament for the Westminster constituency.[3]

Knyvett was already a Member of Parliament in 1605, and had been a member of the Privy Chamber of Queen Elizabeth. He also served as one of London's magistrates, and this is the key to his role in the apprehension of Guy Fawkes.[4] Sir Robert Cecil had been elated at the news of the afternoon search led by the Earl of Suffolk. The desperate fellow they encountered, Johnson, seemed a likely suspect, especially as he had mentioned Thomas Percy. This in turn implicated the Earl of Northumberland, as the close bond between the two Percys was well known. The Earl was a man of authority and power, however, even though his forebears had a long history of treachery and infamy, and so Cecil would have to tread carefully. There was no better man than Knyvett for the task, as not only was he an old acquaintance of Robert Cecil, he also had the legal authority needed for searches and arrests. Knyvett, like Doubleday, profited from his exploits on that November night, and in 1607 was made the first Baron Knyvett of Escrick[5] in Yorkshire.

With Guy bound and guarded by armed men, Knyvett made his way immediately to Whitehall Palace. Although it was after midnight, he found Cecil awaiting news. From Knyvett's hurried actions and anxious expression he guessed the news before he spoke, and leaving Knyvett momentarily he sought council with the King. James was clear, he wanted to see the man himself – in the King's mind there was little doubt that he was now about to confront an infernal servant of Satan, and he would show how a King's power would prevail.

At four o' clock on the morning of 5 November 1605, a tall and bloodied, but unbowed, man was led into the personal bedchamber of the King himself, accompanied by armed guards on all sides.[7] Also there were members of the Privy Council who had been present in the palace, including Robert Cecil and the Earl of Suffolk. Guy was stripped before entering the chamber to ensure that he had no concealed weapons upon him, and it was this that led to the questions about the scars on his body at his later interrogation. This examination also left little doubt about the man's Catholicism and zealousness in his faith, as he was found to be wearing numerous symbols of his faith (presumably crucifixes and rosary beads) as well as, much to the astonishment of his captors, a hair shirt.[8] This uncomfortable item was a sign of special piety and worn to remind the wearer of the pains that Christ had been through for them. Thomas Becket had famously been found to be wearing one after being murdered in Canterbury Cathedral on the orders of King Henry II.[9]

King James was a firm believer in divine right. It was clear to him that God had brought about the convoluted chain of events that led to him being placed upon the English throne. He was used to people bowing before him, casting their eyes down in his presence, but this stranger was different. He was proud and defiant when he should have been scared and grovelling for his life. The two men stared into each other's eyes; James was now in no doubt that here was a man who had intended to kill him, here was a man who would have had no compunction in ending the lives of hundreds of people at a stroke. Here, thought the expert on the subject who had written the *Daemonologie*, was one who was more devil than man.

This was a view that quickly prevailed among the population of England. Guy and his fellow conspirators were not fighting for a cause, they were simply agents of evil seeking the destruction of the country itself, and the greatest devil of all was the man who would have put light to the fuse. In a sermon delivered after the news had spread, William Barlow, the Bishop of Rochester, described Guy as a 'blood sucker' and, using a description that would stick, he labelled Guy as 'the devil of the vault'.[10] Guy Fawkes, insisted Barlow, had wanted to pull down the moon and the sun, not from Heaven to Earth, but into the bottomless pit in which he and Satan lived.

From the moment Doubleday had forced him to the floor and bound his hands, just four hours earlier, Guy knew that all that awaited him now was interrogation, pain, torture and then execution. There was no other possible outcome, and so calling to his mind his soldier's spirit, and the examples of countless saints he had read about, he vowed to endure all.

His calm, measured demeanour was menacing, the flickering candles around the royal bedchamber a reminder of how close the man had come to snuffing out their own brief candles. Nevertheless, even though this man was their deadly foe, the King and his chief minister Cecil were impressed by him.

Robert Cecil wrote to Sir Charles Cornwallis in Spain to inform him of the plot, the arrest and the man's responses to their questioning.[11] There is a grudging respect in Cecil's description:

> He [Guy Fawkes] is no more dismayed, – nay, scarce any more troubled, than if he were taken for a poor robbery

on the highway. To the impatient and hurried questions that were put to him with some violence and passion, he answered calmly and firmly that "his name was John Johnson, and that he was a servant of Thomas Percy – that when the King had come to the Parliament House that day, and the Upper House had been sitting, he meant to have fired the match, and fled for his own safety before the powder had taken fire; and that if he had not been apprehended that night, he had blown up the Upper House, when the Kings, Lords, Bishops, and others had been there'.[12]

The King was alarmed at this forthright proclamation and asked Guy, or John Johnson as he thought he was named, why he had wanted to kill him? Guy told the King it was because he was a heretic and the Pope had excommunicated him. Looking the King in the eye once more, Guy solemnly declared that his only sorrow was that he had not been able to carry out his plan.[13]

This insolence was unheard of in the presence of the King, who was after all God's representative on Earth as Henry VIII had asserted. Guy's answers brought a succession of slaps, kicks and punches to his defenceless body, Cecil's letter to Cornwallis admits as much when he talks of questions being put to him with violence and passion, but the captive remained unbowed physically and mentally. Guy may have been thinking of the questioning of Jesus by Pontius Pilate. Pilate asks why he won't answer his questions, and explains that he has the power to release him and the power to crucify him, to which Jesus replies that he would have no power over him unless it was given to him from above.[14]

Guards had now been positioned around the palace, and in the streets leading up to it, and the gates to the building had been locked. In Whitehall, the questioning continued, but Guy continued to amaze the members of the Privy Council present with his courage and sanguinity. One of the councillors was heard to say that in John Johnson they had another Mucius Scaevola.[15]

Gaius Mucius Scaevola was a Roman soldier of legend. Captured by enemy Etruscans, brought before the King, Scaevola declared that he came there to kill his enemy, and he was as ready to die as he was to kill. To show that Romans act bravely and suffered bravely he thrust his hand into a fire and held it there. The king was amazed at this act, and had the soldier released.[16] There was no such hope for Guy. With daylight breaking across London, the King ordered him to be taken away to the Tower of London under the care of the ever watchful, and ever cruel, Sir William Waad.[17]

By the dawn of Tuesday morning, news of the great discovery was already out. Many of the lords and parliamentarians had already started to gather around Westminster, as the opening was due to have taken place at nine o'clock in the morning. Under the circumstances Parliament's opening was prorogued yet again, although a brief meeting was held in the chamber to discuss what had happened. The *Journal of the House of Commons* recorded,

> This last Night the Upper House of Parliament was searched by Sir Tho. Knyvett; and one Johnson, Servant to Mr. Thomas Percy, was there apprehended; who had placed Thirty-six Barrels of Gunpowder in the Vault under the House, with a Purpose to blow King, and the whole Company, when they should there assemble.[18]

Word of the arrest was common knowledge long before the speech in Parliament however, and it had reached the ears of Kit Wright by five o'clock in the morning,[19] while Guy was still being interrogated by the King. The younger Wright brother had been unable to sleep well, for obvious reasons, and had taken to pacing the streets, watching his breath form white plumes in the bracing morning air.

By a strange coincidence, into the picture once more comes Lord Monteagle. Wright must have been surprised to see Monteagle up at the early hour as well, Kit bowing before him as his position demanded. It was a surprise that turned to sickening fear when the baron told him, 'rise and come along to Essex House, for I am going to call up my Lord of Northumberland'.[20]

Instantly aware that something was very wrong, Kit instead made his way to the Duck and Drake Inn where Thomas Wintour was staying, and burst into his room saying 'the matter is discovered'.[21] This news was so alarming that at first Wintour refused to believe it, and sent Kit Wright to Essex House, the palatial London residence of the Earl of Northumberland, to see if he could get more definite information.[22]

Kit Wright never got as far as Essex House, for on the approach he saw a man named John Lepton climb onto his horse, before calling out, 'will your Lordship have any more with me?' On being answered in the negative, Lepton spurred on his horse and rode away up Fleet Street as fast as he could.[23] At this sight, Kit made haste back to the Duck and Drake.

Wright correctly guessed what this meant. Lepton had been talking to members of the Privy Council who had gathered at Essex House to see if the Earl of Northumberland knew of Thomas Percy's whereabouts. He had now been given the task of hunting Percy down. Lepton was a Groom of the Privy Chamber and renowned for his ability as a horseman. So assiduous was he in his task that he eventually, and erroneously, ended up in Scotland on the hunt for the fugitive Percy.[24]

Thomas Wintour understood the news too, and a maudlin mood descended in his chamber. But even now he was not a man to panic. Instructing Wright to find Percy and warn him, he said that he would remain in London to assess the situation and join the others in the Midlands later.

Thomas Percy had taken the precaution of not staying in his own London residence on Gray's Inn Road on the night of the 4th, but instead renting a room known only to his fellow conspirators. It was a wise precaution for a warrant had been issued for his arrest after the initial questioning of Guy Fawkes – as yet Percy was the only person known to have any connection to the would-be regicide John Johnson.

John Lepton and the men of the Privy Council failed to find him, but Percy was instead woken up by Kit Wright bringing him the news he least wanted to hear. Percy dressed quickly, and he and Wright mounted their horses and rode swiftly northwards. Seeing one of his servants, Percy called out, 'I am undone!'[25] Meanwhile, Robert Keyes and Ambrose Rookwood, who had been staying with a Mrs Moore near Temple Bar, were also given the unwelcome news. By whom remains unknown, although it seems likely to have been Thomas Wintour or Kit Wright en route to Thomas Percy, but whoever the messenger was, Keyes and Rookwood soon joined the exodus northwards.[26]

Thomas Wintour resigned himself to his fate, or was possessed of incredible personal bravery, or had an unshakeable conviction in Guy Fawkes' ability to withstand questioning, possibly all three, for now he knew that Thomas Percy was a wanted man, he knew that arrest, and with it torture, could be his fate at any moment. Even so, before dismissing Kit Wright, he had insisted that he would 'stay and see the uttermost'.[27]

Demonstrating audacious, or fatalistic, calm, Wintour now made his way to the gates of Parliament itself. He found pike-carrying guards blocking the entranceways, and was himself blocked by a guard on King's Street. Turning back, Wintour heard one of the guards say, 'There is a treason discovered in which the King and his Lords shall have been blown up'.[28] Declaring himself 'fully satisfied that all was known',[29] a strange choice of words in the circumstances, Thomas Wintour returned to the Duck and Drake, gathered his belongings, mounted his gelding and finally abandoned London.

Guy Fawkes was now the only conspirator of the thirteen still in the capital, but of course he had little say in the matter. The Tower of London was his new home, and while some of the cells within it were relatively luxurious and equipped to receive noble inmates, Guy's chamber in the White Tower was cold, cramped and unsanitary.

His initial questioning was undertaken by the Lord Chief Justice himself, Sir John Popham, helped by the Attorney General Sir Edward Coke,[29] although Sir William Waad lurked nearby itching to begin his work. The stranger, John Johnson, told them of his time as a soldier in Flanders for the Spanish army, and admitted again that he had intended to blow up Parliament on that day, with the King and his lords and bishops within it.[30]

Once again, Guy was blunt and defiant in his answers. When asked what would have happened if the Queen and the royal children had also been present, Guy stated that he would not have helped them, and when asked what he would have done about any Catholics who may have been present and caught up in the explosion, Guy stated that he would have prayed for them.[31]

It is notable that Guy mentions no names other than that of Thomas Percy, which was already known, and that he had met Spinola, William Stanley, Hugh Owen, and Father Greenway (the alias being used by Oswald Tesimond) in Flanders.[32] Guy knew that he was now a breathing corpse, and his last task on this earth would be to keep the identity of his fellow conspirators secret for as long as possible. This would give them a chance to escape from the country, or even to carry out their uprising in the Midlands. In Guy's mind there was still hope for the aim of the plot, that is the restoration of Catholicism to supremacy in England, even though there was no hope for himself.

The document of this initial Tower interrogation, signed by 'Jhon Jhonson' on every page, was an unsatisfactory one for Popham, Coke and Cecil. Could it really be believed that Johnson and Percy had carried out this plot without any help whatsoever? In a letter written on the evening of 5 November, Popham tells Cecil that he had 'pregnant suspicions' of Catholics including, among others, Robert Catesby, Ambrose Rookwood, Robert Keyes, John Grant, Jack Wright, Christopher Wright, and Thomas Wintour.[33] At this stage, however, there is no evidence given, and it seems that Popham is merely naming men who were known Catholics and known as potential troublemakers rather than acting upon any evidence he had prised out of John Johnson.

Darkness closed in on the solitary man lying in his stone-floored cell, but he slept soundly with no dreams of yesterday or tomorrow. Guy Fawkes had resisted his first period of questioning, and his comrades in arms remained free, but for all of them there was much worse to come.

Chapter 22

By Steps, Proceeding to the Worst

Death, be not proud, though some have called thee
Mighty and dreadful, for thou art not so;
For those, whom thou think'st thou dost overthrow,
Die not, poor Death, nor yet canst thou kill me.
John Donne, *Sonnet X*

For Guy Fawkes the night of 5 November 1605 must have been a terrifying one. Despite the brave exterior he maintained he knew that sooner or later torture would be used on him, and that eventually he would be condemned to the only death worthy of a man who had tried to kill his king: being hung, drawn and quartered.

For others in London, however, it was a night of celebration. Word spread about the King's salvation, one that could only have resulted from divine providence. To mark this modern day passover, this time with death passing over the people of England rather than the people of Israel, bonfires were lit across the capital and beyond. It is a ritual that survives to this day with the lighting of communal bonfires on the fifth night of November, and in fact it was compulsory until 1859 under the rules of the Bonfire Observance of 5th November Act of 1605.[1]

The sixth of November saw more questions put to Guy, but while Popham and Coke were the men asking them, they were actually written by King James in person. The King was taking a keen interest in the questioning of the man known as John Johnson, as well he might if he felt that plotters against him were still at large, and had created a list of sixteen questions to put to Johnson.[2] The first of the royal questions, or interrogatories as they were known, shows just how little they knew about Guy at this time:

> 'As what he is, for I can never yet hear of any man that knows him?'[3]

Guy's answer to this question was straightforward and less than revealing:

> 'He saith his name is John Johnson'.[4]

The first night of imprisonment in the White Tower had obviously done nothing to dampen Guy's defiance, and he was unswerving in the adherence to his original story. Even so, there are elements of the questions put to Guy that catch our attention. One such question set by the King, the twelfth question, asks when and where Johnson learned to speak French.[5] Guy's answer is that he learned to speak French firstly in England and then on his last journey overseas,[6] but the question is more interesting than the answer. Just how did they know that Guy spoke French? Having assumed the role of Yorkshire servant John Johnson it is hardly likely that he would have engaged in a French discourse with his captors. It seems to me that this relates to the next question:

> 'What gentlewoman's letter it was, that was found upon him'?[7]

Guy answers that the letter is from a woman married to an Englishman named Bostock in Flanders. As stated earlier, it's an obvious assumption to link this woman with his commander Colonel Bostock who was killed at the Battle of Nieuwpoort. The sequence of questioning makes me conclude that it was this letter that was written in French, proving that Guy could speak the language. We now have a letter in French from a woman he knew in Flanders, that Guy carried with him everywhere he went for more than five years, and that he held close to him on that fateful night of 4 November even though its existence could blow his cover as it contained his real name.[8] This has the hallmarks of a love letter from a woman who meant a great deal to Guy, and whose memory he would always cherish.

Once again, the confession was signed not only in the name of John Johnson, but also by the Earls of Nottingham and Northampton, and by Sir Robert Cecil, the Earl of Salisbury.[9] The presence of these great men of state at the questioning of Guy Fawkes was a mark of the desperation the court as a whole. It was clear to all that there must have been felt by others involved in the plot, if only to finance the acquisition of the property and gunpowder, and these unknown and unseen enemies could at that very moment be planning a new atrocity.

If the earls had felt their mere presence would be enough to subdue Johnson, they were wrong. He had been less than fulsome in his answers, and his obfuscation was buying precious time for whoever had worked alongside him. Things could not continue as they were. King James gave Sir William Waad the permission he had been looking for, writing, 'If he will not otherwise confess, the gentler tortures are to be first used unto him, *et sic per gradus ad ima tenditur*'.[10]

The Latin at the end of the royal instruction means 'and then by steps proceeding to the worst'. The message was clear – the prisoner was to be spared no torture if he would not confess fully and plausibly. This sentence causes controversy even today, with some commentators saying that it was unlikely torture was used, or if it was used that it was used sparingly. This is the danger of projecting modern values onto a seventeenth century reality.

King James was a believer in the efficacy of torture, and in Scotland he had been keen to join in the torture himself when it was applied to Agnes Sampson[11] and possibly others. He also saw no moral difficulty in the administration of torture when it was used upon those who had committed evil acts or who intended to commit evil acts. This was a commonly held view, as James and many in England at that time saw Guy Fawkes as something less than human – something infernal, the devil from the vault. In that circumstance, it would be a weakness to deal with the prisoner as if he were a man like any other, one deserving of respect or compassion.

Nevertheless there were, even then, legal problems around the use of torture. Torture was forbidden within Magna Carta,[12] but in truth Magna Carta was a document that was very little observed and the common law could be circumvented in exceptional circumstances, and especially with the express permission of the sovereign.

The surreptitious use of torture was widespread, although it was then typically denied by officials. Nicholas Owen, for example, was tortured to death, and yet the official line was that he had somehow torn open his own stomach. Father Tesimond's account shows that the government account was little believed:

> Owen's enemies were motivated by a desire to cover up their own cruelty. This [torture] had been inflicted on him in violation of their own laws, which forbid that anyone should be killed by torture. But their stupid and wicked inventions were all in vain. No one, not even our enemies, allowed them probability or gave them credence.[13]

The same spin, to use a fitting modern phrase, was used regarding Guy, yet the evidence of extreme torture was seen not only by comparing his signature before and after torture, but could also be seen months later at the time of Guy's execution when he could barely walk and had to be carried to the scaffold. Once again Father Tesimond was scornful of the official account given in the *King's Book*:

> Here [in the Tower of London] there can be little doubt that he was tortured with excruciating and most refined torments, whatever the little book has to say, which they published about this plot and the confessions of Guy, Thomas Wintour, and other prisoners. Signs of torture were evident at the time of his execution, for he was scarcely able to move.[14]

Given the evidence it seems strange that some commentators still claim that torture was used sparingly, if at all, especially given that torture is still being used illegally and secretively today, as recent court cases relating to Guantanamo Bay and debates over waterboarding show.

The first instruments of torture used upon Guy Fawkes were the manacles. These were chains fastened to the wall that were then attached to the wrists, leaving the prisoner's arms vertically extended. The prisoner stood on a series of wicker steps which was then removed so that the whole of his weight was placed upon his arms, wrist and hands. In Guy's case we hear that he was suspended by his thumbs for hours on end. This was the gentler torture prescribed by the King. Guy would have felt the same sensations related by Father Gerard as he looked back to the time when he himself had been manacled in the tower:

> Thus hanging by my wrists, I began to pray, while those gentlemen standing round asked me again if I was willing to confess. I replied, "I neither can nor will". But so terrible a pain began to oppress me, that I was scarce able to speak the words. The worst pain was in my breast and belly, my arms and hands. It seemed to me that all the blood in my body rushed up my arms into my hands; and I was under the impression at the time that the blood actually burst forth from my fingers and at the back of my hands. This was, however, a mistake; the sensation was caused by the swelling of the flesh over the iron that bound it. I felt now such intense pain that it seemed to me impossible to continue enduring it. It did not, however, go so far as to make me feel any inclination or real disposition to give the information they wanted.[15]

Guy endured the same pain and met it with the same resolve. After being released from the manacles, he was then held in the cell known as the Little Ease. Just four feet high, sixteen inches wide and two feet long,[16] it was designed to prevent prisoners from being able to stand up, lie down, or sit in comfort, and it must have been especially painful for a man of Guy's tall stature. To the terrible trial of the manacles, and the threat of worse to come, were added beatings and deprivation of sleep, light, and food, and yet Guy still refused to be bowed.

On 8 November, Waad wrote to Robert Cecil to report on his prisoner's steadfastness and obstinacy in the face of torture:

> I find this fellow who this day is in a most stubborn and perverse humour, as dogged as if he were possessed. Yesternight I had persuaded him to set down a clear narrative of all his wicked plots from the first entering to the same, to the end they pretended, with the discourses and projects that were thought upon amongst them, which he undertook and craved time this night to bethink him better; but this morning he hath changed his mind and is sullen and obstinate as there is no dealing with him.[17]

Guy was indeed possessed now, his religious fervour strengthened by the ordeal he faced, he had resolved within himself to endure anything. These mortal tortures were dreadful beyond anything that could be imagined, but in his mind he saw only an immortal paradise hastening towards him. He was also resolved not to implicate his fellow plotters and send them to the same fate that was befalling him. With no contact with the outside world, Guy may have believed that Catesby and the others were succeeding with their uprising. In fact, on that very day, 8 November, the plot would come to a pathetic end.

While Guy was being transported to the Tower on 5 November, the Midland contingent of plotters were carrying out their instructions oblivious to the failure of the London action. Everard Digby had made his way to the Red Lion Inn at Dunchurch[18] in preparation for the supposed hunt. Also there was John Grant, who had arranged a supply of arms ready for the insurrection at his Norbrook home and who had travelled to Dunchurch with his brother-in-law John Wintour, brother to Thomas and Robert.

Robert Wintour himself had travelled first to Ashby St. Ledgers and was hosted by Robert Catesby's mother, while he awaited the arrival of her son.[19] Initially reticent to join the plot, he was now convinced of its necessity and its validity, and looked forward to hearing news of the explosion at Westminster. The news, when it did reach him, was not what he had been hoping for.

The London plotters, minus Guy, left the city at differing times, with Catesby, his servant Thomas Bates, and Jack Wright, leaving on the 4th, Thomas Percy, Kit Wright, Ambrose Rookwood, and Robert Keyes leaving on the morning of the 5th, and Thomas Wintour fleeing the capital later that day. Rookwood was renowned as a brilliant and speedy rider, and it was he who first caught up with Catesby and delivered the disastrous news of Guy's capture.

Using a relay of horses that had been ready prepared along the route by Rookwood, the group now covered the miles with furious haste, travelling a hundred miles in a matter of hours.[20] Rookwood himself rode thirty miles in two hours using just one horse, and he reported how Thomas Percy and Jack Wright threw their cloaks into a hedge so they could ride faster.[21] Upon reaching Ashby St. Ledgers, Catesby was unable to bring himself to enter the house and see his mother – or to let his mother see the wild and desperate look upon his face. Instead he sent a message to Robert Wintour to meet him in fields outside the village. There was no time for prevarication and niceties; upon Robert Wintour's arrival, Catesby simply told him, 'Mr Fawkes was taken and the whole plot discovered'.[22]

Even now, Catesby had the strength of character and personality to compel his men to follow his lead. There was no talk of giving up, and they instead rode on to Dunchurch: if they could kidnap Lady Elizabeth from Coombe Abbey then there was still a chance, in their minds, that their Catholic revolution would succeed.

Further bad news awaited the men when they arrived at their rendezvous. They had expected Sir Everard Digby to gather a large group of men for his hunt, after which Catesby would appraise them of his true intentions. Although maybe a little surprised at first, the men would be so enthused by the plan that they would willingly go along with it, relishing the opportunity to fight for their Catholic faith. The reality proved somewhat different.

Digby had gathered together around eighty people,[23] far less than Catesby had hoped for or expected. Nevertheless, they were men of good standing and well equipped, so all was not lost yet. Among their number were some of the leading Catholics of the Midlands, including Henry Morgan, Robert Acton, and the uncle and nephew Humphrey and Stephen Littleton. Humphrey, upon learning the true purpose of the hunt, departed from the gathering at Dunchurch, and he was not the only one. By the time the assembly had moved on from the Red Lion they were already down to around forty in number[24] and their spirits had dropped accordingly.

Thomas Wintour finally joined them that evening, having initially ridden to his brother Robert's Huddington Hall.[25] One of the first acts he was involved in was also the one that would bring the plot to its ignominious end. The men needed fresh horses, and John Grant knew that a stable of warhorses was being kept at Warwick Castle, as he had some of his own horses stabled there.[26] In the still of the night, the castle's stables were stormed by Catesby and the conspirators and the warhorses were stolen, leaving their tired horses behind in their place.[27] On the face of it, this seemed to have been a success, but if Catesby felt buoyed it was not to last. The audacious theft alerted the Worcestershire authorities, and the Sheriff of Worcester Sir Richard Walsh raised a large group of armed men to track the raiders down. Using intelligence passed to him by villagers who had seen the gang he also discovered the names of some of those concerned. This concerned him greatly, for they were no ordinary brigands but men of good families.

The Sheriff sent a report to London, where it arrived at the desk of Sir Robert Cecil. Cecil knew that this action must be linked to a wider plot involving John Johnson in the tower, and so he at last had the names of some of those involved. On 7 November, a warrant was issued for the arrest of Robert Catesby, Ambrose Rookwood, the two Wright brothers, Thomas Wintour, Edward Grant and Robert Ashfield[28] (presumably the last two referred to John Grant and Thomas Bates who may have been using the alias of Ashfield, although the latter may alternatively have been the Wintour relative John Ashfield who had met Catesby at the Irish Boy Inn).

Robert Wintour was the only one who immediately saw the consequences of the raid, telling Catesby that his actions would make a great uproar in the country and damage any hopes they had of clemency from the King if they were arrested. Catesby looked Wintour in the eyes, and in a calm voice retorted, 'Some of us may not look back... what, hast thou any hope, Robin? I assure thee there is none knoweth of this action but shall perish'.[29]

Finally, the hopelessness of his situation had hit Catesby. The plot had utterly failed. People were leaving at every opportunity, an armed guard was tracking them down, and there was no likelihood of them being able to mount an assault upon Coombe Abbey as originally planned. When captured, their torture and execution would be certain, but they still harboured some hope of escape. For now, Catesby and his men continued to head west, probably hoping to reach Wales and then obtain a crossing to Ireland.

By Thursday night, 7 November, the dwindling company of men had made slow progress and stopped for the night at Stephen Littleton's home, Holbeche House in Staffordshire.[30] It was a dark, quiet, fearful night, and one in which more of the men took the opportunity to escape and take their own chances. Among those who left Holbeche House on that night or the following day were Everard Digby and Thomas Bates.[31]

News reached the house that the Sheriff of Worcester was now nearby, and that he had around 700 men at his command.[32] This, then, was to be their final stand, and so depleted were they in numbers that they stood little chance. Realising this, Catesby asked Robert Wintour to make haste and call upon his father-in-law John Talbot at Pepperhill, ten miles away, where he might be able to persuade Talbot to supply him with troops or armaments. This, however, Wintour would not do, saying that Talbot would look after his wife and children when he was dead.[33] Thomas Wintour volunteered to go in his brother's stead, but when he and Stephen Littleton arrived at Pepperhill they were given short shrift, with Talbot simply asking them what they were doing there and ordering them to get hence immediately.

While the two men were gone, a bizarre and disastrous scene

occurred at Holbeche. During their journeys of the last two days, the men had forded rivers, and upon checking their gunpowder they found that it was too damp to be effective. To resolve this problem they poured the gunpowder into pans that were balanced upon other sacks of gunpowder and then placed in front of the fire to dry out. It could be that the men were tired beyond their endurance and simply not thinking straight, but they failed to foresee what happened next. One of the men tripped while carrying a shovel of hot coals, sending one of the coals into a pan of gunpowder. The resulting explosion destroyed much of the room, and many of the men were severely burned.[34] John Grant's face was particularly disfigured, leaving him blinded, and Catesby and Rookwood were also badly injured. Thus it was that the only explosion that took place during the gunpowder plot injured none but the perpetrators themselves.

Thomas Wintour and Stephen Littleton heard the explosion and spurred their horses on. Not far from the house a servant informed Wintour that Catesby, Rookwood and Grant were dead, and urged him to turn his horse around and flee while he still could. It is at this point that Thomas Wintour revealed his true character and bravery. With certain knowledge that the sheriff's men were closing in he told Littleton and the servant that he would stay and bury his friend, whatever might befall him.[35] Stephen Littleton took a more pragmatic view and left at this point, while Robert Wintour had already fled in the aftermath of the explosion.

Upon entering the damaged house, with smoke and dust stinging his eyes, Thomas Wintour discovered that Catesby was not dead after all, and that he remained defiant to the last. Wintour asked those present what they intended to do now, to which they replied that they intended to die on that spot. 'I will take such part as you do',[36] Wintour replied.

At Catesby's suggestion the men now joined together in a silent prayer, until at around eleven o'clock shots from outside alerted them to the presence of the sheriff and his men. Thomas Wintour was the first to exit the house, but was immediately struck by a musket ball through his shoulder, rendering his right arm useless.[37] Jack Wright was next to be shot, receiving a fatal wound, shortly followed by his younger brother Kit. Ambrose Rookwood was then shot and wounded, before Catesby called out to the injured Wintour, 'Stand by me, Mr Tom, and we will die together'.[38]

Wintour replied, 'I have lost the use of my right arm and I fear that will cause me to be taken'.[39]

Catesby, Percy and Wintour placed themselves shoulder to shoulder, after which Catesby took a gold crucifix from around his neck and crossed himself with it. He next cried out to the sheriff's men that he had been the leader of the plot, and that he saw now that it was not God's will that it succeed, but he would not be taken alive and would defend himself to the death.[40]

A shot rang out from behind a tree, and its single bullet passed through both Thomas Percy and Robert Catesby. Despite this injury, his burns, and a pike wound he had also received, Catesby dragged himself back into the house, where in his last act he took down a picture of the Virgin Mary and kissed it. The leader of the gunpowder plot was dead.[41]

With Catesby's death, the resistance was all but ended. Thomas Wintour tried to fight on with one arm but suffered sword cuts and a pike wound to his stomach before being captured[42]. Sir Everard Digby and Bates, who were hiding with their horses in nearby woods, were found by the sheriff's men who had followed hoofprints in the mud.[43] Francis Tresham, who had conspicuously not left London and joined the Midlands rebellion, was arrested on 12 November.[44] Robert Wintour and Stephen Littleton spent two months in hiding at properties belonging to Humphrey Littleton, and were finally arrested at Hagley Hall, Worcestershire, on 9 January 1606 after being betrayed by the cook.[45]

On 8 November the gunpowder plot reached its ignoble end, and by the end of the day all thirteen conspirators were either dead, captured, or on the run eventually to be captured. As yet this was unknown to Guy Fawkes in the Tower, but that evening he was facing an ordeal of his own. Guy was being subjected to the worst torture device in use at that time: the rack. Limbs would be stretched, joints popped, sinews snapped, bones, body and spirit broken.

Chapter 23

A Prey for the Fowls of the Air

What's this flesh? A little cruded milk
Fantastical puff-paste. Our bodies are weaker than those
Paper prisons boys use to keep flies in; more contemptible,
Since ours is to preserve earth-worms.
John Webster, *The Duchess of Malfi*

The events at Holbeche House on 8 November had advanced rapidly
from defiance to desperation, and then from farce to tragedy. This,
without doubt, is the day that drew a line through any threat posed by
the gunpowder plot, but it was not the end of suffering for those
involved – and for many of those on the periphery who were caught
up in its aftermath.

A letter sent from Sir William Waad to Robert Cecil on the ninth
of November makes it clear that he had started using the rack upon
Guy Fawkes – and it was having its desired effect:

> I have prevailed so much at the length with my prisoner,
> by plying him with the best persuasions I could use, as he
> hath faithfully promised me by narration to discover to
> your Lordship only all the secrets of his heart, but not to
> be set down in writing. Your Lordship will not mislike the
> exception, for when he hath confessed himself to your
> Lordship I will undertake he shall acknowledge it before
> such as you shall call, and then he will not make dainty
> to set his hand to it... Thus in haste, I thank God my poor
> labour hath advanced a service of this importance.[1]

Under torture Guy had finally agreed to reveal the truth, as he saw it, about the plot, but he would only pass this on to Robert Cecil in person. Presumably Guy was holding onto the hope that in this way he wouldn't implicate others, or at least that he wouldn't provide evidence with his name upon it that could be used in a trial. Not to worry, Waad was saying, once he's told you this in person, I'll torture him upon the rack a little more until he has no option but to sign his name.

By 7 November, the mask of John Johnson had slipped and they now knew him as Guido Fawkes, the man who had taken part in the Spanish treason, but he had not yet named his fellow conspirators. By 9 November, under the influence of the rack, he starts to put names to some of those in the plot, including Robert Catesby, Jack and Kit Wright, Thomas Wintour, Robert Keyes and Francis Tresham.[2] This confession of the ninth is notable for one other thing: it contains one of the most famous signatures in British history.

Guy's confession of 9 November has a barely legible 'Guido' inscribed upon it. It is faint and very shaky, baring little relation to his usual signature.[3] It is the signature of a man who has been tortured to within an inch of his life, and Father Gerard, himself no stranger to torture within the Tower, reported that Guy fainted after scratching his name onto the paper.[4]

The rack was an instrument so terrible that the mere sight or mention of it was enough to make most men confess before being subjected to its punishments. The official account given in the *King's Book* states that this applied to Guy as well:

> The next morning being carried to the Tower, he did not there remain above two or three days, being twice or thrice, in that space, re-examined, and the rack only offered and showed to him, when the mark of his Roman fortitude did visibly begin to wear and slide off his face; and then did he begin to confess part of the truth, and thereafter, to open the whole matter.[5]

This was propaganda of the most preposterous kind, and Guy's tortured signature is evidence that still screams out today. Hanging by the manacles was beyond the endurance of most, but Guy showed incredible fortitude. He resisted the rack too as far as he could, but it was an instrument that broke people mentally as well as physically. The prisoner's hands were tied to one crank, and his feet to another, so that their turning stretched the body. It was not just the searing pain but the terrible snapping and popping noises that made it unbearable. It was an instrument that Waad revelled in.

What really mattered to Waad and Cecil was that he was finally producing names, but just which names were they looking for? By the time that Cecil questioned Guy face to face, 9 November, the other conspirators were either dead or captured. Cecil, however, was looking to add other names to the list of transgressors and by doing so bring some of his most despised enemies to a kind of justice.

On 10 November, Cecil wrote to Sir Thomas Edmondes, the ambassador in Brussels, again:

> For as much as by daily examinations [of Guy] it doth appear that there is great cause to suspect that [Hugh] Owen hath been made privy to this horrible conspiracy, I think it very expedient now for his Majesty's service that you do inform the Archduke of it, and put him to the trial of the sincerity of his extraordinary professions towards his Majesty, by showing the horribleness of the fact and requiring at his hands whether he would not give order to make stay of the said Owen in some place of safety, until it may further appear what cause we shall have to charge him with in this action, and then to leave it to the Archduke's own judgement upon the proofs thereof, what course he shall think fit to hold with him.[6]

Cecil was being rather economical with the truth, for although Guy had admitted meeting Hugh Owen in the low countries he had not implicated him in the plot in any way. Cecil hoped by this lie to have Owen extradited to England, but he was unsuccessful.

Guy's deposition of 9 November is of interest for more than just its signature, as it reveals the name of another man that Cecil was hoping to implicate in the plot, one not often associated with it:

> He confesses also that there was speech amongst them to draw Sir Walter Ralegh to take part with them, being one that might stand them in good stead, as others in like sort were named.[7]

Sir Walter Ralegh never shook off the suspicion of being involved in the treason and was asked about it at the 1618 trial that led to his execution.

Guy faced many other interrogations throughout November, December and January, but his signature is surer and firmer in these other depositions, so the use of the rack must have been scaled back if not stopped altogether.

By now the Tower of London was filling up with conspirators and those unlucky enough to have some kind of link to it. Thomas Wintour's confession of 23 December is the most detailed account of the plot, but the signature on this document has also attracted great interest throughout the centuries. Its notoriety comes because Thomas signed it with the surname 'Winter' rather than 'Wintour',[8] leading some to claim that it is a forgery, possibly created by Robert Cecil's forger-in-chief Thomas Phelippes.[9] It seems unlikely, some might say impossible, that a master forger with decades spent at his craft should make such a simple error as to copy the handwriting perfectly and yet spell the name wrong. The evidence within Wintour's confession is also corroborated by other confessions and sources, so I have no doubt that it is genuine. The spelling of words and names was fluid in the Tudor and Stuart period, so Wintour may have used an alternate spelling on other documents unknown to us.

Another notable confession was that given by Thomas Bates. Being of lowly birth, he hoped that he would be spared execution if he could show that his was a servile role. He may have been encouraged in this hope by Robert Cecil, as long as he was careful to provide the names that the Secretary of State wanted. In his confession of 4 December 1605, Bates implicates Father Greenway (alias Oswald Tesimond):

> He [Bates] thereupon went to confession to a priest named Greenway, and in confession told Greenway that he was to conceal a very dangerous project of work. That his master Catesby and Thomas Winter had imported unto him, and that he being fearful of it, asked the communal of Greenway, telling the said Greenway (which he was not desirous to hear) their particular intent and purpose of blowing up the Parliament house, and Greenway the priest thereto said, that he would take no notice thereof but that he the said examinate should be secret in that which his master had imported unto him, because it was for a good cause, and that he willed this examinate to tell no other priest of it. Saying moreover that it was not dangerous unto him, nor any offence to conceal it, and thereupon the said priest Greenway gave this examinate absolution. And he received the sacrament in the company of his master Robert Catesby and Thomas Winter.[10]

When Bates later realised that he had been given false promises and his hopes were in vain, that he would in fact face the same fate as the others, he repented greatly of this statement, saying that his report of Greenway was false, and that he hoped the Lord would pardon him for the weakness he showed when his interrogators were offering him his life.[11]

Another recantation came from Francis Tresham in a letter written just before his supposed death on 23 December 1605. It was given to his faithful servant William Vavasour, and then delivered to his wife Anne before reaching the hands of Robert Cecil in March.[12] In his original deposition made the day after his arrest,[13] Tresham implicated Father Henry Garnet, the head of England's Jesuits, using the name of

Walley which was one of the many aliases that he took. In the later letter however, Tresham writes,

> Now, my Lords, having bethought myself of this business (being too weak to use my own hand in writing this), which I do deliver here upon my salvation to be true as near as I can call to mind, desiring that my former confession may be called in, and that this may stand for truth. It was more than I knew that Master Walley was used herein. And to give your Lordships proof besides my oath, I had not seen him in sixteen years before, nor ever had message or letter from him, and to this purpose I desired Master Lieutenant to let me see my confession, who told me I should not unless I would enlarge it, which he did perceive I had no meaning to do.[14]

This letter is problematic, as is Tresham's arrest and death. It seems incredible that Tresham's servant was allowed access to him in his cell, and we know that his wife Anne was allowed free access to him too, along with her maid Joan Sisor.[15] It is also unique among the conspirators that Tresham's land and property were not forfeit, in effect taken by the state, after his death, but instead passed onto his mother Muriel Tresham so that they could be later passed onto his son.[16] Equally strange is that Tresham was allowed to roam free for three days after Guy had named him as a conspirator in his confession of 9 November.[17] Perhaps oddest of all, however, is the manner of Tresham's death, if indeed he did die at this time.

Unlike the other conspirators, Tresham was not killed in action and nor was he executed, that much is for certain. The official account, given by Sir William Waad to Sir Robert Cecil, is that he died of a stranguary, a painful blockage of the bowels, in his Tower of London cell at two o'clock on the morning of 23 December.[18] Some say that this death was the result of poisoning to stop him revealing too much, possibly about Cecil, but there is intriguing evidence that Tresham's death may have been faked, and that he was allowed to leave the Tower and start a new life.

Tresham was granted a passport by Robert Cecil on 2 November 1605,[19] a time when Cecil had the Monteagle letter in his possession and would surely have suspected Tresham's involvement in either the plot or the letter. From Tresham's time in the Tower, we also have a strange letter from the Lieutenant, Waad, to Cecil on 15 December about Tresham's health: 'If he [Francis Tresham] escape it must be by great care and good providence that he may die of that kind of death he most deserveth'.[20]

This could be Waad opining that if Tresham survived his illness then he deserved to be executed, but could there be another meaning sent from one man to another who were both well versed in the use of codes and cyphers? Was Waad actually saying that Tresham deserved to escape a traitor's death, but they must take great care when arranging it?

That same month Dudley Carleton wrote to Sir Thomas Edmondes in Brussels, saying he had seen two suspicious looking people in Calais. They were obviously English people who did not wish to be recognised and had stolen across the Channel, and, most tellingly, 'one of them looked like Francis Tresham'.[21]

If Tresham was allowed to escape, or assisted to escape, then it is surely a sign that he was an agent of Cecil's, and that Cecil may have been rewarding Tresham for the letter he sent to Lord Monteagle in an attempt to prevent the plot from taking place. Father Francis Edwards, the gunpowder scholar, was of the belief that Tresham did escape from the Tower, and that he was then sheltered at the English embassy in Madrid, living under the assumed name of Matthew Bruninge in a seventeenth century version of a witness protection programme. There is certainly some similarity between Bruninge's handwriting, as seen in letters to Thomas Wilson, Cecil's secretary and veteran intelligencer, and the handwriting of Francis Tresham.[22] Whether Tresham survived or not is a fascinating conundrum that may one day be solved, but what is undisputed is that he avoided the fate awaiting Guy Fawkes and others at the close of January 1606.

The trial of Guy Fawkes took place at Westminster Hall on 27

January 1606. He was brought by boat from the Tower of London to Westminster alongside Thomas, Robert and John Wintour,[23] Robert Keyes, John Grant and Sir Everard Digby. Thomas Bates was already waiting for them, his lower social position meaning that he'd been kept in the Westminster Gatehouse rather than in the Tower.[24]

After waiting half an hour in the Star Chamber, Guy and his fellow accused were brought into the Hall and placed upon a raised platform so they could more easily be seen. Among those watching eagerly for a sight of the evil men that had been so talked about across London were Queen Anne and Prince Henry, who had been hours away from death two months earlier.

This was to be a show trial, as everyone knew; there was no question of guilt or innocence. While waiting for the trial to begin, Guy and the conspirators showed incredible calm, muttering almost silently as they moved bead after bead on their rosaries. They had resigned themselves to death, they had no choice.

Sir Edward Phelips, a lawyer and future Master of the Rolls, was the first to address the court, calling the plot, 'Of such horror and monstrous nature, that before now, the tongue of man never delivered... nor the malice of hellish or earthly devil ever practised'.[25]

As well as indicting the accused men, Phelips also stated that the Jesuit movement shared the guilt, and named Fathers Garnet, Gerard and Tesimond[26] as prime movers in the plot. This was a theme continued by the next man to take the stand for the prosecution, the Attorney General Sir Edward Coke. Coke bemoaned the fact that the priests behind the plot were not yet on trial, angrily stating,

> I never yet knew a treason without a Romish priest; but in this there are many Jesuits, who are known to have dealt and passed through the whole action... So that the principal offenders are the seducing Jesuits; men that use the reverence of religion, yea, even the most sacred and blessed name of Jesus, as a mantle to cover their impiety, blasphemy, treason, and rebellion, and all manner of wickedness.[27]

A PREY FOR THE FOWLS OF THE AIR

After the men's confessions had been read in court the accused were asked if they accepted the charges against them. To the astonishment of the court officials, Guy, who was last to speak, denied the indictment, saying,

> We have never dealt with the Jesuits in this business. Nor did they ever persuade or urge us to undertake it. This is as false as it is true that we alone began and ended the business. So I say that all reference in the indictment to our meetings with them, and the advice and consent they gave us in this, is something entirely new. We never heard of it, and I deny it here and now as completely false. For this reason, I reject the indictment, and in no wise admit it is true![28]

Guy's words were in vain, but he had said what he needed to say, and had remained defiant in front of those who held his life in his hands. All that remained now was for Coke to pronounce the sentence, in all its horror and inevitability:

> To be drawn to the place of execution from his prison as being not worthy any more to tread upon the face of the earth whereof he was made: also for that he hath been retrograde to nature, therefore is to be drawn backward at a horse-tail... He must be drawn with his head declining downward, and lying so near the ground as may be, being thought unfit to take the benefit of the common air. For which cause also shall he be strangled, being hanged up by the neck between Heaven and Earth, as deemed unworthy of both, or either; as likewise, that the eyes of men may behold, and their hearts condemn him. Then he is to be cut down alive, and to have his privy parts cut off and burnt before his face, as being unworthily begotten, and unfit to leave any generation after him. His bowels and inlayed parts taken out and burnt, who inwardly had

conceived and harboured in his heart such horrible treason. After, to have his head cut off, which had imagined the mischief. And lastly, his body to be quartered, and the quarters set up in some high and eminent place, to the view and detestation of men, and to become a prey for the fowls of the air.[29]

Guy knew this sentence would be passed, yet terror still gripped him at the moment those dread words were said to his face. Sir Everard Digby, who was tried subsequently to the other seven accused on account of his rank, found the courage to say that he would go more cheerfully to the gallows if he heard any of the lords say they forgave him. They responded, 'God forgive you, and we do'.[30] It was a brief moment of compassion and humanity on a day of vindictive formality.

Digby was the last to be tried and the first to be executed. He was dragged from the Tower to the courtyard of St. Paul's Cathedral at first light on 30 January 1606. After making his final prayers, Digby was led to the scaffold. It was customary for the prisoner to be hung until half-unconscious and nearly dead before cutting them down, thus alleviating the suffering to come. Digby's executioner however, whether acting on orders or through their own sadism, cut him down almost immediately so that he would suffer more when he came to be castrated and disembowelled. Digby banged his head when cut down, which may have stunned him a little, but it is said that when his heart was ripped out with the traditional cry of 'behold the heart of a traitor', he had enough life in him still to call back, 'Thou liest!'[31]

Also executed that day were Robert Wintour, John Grant, and Thomas Bates. Guy had one more sleepless night to endure, spending it in prayers for a quick and merciful end, and for the eventual success of the cause he so vehemently believed in. Guy had a much longer ride to endure on 31 January, as he was to be executed at Westminster Yard, in the shadow of the building he had hoped to destroy. A huge crowd had gathered throughout the day, a day that had already seen Thomas Wintour, Robert Keyes and Ambrose Rookwood hung, drawn and quartered to the cheers of most in the crowd (although there were also silent supporters of the Catholic cause, including priests saying prayers for the dying and dead).

Being dragged on a wooden bracket behind a horse for two miles exacerbated the injuries Guy had received upon the rack, so that he was barely capable of standing by the time he reached the scaffold. This was the man the crowd had come to see, the devil himself, the gunpowder monster Guido Fawkes.

It is fitting that the man who would have lit the fuse that would have changed history forever, the first of the conspirators to be arrested, was the last to be executed. His weakness was such that he had to be helped to climb the scaffold, and yet he insisted on climbing to the top rung. There he said one final prayer, and thought of his mother and father, of the sisters and others he had loved and would never see again.

The supports were removed and within seconds there was a cracking noise. Guy's body had been unable to support his own weight, his neck had broken and he died instantly. His last prayer had been answered, Guy had escaped the torture and humiliation of being hung drawn and quartered. Nevertheless, his body was quartered after death and his head stuck on a spike on London Bridge[32] so that all could see Guy Fawkes – the man who had tried to kill the King and all his government, now a feast for the crows and an object of scorn and hatred for evermore.

Epilogue

Guy Fawkes' head was displayed to the elements and the public, and this fate befell others within the conspiracy too. Catesby's death at Holbeche House did not spare him the wrath of the government: an order was sent by the Privy Council for his body to be exhumed from the grave, after which has corpse was hung, drawn and quartered. His head was placed on a pike, not on London Bridge, but atop the Parliament building itself, alongside the head of Thomas Percy.[1]

Lord Harrington, the protector of the Lady Elizabeth at Coombe Abbey, would remark upon a similarity between the severed heads of Fawkes, Catesby and the other conspirators, saying they each had a mark of evil on their foreheads, and 'more terrible countenances were never looked upon'.[2] Of course there wasn't an actual mark on their foreheads, but what Harrington referred to was the stain of Catholicism upon them.

While much of the country celebrated the execution of Guy and his cohorts, for others it was the start of a period of terror. On 27 November, a wave of arrests saw the detention of Catholic Lords Montague, Mordaunt and Stourton, along with the arrest of the Earl of Northumberland, and his brothers Sir Allan and Sir Josceline Percy.[3] Montague, Mordaunt and Stourton all fell under suspicion because they had stayed away from the opening of Parliament, and for that they were all convicted of treason, given fines ranging from £6,000 to £10,000, and imprisoned.[4] Lord Montague was released quite quickly, despite his known meeting with Catesby, but Lord Stourton would not be freed until 1608, and Mordaunt died in the Fleet gaol in 1609.[5]

It seemed incredible to the likes of Cecil, Coke and Popham that the plotters could have had no leader within the nobility, a figurehead who would become de facto King if their plan succeeded. Suspicion fell squarely upon the Earl of Northumberland, as he had Catholic sympathies as well as royal blood, and could trace his lineage back to King Henry II. He was also under suspicion because of his close ties to Thomas Percy, and his meeting with Percy on 4 November was seen as especially damning evidence. Percy was put on trial for treason on three counts:[6] seeking to be the head of the Catholics, admitting Thomas Percy to the Gentleman Pensioners without making him take the oath of supremacy, and sending a warning to Thomas Percy.

The Earl of Northumberland was lucky to escape with his life, particularly as his deafness and stutter made him a less than impressive figure during his trial. He was instead stripped of all his titles, fined the huge sum of £30,000, later reduced to £11,000, and committed to the Tower of London where he would spend the next fifteen years.[7]

Those on the periphery of the plot could also expect little mercy. Stephen Littleton, who had fled from his home Holbeche House, was executed at Stafford alongside Henry Morgan.[8] Stephen's uncle Humphrey Littleton, for the crime of hiding his nephew, was also executed, along with two of his servants, Perks and Burford.[9]

By mid-January, with the help of Thomas Bates's later recanted confession, it was time to target the Jesuits. On 15 January 1506 a proclamation was issued against Father Garnet, Father Gerard, and Father Tesimond. This notice, pinned up at prominent locations across the country, warned that any person found harbouring the priests, or concealing information regarding their whereabouts, would be deemed no less guilty 'than those that had been actors and counsellors of the main treason itself'.[10]

Father Gerard, a seasoned veteran at escaping perilous situations, managed to escape to the continent within days. Things looked more worrying for Father Tesimond (Father Greenway), as he was apprehended on a London street while reading his own proclamation notice. A man seized him by the arm; Tesimond protested his innocence but allowed himself to be led away. Tesimond, however, had learned well at the same York school that Guy Fawkes and the Wright brothers attended. Once in a quiet alleyway, Tesimond turned on the man who had apprehended him and being bigger and stronger soon got the better of him and escaped.[11] Hiding at the bottom of a boat underneath a pile of pig carcasses, Father Tesimond also reached the safety of the continent.

Father Henry Garnet was not so fortunate. The man who had nothing to do with the organising of the gunpowder plot, who had tried his hardest not to hear about it, and who had often preached on behalf of a peaceful solution, was arrested, tortured, and, on 3 May 1606, hung, drawn and quartered.[12] It was said that Garnet's blood splattered a husk of corn, upon which his face appeared. This miraculous piece of corn was placed inside a silver reliquary, and the story of its existence became widespread, much to the annoyance of the government who tried to have it suppressed.[13]

Also rounded up and executed at this time were Jesuits with little or no relation to the plot, including Guy's former schoolmate Father Oldcorne. Nicholas Owen, the maker of priest holes, was arrested and tortured to death, and Father Strange, another Jesuit with no connection at all to the gunpowder conspiracy, was tortured so severely that he spent the remaining thirty-three years of his life 'in extreme debility and severe suffering'.[14] Even servants were under suspicion, as shown by the arrest of James Johnson, servant to Anne Vaux (who was herself questioned) at White Webbs. James knew nothing of the plot, and yet he too was tortured until he was left permanently disabled.[15]

The gunpowder plot caused widespread revulsion among the English populace, stirred up by anti-Catholic pamphlets as well as by the rhetoric of people like Sir Edward Coke. It had a long-lasting effect on how Catholics were perceived in the country. In 1613, a bill was defeated in Parliament that would have made it compulsory for Catholics to wear red hats or multi-coloured stockings so that they could always be identified.[16] Such anti-Catholic measures were not confined to the seventeenth century, as Catholics were barred from voting until 1829, and even today Catholics are not allowed a place in the line of succession to the throne.

Guy Fawkes had wanted to raise the Catholic faith in England to a position of glory once more, but in that aim he failed utterly. The actions of Guy, Catesby and the other plotters set back the Catholic cause and led to renewed persecutions, both financial and physical.

EPILOGUE

Guy himself became a hate figure, a demon incarnate, and yet in recent decades he has started to acquire a rather different reputation. While impossible to condone the atrocious act he would have undertaken, people are recognising at least that he was a man of courage and conviction, rather than being a mercenary motivated by thoughts of earthly rewards. He is now often proclaimed, jocularly, as 'the last person to enter Parliament with honest intentions'. Guy Fawkes has also become a figurehead for modern day anarchists and libertarians, and for contemporary protesters in support of a plethora of causes. Guy Fawkes masks are now seen at protests across the world, peaceful and not so peaceful, worn by those who share his sense of passion for following a belief.

So we return to the question posed at the start of this book: was the real Guy Fawkes a fool, a fanatic, or a freedom fighter? He was a dangerous combination of all three; a man who believed completely in the validity of his actions while at the same time being a slave to fortune. Guy saw himself and those of his faith, those he loved, as being persecuted; he recognised no hope in education, saw no chance of social change; in Guy's mind peaceable solutions had been tried, and had failed. Marginalised people like Guy Fawkes can become tigers backed into corners, and throughout the centuries some of them, like Guy, have enacted, or attempted to enact, extreme and violent solutions of their own. As Guy Fawkes himself said on the day after he was captured, 'A desperate disease requires a dangerous remedy'.[17]

The deep emotions that drove Guy to contemplate cold-blooded atrocities will always be present in a dark corner of the human spirit, which is why the story of Guy Fawkes is as important and relevant today as it has ever been.

Notes

Prologue
1. This was the conclusion of explosives expert Dr Sidney Alford. See chapter fifteen.

Chapter 1
1. Pettegree, Andrew, *Brand Luther*, p. 70
2. Loughlin, Susan, *Insurrection: Henry VIII, Thomas Cromwell and the Pilgrimage of Grace*, p. 18
3. Hargrave, William, *History and Description of the Ancient City of York*, p. 127
4. Elton, Geoffrey Rudolph, *The Tudor Constitution: Documents and Commentary,* p. 192
5. Palliser, David Michael, *The Reformation in York, 1534-1553, Issue 40,* pp. 8-9
6. Palliser, Davide Michael, *Tudor York*, p. 262
7. Ritchie, Carson I.A., *The Ecclesiastical Courts of York*, p. 57
8. State Papers, SP14/216/19, *Examination of John Johnson in Response to Interrogatories, 6 November 1605*
9. Baptismal record of Guy Fawkes, now in the archive collection of York Minster
10. Longley, Katherine M., *Recusant History 1973, volume 12*

Chapter 2
1. The original can now be seen at Hatfield House, Hertfordshire, built by Sir Robert Cecil.
2. Known to history as Lady Jane Grey, she should more accurately be styled Queen Jane. While she was never crowned, she was legally named as successor to King Edward VI and proclaimed queen upon his death (for other examples of monarchs who were not crowned, we have only to look back as far as King Edward VIII). History also remembers her as the 'nine-day Queen', but while she reigned for nine days after the public declaration of her as queen, she had been proclaimed ruler by the Privy Council four days earlier
3. Haigh, Christopher, *The English Reformation Revised,* p. 175
4. Deiter, Kristen, *The Tower of London in English Renaissance Drama: Icon of Opposition,* p. 51
5. For a full translation of the 1570 Papal Bull, 'Regnans in Excelsis', see: www.papalencyclicals.net/Pius05/p5regnans.htm
6. Allen, Cardinal William, *An Admonition to the Nobility and People of England and Ireland*, p. xi
7. Butler, Alban, *Lives of the Saints: August,* p. 68

NOTES

8. Lingard, John, *The History of England, from the First Invasion by the Romans to the Commonwealth, Volume VI*, p. 30

9. Whitelock, Anna, *Elizabeth's Bedfellows: An Intimate History of the Queen's Court*, p. 304

10. Strachey, Lytton, *Elizabeth and Essex: A Tragic History*, pp. 261-3

11. Lemon, Rebecca, *Treason by Words,* p. 80

Chapter 3

1. Kotar, S.L. and Gessler, J.E., *Smallpox: A History*, p. 10

2. Brandon, Ed and David, *Curiosities of York,* p. 26

3. A lease of 8 July 1579 confirms Edith Fawkes as leaseholder of: 'a dwelling house or tenement in Stonegate within the City of York... Bounding on the south side upon the tenement of John Brockett Public Notary', *Dean and Chapter Register of Leases 1543-87 - f 304r ll 22-2,* ms. in York Library

4. As confirmed by the burial of an unnamed 'servant of Mr Brocket' in 1574, recorded in the parish register of St. Helen's Church, Stonegate, York

5. 'The nine-men's-morris is filled up with mud, and the quaint mazes in the wanton green, For lack of tread are indistinguishable' (*A Midsummer Night's Dream*, Act II Scene I, lines 83-5)

6. Maynard, Jean Olwyn, *Margaret Clitherow*, p.15

7. For more on the history of St. Peter's School, see: www.stpetersyork.org. uk/st_peters/about/history_of_st_peters

8. Morley, Paul, *The North: and Almost Everything in it*, p. 93

9. Johnston, A.F. and Rogerson, M, *Records of Early English Drama: York*, p. 418

10. Raine, A., *A History of St Peter's School, York AD 627 To the Present Day*, p. 85

11. Drysdale, R., *Over Ancient Ways: A Portait of St Peter's School, York*, p. 16

12. Morris, John, *The Troubles of our Catholic Forefathers Related by Themselves*, p. 143

Chapter 4

1. *Daily Telegraph*, 31 October 2015

2. Ibid.

3. Wagner, John A. and Schmid, Susan Walters, *Encyclopedia of Tudor England, Volume 1*, p. 889

4. Edward Fawkes' burial record is at St. Michal-le-Belfrey Church, York, but it shows that he was interred at the adjacent York Minster

5. Rosenthal, Alexander S., *Crown under Law: Richard Hooker, John Locke, and the Ascent of Modern Constitutionalism*, p. 7

6. *York Archbishop's Registers, 1519-1588*, University of York archives

7. Dethridge, David, *Great Anglican Divines – Edmund Grindal*, Cross Way, Winter 1985 issue

8. Brook, Benjamin, *The Lives of the Puritans*, p. 282

9. *The Journal of Ecclesiastical History*, April 1965, p. 130

10. Maynard, Jean Olywn, *Margaret Clitherow*, p. 37

11. Mullett, Michael, *Historical Dictionary of the Reformation and Counter-Reformation*, p. 6

12. Garnet, Henry, *Portrait of Guy Fawkes: An Experiment in Biography*, p.163

13. Ibid. p. 165

14. William Shakespeare's will, prepared on 25 March 1616, a month before he died, is in the National Archives, London. It can be read online at: www.nationalarchives.gov.uk/dol/images/examples/pdfs/shakespeare.pdf

15. Camm, Bede, *Forgotten Shrines: An Account of Some Old Catholic Halls and Families in England*, p. 147

Chapter 5

1. State Papers, SP14/216/18, *Interrogatories of James I for John Johnson*, 6 November 1605

2. State Papers, SP14/216/17, *Examination of John Johnson*, 6 November 1605

3. Morris, T.A., *Europe and England in the Sixteenth Century*, p. 333

4. Butler, Alban, *Lives of the Saints: August,* p. 225

5. Morris, John, *The Catholics of York Under Elizabeth*, p. 345

6. Longley, Katherine, *Saint Margaret Clitherow*, p. 178

7. Ibid. p. 68

8. See the diagram linking 'Conspirators' Relationships' at the front of Antonia Fraser's *The Gunpowder Plot: Terror and Faith in 1605*

9. Flower, William, *The Visitation of Yorkshire in the Years 1563 and 1564*, p. 333

10. Lake, Peter and Questier, Michael, *The Trials of Margaret Clitherow*, p. 17

11. Maynard, Jean Olwen, *Margaret Clitherow*, p. 27

12. Doran, Susan and Jones, Norman, *The Elizabethan World*, p. 137

13. 'Sufferings of Mrs. Foster at York'*, The Gentleman's Magazine, Volume 167, 1840*, p. 465

14. Hildyard, Christopher, *The Antiquities of York City, and the Civil Government Thereof*, p. 82

15. *Recusant History, Volume 20, 1991*, p. 419

16. Butler, Alban, *Lives of the Saints, Volume 1*, p. 469

17. Lake, Peter and Questier, Michael, *The Trials of Margaret Clitherow*, p. 87

18. Maynard, Jean Olwen, *Margaret Clitherow*, p. 59

19. Lake, Peter and Questier, Michael, *The Trials of Margaret Clitherow*, p. 107

20. Margaret Clitherow had inherited property in Davygate, York, upon the death of her mother in 1585. After Margaret's killing it was acquired by Henry May

NOTES

Chapter 6

1. Father Oswald Tesimond wrote of Guy: 'He was also – something decidedly rare among soldiery, although it was immediately evident to all – a very devout man, of exemplary life and commendable reticence.' Edwards, Father Francis (ed.), *The Narrative of Oswald Tesimond Alias Greenway*, p. 69

2. A letter on Guy's behalf from his cousin Father Richard Collinge, written in 1599, says that Guy 'hath left a pretty living here in this country which his mother being married to an unthrifty husband since his departure I think hath wasted away.' Garnet, Henry, *Portrait of Guy Fawkes*, p. 46

3. For details of Denis Bainbridge's family, see *Wills & Administrations from Knaresborough Court Rolls 1506-1858, volume 1*, pp. 179-80

4. Pullein, Catherine, *The Pulleyns of Yorkshire*, p. 94

5. A guise that survived even after the start of his interrogations in the Tower of London

6. Guy was sent to Spain in 1603 to speak to King Philip III, son of the man who had ordered the original Armada to England

7. Aveling, Hugh, *The Catholic Recusants of the West Riding of Yorkshire 1558-1790*, p. 217

8. See note 2 above. Father Collinge also referred to Bainbridge as a man who was 'ornamental' rather than 'useful'

9. The Claro Community Archaeology Project continue to work on this, and their activities include the use of digs and water divination

10. *A List of the Roman Catholics in the County of York in 1604*, ms. in the Bodleain library, Oxford (part of the Rawlinson Manuscripts, reference B. 452)

11. *The Yorkshire Archaeological Journal, Volume 69*, p.180

12. *Wills and Administrations from Knaresborough Court Rolls, Volume One*, p. 180

13. For the online record of the marriage, see familysearch.org/pal:/MM9.2.1/MZMK-RB1

14. *A List of the Roman Catholics in the County of York in 1604*, ms. in the Bodleain library, Oxford (part of the Rawlinson Manuscripts, reference B. 452)

15. Peacock, Edward (ed.), *A List of the Roman Catholics in the County of York in 1604*, p. 121

Chapter 7

1. The 'Curse of Cowdray' has been passed down orally, and latterly in books, since the sixteenth century, and while it takes varied forms it always centres upon the destruction of the family through fire and water

2. Sir Henry Owen was the son of Sir David Owen, who was himself the illegitimate son of Owen Tudor, founder of the Tudor dynasty, and therefore uncle of King Henry VII, the father of Henry VIII

3. Coudreye had been the family seat of the Bohun family since it was built in the late thirteenth century. It came into the Owen family after the death of Mary Bohun, who was the first wife of Sir David Owen
4. Sir Anthony had already been given several positions in court by Queen Mary, and his wife Magdalen Dacre was one of the ladies in Queen Mary's wedding procession
5. King Henry VIII stayed at Cowdray on three occasions (1538, 1539, and 1545), and it was also visited by his son Edward VI (1552) and his daughter Elizabeth I (1591)
6. The 1581 act, the 'Act to retain the Queen's Majesty's subjects in their obedience' also made it possible to imprison anyone who heard a Catholic mass for a year, and to keep them in prison until they paid their fine
7. Garnet, Henry, *Portrait of Guy Fawkes,* p.168
8. Ibid., pp. 169-70
9. For this calculation, and to see other possible conversion amounts see www.measuringworth.com
10. Garnet, Henry, *Portrait of Guy Fawkes,* p. 171
11. The claim of the second marquis came after he was arrested and interrogated following the failure of the gunpowder plot, so his remarks can be seen as an attempt to mitigate any knowledge he had of Guy Fawkes
12. Cooper, M., *Memoirs of the Life of Robert Devereux, Earl of Essex*, pp. 23-5
13. Although Catesby avoided execution for his minor role in the Essex rebellion, his heavy fine meant that he had to sell his manor house at Chastleton in Oxfordshire
14. Lingard, John, *The History of England, Volume IV*, p. 345
15. Queen Mary reigned from 1553 until her death in 1558. A popular monarch initially, she soon became known for her cruel treatment of Protestants, and gained the name of 'Bloody Mary' for having over 280 Protestants burned at the stake during her reign
16. McDermott, James, *England and the Spanish Armada*, p. 280
17. Archer, Jayne Elisabeth and Knight, Sarah, *The Progresses, Pageants and Entertainments of Queen Elizabeth I*, pp. 189-205
18. Archer, Jayne Elisabeth and Knight, Sarah, p. 190
19. Ambrose Rookwood became one of Guy's fellow gunpowder conspirators
20. Connelly, Roland, *The Women of the Catholic Resistance in England, 1540-1680*, p. 132
21. Montague's letter to the Earl of Dorset is dated 13 November 1605. Getting his excuses in early did not prevent the viscount from being arrested and imprisoned, although he was later released without charge
22. Scott, Sir Sibbald David, *Viscount Montague's Book of Orders and Rules*, p. 22
23. Robert Catesby was distantly related to the second viscount, whose mother

was born Dorothy Catesby. Robert Catesby also famously, if obliquely, warned Viscount Montague to stay away from Parliament on 5 November 1605, as we shall see later

Chapter 8

1. State Papers, SP14/216/17, *Examination of John Johnson, 6 November 1605*
2. Ibid. (answer number three)
3. Thomas Percy entered Cambridge University in 1579
4. Robert Catesby entered Oxford's Gloucester Hall College in 1586, and was one of a number of Catholic students there even though it was impossible for them to graduate unless they forswore their faith by taking the Oath of Allegiance. Gloucester Hall is the present-day Worcester College, Oxford
5. Before the 1530s reformation, monasteries, nunneries and the church owned around half of all the land and property in London: for example, Covent Garden was once a convent garden
6. Although King Henry VIII made the stews of Bankside in Southwark illegal on 13 April 1546 this doesn't seem to have stopped prostitution in the area
7. Ward, Joseph P., *London: A Social and Cultural History, 1550-1750*, p. 43
8. Maynard, Jean Olwen, *Margaret Clitherow*, p. 51
9. *Proceedings and Ordinances of the Privy Council of England, Volume 6*, p. cxxix
10. Walsingham's double agents Gilbert Gifford and Thomas Phelippes had been placed by him inside Chartley Castle, where Mary was imprisoned, and on his instructions they encouraged the plot and intercepted Mary's coded messages
11. Francis Tresham, Thomas Percy, and even Robert Catesby have all been accused of being agents for Cecil over the centuries, with some accusations and theories more plausible than others
12. Fraser, Antonia, *The Gunpowder Plot*, p. 123
13. In 1597 Ben Jonson's play *The Isle of Dogs*, co-written with Thomas Nashe, caused such offence to the court that he was imprisoned. A year later he was imprisoned again, this time for killing the actor Gabriel Spenser in a duel. It is believed that he converted to Catholicism in prison, under the influence of the imprisoned Jesuit priest Father Thomas Wright
14. Thomas Kyd, author of *The Spanish Tragedy* and a former room-mate of Marlowe's, spent time in prison and died a year later in 1594
15. The coroner's inquest of Friday, 1 June 1593, concluded that Marlowe had become involved in a fracas with one Ingram Frizer, who we now know to have been a government agent, and that Frizer killed Marlowe in self-defence. Frizer was found not guilty of murder and freed
16. Hugh Owen was born in Caernarvonshire in Wales; he sometimes used Welsh in the coded letters that he sent

Chapter 9

1. Richard Collinge was the nephew of William Harrington, who was the cousin of Guy's father Edward. William Harrington was arrested in 1581 for harbouring the fugitive Jesuit priest Edmund Campion. Campion was hung, drawn and quartered in December of that year, and canonised as a martyr, alongside St. Margaret Clitherow, in 1970

2. Morris, John (ed.), *The Condition of Catholics Under James I: Father Gerard's Narrative of the Gunpowder Plot*, pp. 57-8

3. Although the passing of time leaves the records far from complete, some of Guy's records of service in Flanders and elsewhere can be found in the Royal Archives in Brussels

4. This was one of the questions posed by King James, see SP14/216/18, *Interrogatories of James I for John Johnson, 6 November 1605.* Undoubtedly they wanted to connect Johnson, as they then knew Guy Fawkes, to the activities of Catholic exiles such as Hugh Owen and Robert Stanley in France and Flanders, but Guy was wise to this

5. State Papers SP14/216/9, *Examination of John Johnson in Response to Interrogatories, 6 November 1605*

6. He also reigned as King Charles I of Spain. With Spanish lands in America and Asia also under his control, his empire was described as 'the empire on which the sun never sets'. He was succeeded by Philip II

7. *Journal of the Cork Historical and Archaeological Society 1939*, p. 44

8. Falls, Cyril, *Elizabeth's Irish Wars*, pp. 128-9

9. At the Battle of Bunamargey Abbey, 1 January 1585, when he was surprised by the enemy and had no time to don his armour

10. Froude, James Anthony, *History of England from the Fall of Wolsey to the Defeat of the Spanish Armada*, p. 187

11. Dutton, Richard, Findlay, Alison Gail, and Wilson, Richard, *Theatre and Religion: Lancastrian Shakespeare*, p. 137

12. Sir Philip Sidney developed gangrene in a thigh wound, and died twenty-six days later aged 31

13. Fraser, Antonia, *The Gunpowder Plot,* pp. 72-3

14. The Jesuit Cardinal William Allen made a defence of Stanley's actions in a lengthy epistle entitled 'Concerning the yielding up of the city of Deventer, unto his Catholic Majesty, by Sir William Stanley Knight. Wherein is shown both how lawful, honourable and necessary that action was: and also that all others, especially those of the English nation, that detain any towns, or other places, in the low countries, from the King Catholic, are bound, upon pain of damnation, to do the like'

15. Haynes, Alan, *The Gunpowder Plot*, p. 21

16. Garnet, Henry, *Portrait of Guy Fawkes*, p. 46

NOTES

17. Ibid., p. 48
18. A fourteen-day siege was ended by a lightning assault by the Spanish. In under an hour they had conquered the Calais stronghold, losing just nineteen men, while the defending French lost around a thousand
19. Loomie, Father Albert J., *Guy Fawkes in Spain*, p. 23
20. Bostock took command when Sir William Stanley left the regiment to pursue negotiations with Spain aimed at getting them to launch another invasion of England
21. Van der Hoeven, Marco (ed.), *Exercise of Arms: Warfare in the Netherlands, 1568-1648*, p. 106
22. King James himself ordered that Guy be asked where the scars on his chest came from, as revealed in State Papers SP14/216/18. Guy responded with the unlikely explanation that they had resulted from a bout of pleurisy
23. Edwards, Father Francis (ed.), *The Narrative*, p. 69
24. Edwards, Father Francis (ed.), *The Narrative*, p. 68
25. State Papers, SP14/216/9, *Examination of John Johnson in Response to Interrogatories, 6 November 1605*

Chapter 10
1. The trials lasted two years and implicated seventy people, from lowly midwives to the Earl of Bothwell
2. *A True Discourse of the Apprehension of Sundrye Witches lately taken in Scotland: Whereof some are Executed, and some are yet Imprisoned*, p. 13
3. Strickland, Alice, *Lives of the Queens of England*, p. 326
4. Ibid.
5. Levack, Brian P. (ed.), *The Oxford Handbook of Witchcraft in Early Modern Europe and Colonial America*, p. 302
6. King James's *Daemonologie* is now held in the British Library, London
7. King James VI of Scotland had four regents governing for him during his childhood. As an indication of how violent and unpredictable the Scottish court was at that time, two of the regents were assassinated, one executed, and one is presumed to have died of poisoning
8. Wagner, John (ed.), *Historical Dictionary of the Elizabethan World*, p. 262
9. Weir, Alison, *Mary Queen of Scots: and the Murder of Lord Darnley*, p. 190
10. Ibid., p. 251
11. John of Gaunt was himself the son of a King, Edward III
12. A copy can be read at the British Library, London
13. Tallis, Nicola, *Crown of Blood*, p. 274
14. Margaret Tudor married King James IV of Scotland, and ruled as Queen of Scotland from 1503 until 1513
15. Fraser, Antonia, *The Gunpowder Plot*, p. 5

16. Childs, Jessie, *God's Traitors*, p. 280

17. Original manuscripts of the letters are at Hatfield House, or see Bruce, John (ed.), *Correspondence of King James VI of Scotland with Sir Robert Cecil and others*

18. As well as serving as Northumberland's intermediary with King James, Thomas Percy was also constable of Alnwick Castle and in charge of the earl's estates. The earl later gained him a position as one of the King's bodyguards. Little wonder that some have conjectured that he may have been an illegitimate half-brother to the earl

19. Edwards, Father Francis (ed.), *The Narrative*, pp. 58-9

20. Loomie, Father Albert J., 'King James I's Catholic Consort', *Huntington Library Quarterly 34*, pp. 303-16

21. Guy was on the diplomatic mission that became known as the Spanish Treason – see Chapter 11

22. Edwards, Father Francis (ed.), *The Narrative*, pp. 52-3

Chapter 11

1. Fraser, Antonia, *The Gunpowder Plot*, p. xxvii

2. Father Garnet was executed due to his supposed links to the gunpowder plot

3. Coffey, John, *Persecution and Toleration in Protestant England 1558-1689*, p. 117

4. One of the strangest anomalies of Baldwin's life is that he died of natural causes aged 69. One of the English authorities' most vilified and sought-after Catholics, he was arrested twice, in 1594 and 1610, but despite spending more than eight years imprisoned the authorities could prove no charge against him and he was freed both times

5. Thomas James also wrote a book entitled *The Jesuits' Downfall* in 1612, in which he looked at the Gunpowder Plot and the impact it had upon Jesuits in England

6. Fraser, Antonia, *The Gunpowder Plot*, p. 48

7. Childs, Jessie, *God's Traitors*, p. 280

8. Loomie, Father Albert J., *Guy Fawkes in Spain,* p. 20

9. Thomas Wintour was the only major conspirator captured alive at the siege of Holbeche House after the failure of the plot, and so his confessions at the Tower of London form key evidence alongside the confessions of Guy Fawkes

10. State Papers, SP14/216/16, *Examination of Guido Fawkes, 25 November 1605*

11. Spanish state paper E840/129

12. Father Hill had presented the petition to the King in York, during his journey from Scotland to London

13. The letter of Guy Fawkes is now contained in the Spanish state papers. For further details, see Loomie, Father Albert J., *Guy Fawkes in Spain,* p. 22

14. Ibid.

15. Loomie, Father Albert J., *Toleration and Diplomacy: The Religious Issue in Anglo-Spanish Relations*, p. 12

16. Morrill, John (ed.), *The Oxford Illustrated History of Tudor and Stuart Britain*, p. 417

17. Howell, Thomas Bayly, *A Complete Collection of State Trials and Proceedings for High Treason and other Crimes and Misdemeanours from the Earliest Period to the Year 1783*, pp. 62-3

18. Sir Walter Ralegh spent thirteen years in the Tower before being pardoned in 1616. It is noteworthy that both Thomas Wintour and Guy Fawkes were asked whether Ralegh had been involved in the early planning of the gunpowder plot. A positive answer to that question would undoubtedly have seen Ralegh lose his head

19. Stuart, Arbella, *The Letters of Lady Arbella Stuart*, p. 45

20. Britton, John, and Brayley, Edward Wedlake, *Memoirs of the Tower of London*, p. 132

21. Sharpe, J.A., *Remember, Remember*, p. 45

Chapter 12

1. No record survives of Catesby's birth or baptism, although given the strong recusancy of his parents they may not have registered his birth officially, choosing instead to have him baptised surreptitiously by a Catholic priest. Nevertheless, 1572 is uniformly accepted as the year of his birth

2. Owen Tudor's marriage, far in excess of what his social standing entitled him to expect, to Catherine of Valois, widow of King Henry V, was the rock on which the royal Tudor dynasty was founded

3. Sir William Catesby served Richard III as Chancellor of the Exchequer and Leader of the House of Commons

4. Catesby was the cat of the poem (Sir Richard Ratcliffe and Francis Lovell are the others referred to), the writing of which led to Collingbourne being hung, drawn and quartered for treason in the same year

5. Wagner, John A., *Encyclopedia of the Wars of the Roses*, p. 49

6. We'll read later how this Catholic network, spread across the Midlands, was central to Robert Catesby's plan to seize control of England after the initial explosion under the House of Lords

7. It seems likely that Catesby was actually 32 or 33 at the time of the plot, not 34

8. Edwards, Father Francis (ed.), *The Narrative*, p. 54

9. Hall, Campion, *The Reckoned Expense: Edmund Campion and the Early English Jesuits*, p. 52

10. Haynes, Alan, *The Gunpowder Plot*, p. 48

11. The records are held at St. Mary the Virgin's Church, Chastleton

12. Childs, Jessie, *God's Traitors*, p. 273

13. Wagner, John A. and Schmid, Susan Walters, *Encyclopedia of Tudor England, Volume 1*, pp. 1091-2
14. Sharpe, J.A., *Remember, Remember*, p. 30
15. Gerard, Father John, *The Autobiography of a Hunted Priest*, pp. 170-1
16. Ibid., p. 171
17. Anne Vaux was the daughter of William Vaux, Baron Harrowden, who had been tried alongside Sir William Catesby for hiding Father Edmund Campion. Anne had a network of houses specifically to be used for harbouring Catholic priests. Foremost among them was White Webbs, which became home to Father Henry Garnet and in which she lived under the alias of Mrs Perkins. She was related to Francis Tresham, and White Webbs was often visited by the gunpowder conspirators
18. Edwards, Father Francis (ed.), *The Narrative*, p. 61
19. Ibid.
20. Plowden, Alison, *The Elizabethan Secret Service*, p. 143
21. Haynes, Alan, *The Gunpowder Plot*, p. 47
22. Fraser, Antonia, *The Gunpowder Plot*, p. 99
23. Ibid., pp. xxv
24. Monteagle's letter is reproduced in full in *The Gentleman's Magazine, Volume XIV, 1840*, p. 632

Chapter 13
1. Fraser, Antonia, *The Gunpowder Plot*, p. 99
2. Thomas Wintour never revealed who had asked him to undertake his mission to Spain, only hinting that they were friends who had been connected to the Essex rebellion, but it is commonly accepted that the instigators of the trip were Robert Catesby and Lord Monteagle
3. Haynes, Alan, *The Gunpowder Plot*, p. 47
4. Morgan, George Blacker, *The Great English Treason*, p. 80
5. De Fonblanque, Edward Barrington, *Annals of the House of Percy, from the Conquest to the Opening of the Nineteenth Century*, p. 252
6. Fraser, Antonia, *The Gunpowder Plot*, p. 40
7. Thomas Percy and his wife Martha had periods of separation, and in 1605 Martha and her daughter (the one betrothed to Robert Catesby's son) were living on an annuity being paid to them by a man who turns up frequently in the story of the gunpowder plot – Lord Monteagle
8. Morris, John (ed.), *The Condition of Catholics under James I*, p. 57
9. Ibid., p. 58
10. Haynes, Alan, *The Gunpowder Plot*, p. 50
11. We shall see later how Guy Fawkes had an opportunity to kill King James at a society wedding in 1604

NOTES

12. Edwards, Father Francis (ed.), *The Narrative*, pp. 54-5
13. See State Papers, SP14/216/114, *Confession of Thomas Wintour*
14. Ibid.
15. Haynes, Alan, *The Gunpowder Plot*, p. 50
16. State Papers, SP14/216/114, *Confession of Thomas Wintour*
17. Ibid.
18. Ibid.
19. Wintour had been badly injured in the siege at Holbeche House that claimed the lives of Catesby and many of the other conspirators, and it was his injury that allowed him to be taken alive and then interrogated by Sir Robert Cecil's men
20. The Constable of Castile was Juan Fernandez de Velasco, the Duke of Frias. He was a central figure in the negotiation and signing of the Treaty of London, sealing peace between Spain and England, in August 1604
21. State Papers, SP14/216/114, *Confession of Thomas Wintour*

Chapter 14
1. Haynes, Alan, *The Gunpowder Plot*, p. 21
2. We find 'Mr Faukes of Yorkshier' listed as a member of Lord Arundell's Company of the English Regiment as late as the autumn of 1605, even though Guy was in England then. See State Papers, SP77, Bundle 7, Part I, ff. 329r.-32v
3. State Papers, SP14/216/114, *Confession of Thomas Wintour*
4. Ibid.
5. Ibid.
6. Fraser, Antonia, *The Gunpowder Plot,* p. 69
7. State Papers, SP14/216/114, *Confession of Thomas Wintour*
8. Ibid.
9. Edwards, Father Francis (ed.), *The Narrative*, p. 61
10. State Papers, SP14/216/114, *Confession of Thomas Wintour*
11. Sadler, Geoffrey, *Foul Deeds and Suspicious Deaths in and around Chesterfield*, p. 12
12. Haynes, Alan, *The Gunpowder Plot*, p. 46
13. Edwards, Father Francis (ed.), *The Narrative*, p. 208
14. State Papers, SP14/216/114, *Confession of Thomas Wintour*
15. Lady Elizabeth Stuart was being raised at Coombe Abbey in Warwickshire, a place Catesby knew well. She was the second child of King James and Queen Anne. The plotters assumed that Prince Henry would be killed in the blast they planned as well as his father, and the third child, Charles, was a sickly infant and considered unsuitable for what they had in mind
16. State Papers, SP14/216/114, *Confession of Thomas Wintour*

Chapter 15
1. Haynes, Alan, *The Gunpowder Plot*, p. 54
2. Northumberland's wholly unsuitable selection of Thomas Percy as a Gentleman Pensioner, and his failure to make him take the oath of supremacy, was later used as evidence to prove the earl's complicity in the gunpowder plot.
3. John Whynniard was among the party, along with Lord Monteagle and the Earl of Suffolk, who made the first search of the cellars underneath Parliament
4. Anstruther, Godfrey, *Vaux of Harrowden: A Recusant Family*, p. 184
5. Edwards, Father Francis (ed.), *The Narrative*, p. 198
6. Gerard, Father John, *The Autobiography of a Hunted Priest*, p. 51
7. Gardiner, Samuel Rawson, *What Gunpowder Plot Was*, p. 86
8. Donaldson, Peter, *The History of Sir William Wallace*, p. 61.
9. Fraser, Antonia, *The Gunpowder Plot*, p. 74
10. Garnet, Henry, *Portrait of Guy Fawkes: An Experiment in Biography*, p.135
11. The very first response of Guy Fawkes to his interrogators on 6 November 1605, was 'He saith his name is John Johnson', see State Papers, SP14/216/19
12. This was the conclusion of explosives expert Dr Sidney Alford in the *New Civil Engineer* and in the 2005 BBC docu-drama *The Gunpowder Plot: Exploding the Legend*
13. Evelyn, Helen, *The History of the Evelyn Family*, p. 18
14. State Papers, SP14/216/114, *Confession of Thomas Wintour*
15. Haynes, Alan, *The Gunpowder Plot*, p. 55
16. State Papers, SP14/216/114, *Confession of Thomas Wintour*
17. Ibid.
18. Edwards, Father Francis (ed.), *The Narrative*, p. 72
19. State Papers, SP14/216/114, *Confession of Thomas Wintour*
20. Edwards, Father Francis (ed.), *The Narrative*, p. 75
21. Simons, Eric N., *The Devil of the Vault*, p. 80

Chapter 16
1. Candlemas marks the fortieth day of the Christmas season, and was celebrated by Catholics as the Feast of the Purification of the Blessed Virgin Mary and of the Presentation of our Lord Jesus. Falling on 2 February it is the end of the Christmas period
2. Jesse, John Heneage, *Literary and Historical Memorials of London – Volume 2*, p. 175
3. Simons, Eric N., *The Devil of the Vault*, p. 85
4. State Papers, SP14/216/114, *Confession of Thomas Wintour*
5. Ibid.
6. Ibid.
7. Edwards, Father Francis (ed.), *The Narrative*, p. 84

NOTES

8. Ibid., p. 85

9. State Papers, SP14/216/114, *Confession of Thomas Wintour*

10. Edwards, Father Francis (ed.), *The Narrative*, p. 83

11. Morris, John (ed.), *The Condition of Catholics under James I*, p. 219

12. The Catherine Wheel in Oxford was opposite St. Mary Magdalene's Church, a site now occupied by Baliol College

13. McCoog, Thomas M., *The Reckoned Expense*, p. 61

14. Edwards, Father Francis, *The Enigma of the Gunpowder Plot, 1605: The Third Solution*, p. 158

15. Edwards, Father Francis (ed.), *The Narrative*, p. 101

16. Edwards, Father Francis, *The Enigma*, p. 63

17. Ibid., p. 64

18. Edwards, Father Francis (ed.), *The Narrative*, pp. 109-10

19. Haynes, Alan, *The Gunpowder Plot*, p. 59

20. Gardiner, Samuel Rawson, *What Gunpowder Plot Was*, pp. 100-1

21. Edwards, Father Francis (ed.), *The Narrative*, p. 86

22. Haynes, Alan, *The Gunpowder Plot*, p. 59

23. State Papers, SP14/216/114, *Confession of Thomas Wintour*

24. Edwards, Father Francis (ed.), *The Narrative*, p. 86

25. Ibid.

26. Gardiner, Samuel Rawson, *What Gunpowder Plot Was*, p. 100

Chapter 17

1. State Papers, SP14/216/114, *Confession of Thomas Wintour*

2. Edwards, Father Francis (ed.), *The Narrative*, p. 102

3. Ibid.

4. Edwards, Father Francis (ed.), *The Narrative*, p. 107

5. State Papers, SP14/216/6, Examination of John Johnson, 5 November 1605

6. Houliston, Victor, *Catholic Resistance in Elizabethan England*, p. 5

7. Edwards, Father Francis (ed.), *The Narrative*, p. 103

8. Davis, John Paul, *Pity for the Guy*, p. 161

9. *Recusant History, Volume 23*, p. 527

10. Ibid.

11. Pendrill, Colin, *Spain 1474-1700: The Triumphs and Tribulations of Empire*, p. 123

12. Haynes, Alan, *The Gunpowder Plot*, p. 72

13. State Papers, SP14/216/6, *Examination of John Johnson*, 5 November 1605

14. Anstruther, Godfrey, *Vaux of Harrowden*, p. 269

15. Haynes, Alan, *The Gunpowder Plot*, p. 73

16. Fraser, Antonia, *The Gunpowder Plot,* p. 124

17. Edwards, Father Francis (ed.), *The Narrative*, pp. 102-3

18. State Papers, SP14/216/6, *Examination of John Johnson*, 5 November 1605
19. Haynes, Alan, *The Gunpowder Plot*, p. 62
20. Edwards, Father Francis (ed.), *The Narrative*, p. 79
21. Ibid., p. 77
22. Ibid.
23. Ibid., pp. 81-2
24. Haynes, Alan, *The Gunpowder Plot*, p. 64
25. Sprott, S.E., *Sir Edward Baynham*, p. 96
26. Haynes, Alan, *The Gunpowder Plot*, p. 68
27. Fraser, Antonia, *The Gunpowder Plot,* p. 134
28. Edwards, Father Francis (ed.), *The Narrative*, p. 82

Chapter 18
1. State Papers, SP14/216/114, *Confession of Thomas Wintour*
2. Ibid.
3. Walls, Ernest, *Shakespeare's Avon*, p. 185
4. Edwards, Father Francis (ed.), *The Narrative*, p. 100
5. *Matthew 10:37*
6. Edwards, Father Francis (ed.), *The Narrative*, p. 101
7. State Papers, SP14/216/127, *Declaration of Robert Keyes*
8. Fraser, Antonia, *The Gunpowder Plot,* p. 135
9. Ibid.
10. Fraser, Antonia, *The Gunpowder Plot,* p. 147
11. Edwards, Father Francis (ed.), *The Narrative*, p. 105
12. Haynes, Alan, *The Gunpowder Plot*, p. 77
13. Collings, Michael R., *Milton's Century*, p. 49
14. Edwards, Father Francis (ed.), *The Narrative*, p. 112
15. Ibid., p. 112
16. State Papers, SP14/216/114, *Confession of Thomas Wintour*
17. *Records of the English Province of the Society of Jesus in the Sixteenth and Seventeenth Centuries, Volume 3*, p. 137
18. Haynes, Alan, *The Gunpowder Plot*, p. 78
19. Collings, Michael R., *Milton's Century*, p. 48
20. It's not known what in particular caused offence in this play by Johnson and Nashe, except that it was called lewd and slanderous. Whatever the reason, Ben Jonson found himself in the Marshalsea Prison in 1597
21. Haynes, Alan, *The Gunpowder Plot*, p. 83
22. *Calendar of State Papers, Domestic Series, of the Reign of Elizabeth, 1601-1603*, p. 111
23. Taylor, E.G.R. (ed.), *The Original Correspondence and Writings of the Two Richard Hakluyts, Volume II*, p. 491

NOTES

24. Anstruther, Godfrey, *Vaux of Harrowden*, p. 274
25. Haynes, Alan, *The Gunpowder Plot*, p. 80
26. Fraser, Antonia, *The Gunpowder Plot*, p. 66
27. Edwards, Father Francis (ed.), *The Narrative*, p. 108
28. State Papers, SP14/216/63, *Testimony of Francis Tresham*
29. State Papers, SP14/216/114, *Confession of Thomas Wintour*
30. Fraser, Antonia, *The Gunpowder Plot*, p. 149
31. Haynes, Alan, *The Gunpowder Plot*, p. 104
32. Edwards, Father Francis (ed.), *The Narrative*, p. 115
33. State Papers, SP14/216 Pt1 (11a)

Chapter 19
1. *The King's Book*
2. Bengtsen, Fiona, *Sir William Waad, Lieutenant of the Tower, and the Gunpowder Plot*, p. 123
3. The letter was from Cecil's spy Captain William Turner, see Chapter 17
4. Fraser, Antonia, *The Gunpowder Plot*, p. 151
5. Edwards, Father Francis (ed.), *The Narrative*, p. 117
6. *The King's Book*
7. Edwards, Father Francis (ed.), *The Narrative*, p. 117
8. Morris, John (ed.), *The Condition of Catholics under James I*, p. 97
9. Scott, Sir Walter, *The Court and Character of King James*, p. 3
10. Anstruther, Godfrey, *Vaux of Harrowden*, p. 274
11. Fraser, Antonia, *The Gunpowder Plot*, p. 151
12. Brown, Sylvia (ed.), *Women, Gender, and Radical Religion in Early Modern Europe*, p. 244
13. Bengtsen, Fiona, *Sir William Waad*, p. 46
14. Edwards, Father Francis (ed.), *The Narrative*, p. 117
15. State Papers, SP14/216/114, *Confession of Thomas Wintour*
16. Ibid.
17. Edwards, Father Francis (ed.), *The Narrative*, p. 119
18. State Papers, SP14/216/114, *Confession of Thomas Wintour*
19. Edwards, Father Francis (ed.), *The Narrative*, p. 118
20. Ibid.
21. See Monteagle's letter to Catesby in Chapter 12.
22. Edwards, Father Francis (ed.), *The Narrative*, p. 54. In his footnote, Father Edwards writes, 'In the translator's view, Catesby's role was that of an agent provocateur, second-in-command to Thomas Percy'
23. Haynes, Alan, *The Gunpowder Plot*, p. 48
24. Ibid., p. 79
25. Fraser, Antonia, *The Gunpowder Plot*, p. 154

26. Gardiner, Samuel Rawson, *History of England from the Accession of James I to the Disgrace of Chief-Justice Coke*, p. 243
27. State Papers, SP14/216/114, *Confession of Thomas Wintour*
28. See note 7 to Chapter 13
29. Edwards, Father Francis (ed.), *The Narrative*, p. 125
30. See Appendix 2 of Edwards, Father Francis (ed.), *The Narrative*. The expert analyst was Joan Cambridge, and her findings were originally published in the Observer in 1967

Chapter 20
1. Morris, John (ed.), *The Condition of Catholics under James I*, p. 97
2. *The King's Book*
3. Ibid.
4. Edwards, Father Francis (ed.), *The Narrative*, p. 119
5. After Guy's arrest and initial questioning, Sir William Waad of the Tower of London reported incredulously to Sir Robert Cecil that the prisoner 'hath taken such rest this night as a man void of all troubles of mind'. (Letter dated 7 November 1605, Cecil papers collection, Hatfield House)
6. Edwards, Father Francis (ed.), *The Narrative*, p. 121
7. State Papers, SP14/216/114, *Confession of Thomas Wintour*
8. Edwards, Father Francis (ed.), *The Narrative*, p. 120
9. Ibid., pp. 119-20
10. Ibid., p. 120
11. State Papers, SP14/216/114, *Confession of Thomas Wintour*
12. Ibid.
13. Morris, John (ed.), *The Condition of Catholics under James I*, p. 106
14. State Papers, SP14/216/100, *Examination of Guy Fawkes 16 November*
15. Haynes, Alan, *The Gunpowder Plot*, p. 93
16. Nicholls, Mark, *Investigating Gunpowder Plot*, p. 163
17. The Earl of Northumberland, by some unfairly suspected of being the leader of the plot, narrowly escaped with his life and was instead given a lengthy prison sentence
18. Edwards, Father Francis (ed.), *The Narrative*, p. 127
19. State Papers, SP14/216/100, *Examination of Guy Fawkes 16 November*
20. *The King's Book*
21. Ibid.
22. Ibid.
23. State Papers, SP14/216/100, *Examination of Guy Fawkes 16 November*
24. *1 Corinthians 13*
25. Gardiner, Samuel Rawson, *What Gunpowder Plot Was*, p. 135
26. Ibid., p. 136

27. It is generally accepted that these items were found upon Guy, although in his confession of 16 November Guy said he had thrown them out of a window, a difficult act to achieve with hands bound
28. Edwards, Father Francis (ed.), *The Narrative*, pp. 127-8

Chapter 21
1. *The King's Book*
2. Edwards, Father Francis (ed.), *The Narrative*, p. 127
3. Merritt, J.F., *The Social World of Early Modern Westminster*, p. 127
4. Haynes, Alan, *The Gunpowder Plot*, p. 94
5. Craig, Sir John, *The Mint*, p. 129
6. State Papers, SP14/216/18, *Interrogatories of James I for John Johnson, 6 November 1605*
7. Haynes, Alan, *The Gunpowder Plot*, p. 95
8. Edwards, Father Francis (ed.), *The Narrative*, p. 129
9. Barlow, Frank, *Thomas Becket*, p. 250
10. James, Anne, *Poets, Players and Preachers*, p. 45
11. An almost identical letter was also sent by Cecil to Sir Thomas Edmondes, the ambassador in Brussels, presumably so both men could ascertain whether the plot had any connection with Spain or with English exiles in Belgium
12. Jardine, David, *A Narrative of the Gunpowder Plot*, p. 103
13. Edwards, Father Francis (ed.), *The Narrative*, p. 128
14. *John 19:11*
15. Edwards, Father Francis (ed.), *The Narrative*, p. 129
16. Cormack, Margaret, *Sacrificing the Self: Perspectives in Martyrdom and Religion*, p. 27
17. Sir William Waad, pronounced 'Wade', was Lieutenant of the Tower of London. A renowned sadist, he insisted on being present every time a prisoner was tortured there
18. 'House of Commons Journal Volume 1: 05 November 1605', in *Journal of the House of Commons: Volume 1, 1547-1629*
19. State Papers, SP14/216/114, *Confession of Thomas Wintour*
20. Ibid.
21. Ibid.
22. Ibid.
23. Ibid.
24. Nicholls, Mark, *Investigating Gunpowder Plot*, p. 11
25. Davis, John Paul, *Pity for the Guy*, p. 187
26. Durst, Paul, *Intended Treason: What Really Happened in the Gunpowder Plot*, p. 126
27. State Papers, SP14/216/114, *Confession of Thomas Wintour*

28. Ibid.
29. Gardiner, Samuel Rawson, *What Gunpowder Plot Was*, p. 17
30. State Papers, SP14/216/6, *Examination of John Johnson, 5 November 1605*
31. Ibid.
32. Ibid.
33. Popham to Cecil, November 5, State Papers, SP14/216/10

Chapter 22
1. Gascoigne, Margaret and Monger, George, *Discovering English Customs and Traditions*, p. 10
2. State Papers, SP14/216/18, *Interrogatories of James I for John Johnson, 6 November 1605*
3. Ibid.
4. State Papers, SP14/216/19, *Examination of John Johnson in Response to Interrogatories, 6 November 1605*
5. State Papers, SP14/216/18, *Interrogatories of James I for John Johnson, 6 November 1605*
6. State Papers, SP14/216/19, *Examination of John Johnson in Response to Interrogatories, 6 November 1605*
7. State Papers, SP14/216/18, *Interrogatories of James I for John Johnson, 6 November 1605*
8. State Papers, SP14/216/19, *Examination of John Johnson in Response to Interrogatories, 6 November 1605*
9. Ibid.
10. Gardiner, Samuel Rawson, *What Gunpowder Plot Was*, p. 26
11. See chapter ten for the account of the torture and confession of Agnes Sampson
12. Clause 29 of Magna Carta states 'nor will we proceed with force against him, or send others to do so'
13. Edwards, Father Francis (ed.), *The Narrative*, p. 199
14. Ibid., p. 129
15. Morris, John (ed.), *The Condition of Catholics under James I*, p. xcviii
16. Mannix, Daniel P., *The History of Torture*, p. 104
17. State Papers, SP14/216/48, *Waad to Salisbury, 8 November 1605*
18. Now a private residence in Dunchurch, Warwickshire known as 'Guy Fawkes House'
19. Haynes, Alan, *The Gunpowder Plot*, p. 97
20. Edwards, Father Francis (ed.), *The Narrative*, p. 130
21. State Papers, SP14/216/136, *Examination of Ambrose Rookwood, 2 December 1605*
22. State Papers, SP14/216/22, *Confession of Robert Wintour*

NOTES

23. Edwards, Father Francis (ed.), *The Narrative*, p. 131
24. Humphreys, John, *Studies in Worcestershire History*, p. 34
25. State Papers, SP14/216/114, *Confession of Thomas Wintour*
26. Edwards, Father Francis (ed.), *The Narrative*, p. 101
27. Ibid., p. 130
28. State Papers, SP14/216/22, *Confession of Robert Wintour*
29. Ibid.
30. Edwards, Father Francis (ed.), *The Narrative*, p. 132
31. Haynes, Alan, *The Gunpowder Plot*, p. 101
32. Edwards, Father Francis (ed.), *The Narrative*, p. 132
33. State Papers, SP14/216/22, *Confession of Robert Wintour*
34. Edwards, Father Francis (ed.), *The Narrative*, p. 133
35. State Papers, SP14/216/114, *Confession of Thomas Wintour*
36. Ibid.
37. Ibid.
38. Ibid.
39. Ibid.
40. Edwards, Father Francis (ed.), *The Narrative*, p. 135
41. Ibid.
42. State Papers, SP14/216/114, *Confession of Thomas Wintour*
43. State Papers, SP14/216/135, *Examination of Everard Digby*
44. Jardine, David, *A Narrative of the Gunpowder Plot*, pp. 120-1
45. Edwards, Father Francis (ed.), *The Narrative*, p. 137

Chapter 23
1. Jardine, David, *A Narrative of the Gunpowder Plot*, p. 135
2. State Papers, SP14/216/54, *Deposition of Guido Fawkes, 9 November 1605*
3. Ibid.
4. Morris, John (ed.), *The Condition of Catholics under James I*, p. ccxxv
5. *The King's Book*
6. Letter dated 10 November 1605, Earl of Salisbury to Sir Thomas Edmondes, Cecil papers collection, Hatfield House
7. State Papers, SP14/216/54, *Deposition of Guido Fawkes, 9 November 1605*
8. See State Papers, SP14/216/114, *Confession of Thomas Wintour*
9. Edwards, Father Francis, *The Enigma of the Gunpowder Plot, 1605: The Third Solution*, p. 222
10. State Papers, SP14/216/145, *Examination of Thomas Bates, 4 December 1605*
11. Edwards, Father Francis (ed.), *The Narrative*, p. 153
12. Ibid, p. 234
13. State Papers, SP14/216/63, *Voluntary Declaration of Francis Tresham*
14. State Papers, SP14/216/211, *Deathbed Declaration of Francis Tresham*

15. Edwards, Father Francis (ed.), *The Narrative*, p. 233
16. Public Record office, E. 124, vol. 3, ff. 63v-5r
17. State Papers, SP14/216/54, *Deposition of Guido Fawkes, 9 November 1605*
18. Anstruther, Godfrey, *Vaux of Harrowden*, p. 331
19. Bengtsen, Fiona, *Sir William Waad*, p. 65
20. Jardine, David, *A Narrative of the Gunpowder Plot*, p. 124
21. Edwards, Father Francis (ed.), *The Narrative*, p. 232
22. Ibid., p. 239-40
23. John Wintour had played no part in the planning or development of the plot, but his partaking in the Midlands uprising was enough to see him placed on trial with his half-brothers Thomas and Robert. He too would be executed as a traitor
24. Haynes, Alan, *The Gunpowder Plot*, p. 111
25. *A Complete Collection of State Trials and Proceedings for High Treason, Volume II*, p. 164
26. Ibid.
27. Ibid., p. 171
28. Edwards, Father Francis (ed.), *The Narrative*, p. 205
29. *A Complete Collection of State Trials and Proceedings for High Treason, Volume II*, p. 184
30. Ibid., p. 194
31. Aubrey, John, *Brief Lives*, p. 101
32. Janes, Regina, *Losing Our Heads: Beheadings in Literature and Culture*, p. 53

Epilogue
1. Haynes, Alan, *The Gunpowder Plot*, p. 104
2. Fraser, Antonia, *The Gunpowder Plot,* p. 195
3. Haynes, Alan, *The Gunpowder Plot*, p. 125
4. Lingard, John, *The History of England, Volume IX,* p. 58
5. Nicholls, Mark, *Investigating Gunpowder Plot*, p. 77
6. Lingard, John, *The History of England, Volume IX,* p. 59
7. Jardine, David, *A Narrative of the Gunpowder Plot*, p. 163
8. Haynes, Alan, *The Gunpowder Plot*, p. 129
9. Caulfield, James, *A History of the Gunpowder Plot*, p. 74
10. Jardine, David, *A Narrative of the Gunpowder Plot*, p. 169
11. Ibid., p. 171
12. Ibid., p. 257
13. Fraser, Antonia, *The Gunpowder Plot,* pp. 268-9
14. Edwards, Father Francis (ed.), *The Narrative*, p. 159
15. Fraser, Antonia, *The Gunpowder Plot,* p. 245
16. Davis, John Paul, *Pity for the Guy*, pp. 236-7
17. Ratcliffe, Susan (ed.), *Oxford Treasury of Sayings and Quotations*, p. 389

Select Bibliography

Ainsworth, William Harrison, *Guy Fawkes, or, The Gunpowder Treason; An Historical Romance* (Richard Bentley, 1841)

Alford, Stephen, *The Watchers: A Secret History of the Reign of Elizabeth I* (Penguin, 2013)

Anstruther, Godfrey, *Vaux of Harrowden: A Recusant Family* (R.H. Johns, 1953)

Aubrey, John, *Brief Lives* (Boydell & Brewer, 1982)

Bengtsen, Fiona, *Sir William Waad, Lieutenant of the Tower, and the Gunpowder Plot* (Trafford Publishing, 2005)

Brown, Sylvia Monica, Women, Gender, and Radical Religion in Early Modern Europe (Brill, 2007)

Caulfield, James, *A History of the Gunpowder Plot with Several Historical Circumstances Prior to that Event* (Verner and Hood, 1804)

Childs, Jessie, *God's Traitors: Terror and Faith in Elizabethan England* (Oxford University Press, 2014)

Cooper, John, *The Queen's Agent: Francis Walsingham at the Court of Elizabeth I* (Faber & Faber, 2012)

Davies, Robert, *The Fawkes's of York in the Sixteenth Century* (J.B. and J.G. Nichols, 1850)

Davis, John Paul, *Pity for the Guy* (Peter Owen, 2009)

Donaldson, Ian, *Ben Jonson: A Life* (Oxford University Press, 2011)

Doran, Susan and Jones, Norman, *The Elizabethan World* (Routledge, 2014)

Edwards, Father Francis (ed.), *The Narrative of Oswald Tesimond Alias Greenway* (The Folio Society, 1973)

Fraser, Antonia, *The Gunpowder Plot: Terror and Faith in 1605* (Weidenfeld & Nicolson 1996)

Gardiner, Samuel Rawson, *What Gunpowder Plot Was* (Longmans, Green & Co., 1897)

Garnet, Henry, *Portrait of Guy Fawkes: An Experiment in Biography* (Robert Hale, 1962)

Gerard, Father John, *The Autobiography of a Hunted Priest* (Ignatius Press, 2012)

Gerard, John, S.J., *What was the Gunpowder Plot? The Traditional Story Tested by Original Evidence* (Osgood, McIlvaine & Company, 1897)

Guy, John, *My Heart Is My Own: The Life of Mary Queen of Scots* (Harper, 2004)

Hanson, Neil, *The Confident Hope of a Miracle: The True History of the Spanish Armada* (Corgi, 2004)

Haynes, Alan, *The Gunpowder Plot* (Sutton Publishing, 2005)

Hogge, Alice, *God's Secret Agents* (Harper, 2006)

James, Anne, *Poets, Players and Preachers: Remembering the Gunpowder Plot in Seventeenth-Century England* (University of Toronto Press, 2016)

Jardine, David, *A Narrative of the Gunpowder Plot* (John Murray, 1857)

Lake, Peter and Questier, Michael, *The Trials of Margaret Clitherow: Persecution, Martyrdom and the Politics of Sanctity in Elizabethan England* (Bloomsbury, 2011)

Lemon, Rebecca, *Treason by Words: Literature, Law and Rebellion in Shakespeare's England* (Cornell University Press, 2007)

Loades, David, *The Cecils* (Bloomsbury, 2009)

Loomie, Father Albert J., *Guy Fawkes In Spain: The 'Spanish Treason' in Spanish Documents* (University of London Institute of Historical Research, 1971)

MacCulloch, Diarmaid, *Reformation: Europe's House Divided 1490-1700* (Penguin, 2004)

Magee, Brian, *The English Recusants* (Burns, Oates & Washbourne, 1938)

Matusiak, John, *James I: Scotland's King of England* (The History Press, 2015)

Maynard, Jean Olwyn, *Margaret Clitherow* (Catholic Truth Society, 2003)

McCoog, Thomas M. (ed.), *The Reckoned Expense: Edmund Campion and the Early English Jesuits* (Boydell & Brewer, 1996)

McDermott, James, *England and the Spanish Armada: The Necessary Quarrel* (Yale University Press, 2005)

Morrill, John (ed.), *The Oxford Illustrated History of Tudor and Stuart Britain* (Oxford University Press, 1996)

Morris, John (ed.), *The Condition of Catholics Under James I: Father Gerard's Narrative of the Gunpowder Plot* (Longmans, Green & Co., 1871)

Nicholls, Mark, *Investigating Gunpowder Plot* (Manchester University Press, 1991)

Pullein, Catherine, *The Pulleyns of Yorkshire* (J. Whitehead & Son, 1915)

Riggs, David, *The World of Christopher Marlowe* (Faber & Faber, 2014)

Sharpe, J.A., *Remember, Remember: A Cultural History of Guy Fawkes Day* (Profile Books, 2005)

Sidney, Philip, *A History of the Gunpowder Plot: The Conspiracy and its Agents* (Religious Tract Society, 2004)

Strachey, Lytton, *Elizabeth and Essex: A Tragic History* (I.B. Tauris, 2012)

Tallis, Nicola, *Crown of Blood: The Deadly Inheritance of Lady Jane Grey* (Michael O'Mara Books, 2016)

Telford, Linda, *Tudor Victims of the Reformation* (Pen & Sword, 2016)

Weir, Alison, *Mary Queen of Scots: and the Murder of Lord Darnley* (Random House, 2008)

Wells, Stanley, *Shakespeare & Co.* (Penguin, 2007)

Wilson, A.N., *The Elizabethans* (Random House, 2011)

Winsham, Willow, *Accused: British Witches Throughout History* (Pen & Sword, 2016)